The Failure of Louis XIV's Dutch War

Louis XIV as Mars sculpture in stucco
by Antoine Coysevox, 1673, Salon de Guerre, Versailles
(courtesy of Georges Giraudon)

споспоспо

The Failure of
Louis XIV's Dutch War

by
Carl J. Ekberg

The University of North Carolina Press
Chapel Hill

© 1979 The University of North Carolina Press
All rights reserved
Manufactured in the United States of America
ISBN 0-8078-1347-8
Library of Congress Catalog Card Number 78-21955

Library of Congress Cataloging in Publication Data

Ekberg, Carl J
  The failure of Louis XIV's Dutch War.

  Bibliography: p.
  Includes index.
    1. France—Foreign relations—1643–1715.   2. Louis
XIV, King of France, 1638–1715.   3. Dutch War, 1672–1678.
I. Title.
DC127.3.E38   944'.033   78-21955
ISBN 0-8078-1347-8

For Gloria and Vanessa

Affairs of state without men are dead letters, and our goal is rightly to make these affairs comprehensible by bringing the men to life.

Albert Sorel
*Nouveaux essais d'histoire
et de critique*

Contents

	Preface	[xiii]
	Chronology	[xvii]
I	Louis XIV's Politics: Motives, Men, and Issues	[3]
II	The King's Campaign: Maastricht, Trier, and Alsace	[13]
III	Ordeal in Germany: A Shadow on Turenne's Glory	[48]
IV	The Cologne Conference: Honoré Courtin's Disenchantment	[77]
V	War with Spain: An Old Conflict Renewed	[110]
VI	The End of the Dutch War: Louis XIV's First Setback	[129]
VII	Charles II and Louis XIV: The Manipulator Manipulated	[151]
VIII	Louis XIV and France	[172]
	Notes	[185]
	Bibliography	[211]
	Index	[221]

∽∽∽

Illustrations

Louis XIV   frontispiece
Marquis de Pomponne   [12]
Vicomte de Turenne   [50]
Honoré Courtin   [78]
Marquis de Louvois   [128]

Maps

The United Provinces in 1672   [xii]
Louis XIV's Campaign; May–October 1673   [47]
Turenne's Campaign; June–November 1673   [76]

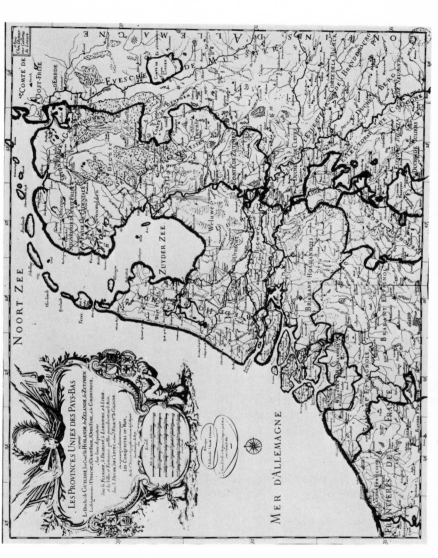

The United Provinces in 1672, with Maastricht (Maestricht) at bottom-center (*courtesy of the Bibliothèque Nationale*)

Preface

At the beginning of this century, Ernest Lavisse in his great *Histoire de France* remarked that our knowledge of the political and military history of the first half of Louis XIV's reign was superficial. At about the same time, the young Georges Pagès, who became the doyen of political historians of the Old Regime for the next generation of French scholars, made much the same observation. He wrote in *Revue d'histoire moderne et contemporaine* that the period 1661–88 was to him the most interesting phase of Louis's reign, and then noted that relatively little was known about it. After Lavisse published *Histoire de France* in 1911, Pagès, Gaston Zeller, Camille Picavet, Bertrand Auerbach, and others selectively rummaged through the mass of documents in the archives of the French foreign ministry and wrote the studies upon which our knowledge of Louis's foreign policy is still largely based. As recently as 1960, however, Victor-L. Tapié, who had studied with Pagès, felt justified in remarking, in *Bulletin de la société d'étude du XVIIe siècle*, that our knowledge of this subject remains cursory and shallow. Three generations of French historians thus agreed that Louis XIV's reign, and particularly the first half of that reign, was a rich but neglected field for the student of international relations.

French historians of the Old Regime now often scorn the study of politics as *histoire événementielle*, and despite the work being done by European and American scholars, Tapié's remark is almost as true today as it was eighteen years ago. The French continue to publish the important series, *Recueil des instructions données aux ambassadors et ministres de France*, and Georges

Dethan ably directs publication of *Revue d'histoire diplomatique*, but most French scholars no longer consider the foreign affairs archives worthy of study. Yet it is a fact that Louis XIV considered foreign policy and military matters his special spheres of responsibility, and that the best avenue we have for approaching him as a man and a statesman is through the foreign affairs archives at the Quai d'Orsay and the war archives at Vincennes. The dispatches in these depositories provide the best continuous (and perhaps most intimate) record we have of Louis's thoughts and doubts, his triumphs and failures. Insofar as one can penetrate the mind of one of the Old Regime's most powerful and influential men, this is best done by scrutinizing documents that he either wrote himself or closely oversaw in their drafting.

This study is focused upon Louis's foreign policy during roughly one year, 1673, of the Dutch War (1672–78/79). Anyone who wades into the sea of extant documents from Louis's reign must choose some method of setting limits to his researches; as always, the historian must select. The period 1672–74 is remarkable both for the bulk and the intensity of the king's communications with his subordinates within the royal government. Not only did Louis exchange an unusually large number of letters, dispatches, and memoranda with his ministers, diplomats, and generals at this time, but these documents often have an urgency and animation that tell us something of moment was taking place. The first years of the Dutch War are one of the pressure points of Louis's reign, where the historian can most clearly feel the pulse of the ruler and his government. To examine events very closely in the light of large questions is often the most fruitful way for the historian to proceed. This study is narrow in scope, but the problem it treats —the evolution of a limited war into a great war—is deep and universal.

Even in a monographic study, one incurs many debts. I must thank French studies, and Maurice Lee, Jr., who helped me to understand seventeenth-century English politics. Joseph Klaits, Andrew Lossky, and Paul Sonnino read the manuscript of this work with great care, and their remarks helped me avoid many errors of fact and interpretation; those that remain are wholly my responsibility. My greatest debt is to Herbert H. Rowen, who has worked for ten years to clarify my writing—and thus my thinking—on early modern politics. Moreover, he gave unstintingly of his time to aid and encourage me at every stage of my work.

I wish to express my gratitude to Rutgers University, Illinois State University, and the U.S. Steel Foundation for their financial assistance that allowed me to pursue my research in France. Library staffs of many institutions, French and American, have rendered me invaluable assistance over the years, and I wish especially to thank Garold Cole of the Illinois State University Library for his aid with bibliographical questions and with the problems of obtaining needed reference materials. I am also happy to acknowledge the assistance of the secretaries in the Department of History at Illinois State University, led by Dorothy Haeffle, who helped me in typing the early drafts of this study.

Parts of this work that previously appeared in *French Historical Studies*, *Military Affairs*, and the *European History Review* are reproduced with their permission.

A Note on Dates and Sources

By the mid-seventeenth century the Julian calendar was ten days behind the Gregorian calendar. Most European countries, but not Russia, Sweden, or England, had adopted the new calendar. Foreigners residing in England, such as the Venetian and French ambassadors, used the "new style" of their governments in their correspondence. In their letters, Englishmen employed on the Continent as ambassadors or envoys gave either both dates or conformed to the new-style Gregorian calendar. Thus, except where noted (o.s.), all dates in this study are given in the new style.

This study is based principally upon French archival sources. The correspondence of the period, as it comes down to use in the archives, appears in three forms: dispatches that were sent and received, many of which were collected and preserved; *minutes*, or rough drafts of the dispatches, which often show the corrections, deletions, and additions that were incorporated before the final drafting of the dispatches; and *copies du temps*, which are copies made by the royal *commis* of incoming and outgoing dispatches. Often one will find a dispatch in two forms, occasionally in all three. I have used all three forms of correspondence in this study and have seen fit to distinguish them in the notes only when such a distinction is necessary to make a point.

Chronology

1648   Spain and the Dutch make a separate peace; Spain recognizes independence of the Dutch Republic and cedes it some territory beyond the seven northern provinces (including Maastricht) that will henceforth be known as the Generality Lands. Peace of Westphalia: France acquires (Treaty of Münster) sovereignty of Metz, Toul, Verdun, the Hapsburg landgravate of Upper and Lower Alsace, and the governorship (*Landvogtei*) of the ten Alsatian cities (the Decapolis).

1658   Leopold von Hapsburg elected holy Roman emperor, but France maintains influence in the empire through Mazarin's sponsorship of League of the Rhine, designed to protect "German liberties" from Hapsburg power.

1659   Peace of the Pyrenees: Spain cedes to France certain strategic fortresses in Flanders and Artois and returns Roussillon and Cerdagne (Spanish since 1492); marriage arranged between Louis XIV and Maria Teresa, eldest daughter of Philip IV of Spain.

1660   Marriage of Louis XIV and Maria Teresa (Marie Thérèse), who renounces her right to inherit Spanish possessions in return for dowry of 500,000 écus (never paid).

1661   Death of Cardinal Mazarin.

1663   Renewal of League of the Rhine.

1665–67   Second Anglo-Dutch War; France is half-hearted ally of the Dutch. Ended by Treaty of Breda, which conveys New Netherlands in America to England.

1667   Last renewal of League of the Rhine.

1667–68   War of Devolution: Philip IV of Spain had died in 1665, and Louis XIV claims for his wife parts of the Spanish Netherlands on the basis of local law of inheritance (Marie Thérèse was only surviving child of Philip IV's first mar-

[xvii]

riage). At Peace of Aix-la-Chapelle, France acquires 12 fortresses along its northern frontier.

1668   Secret partition treaty between Louis XIV and Leopold I, designed to govern division of Spanish empire upon the death of Carlos II. Triple Alliance of England, Sweden, and Dutch Republic, ostensibly for preventing further French expansion into the Netherlands.

1670   Louis XIV occupies the whole of Lorraine. Louis and Charles II of England sign secret Treaty of Dover in preparation for attack upon the Dutch Republic.

1671   Death of Hugues de Lionne.

1672   *April*: Sweden signs treaty with France, agreeing to aid Louis with an army should war develop in Germany. Louis begins attack on Dutch Republic.
May: Elector Frederick William of Brandenburg commits himself by treaty to send an army to assist the Dutch.
June: The Dutch flood their polders, sealing off Amsterdam and The Hague. Abortive negotiations between French and Dutch in Doesburg.
July: William of Orange appointed stadtholder of Dutch Republic.
August: Johan and Cornelis de Witt murdered by Orangist mob at The Hague.
December: Luxembourg's attempt to attack Amsterdam across ice of the frozen polders fails.

1673   *January–February*: Turenne's campaign in Westphalia; he easily drives back Brandenburgers and Imperials.
1 May: Louis XIV begins his summer campaign.
June: Cologne Peace Conference begins.
21 June: Elector Frederick William of Brandenburg concludes Treaty of Vossem with France, thereby abandoning the war temporarily.
30 June: Maastricht capitulates to Louis XIV.
July: Louis marches into Lorraine and orders Turenne to march his army into Main Valley.
23 July: French troops ordered to occupy electorate of Trier.
21 August: Naval battle of Texel (Kijkduin); the Dutch fleet holds off the combined Anglo-French fleet.
24 August: Louis XIV begins march into Alsace.
28 August: Louis imposes French garrisons on the Alsatian cities.
28–30 August: Alliance of The Hague; the Austrian and Spanish Hapsburgs, Dutch Republic, and duke of Lorraine join in a military alliance to confront Louis XIV.

28 August –7 September: French army successfully besieges city of Trier.

12 September: Prince of Orange retakes Naarden from French.

15 September–15 October: Montecuccoli outmaneuvers Turenne along Main River.

13 October: Louis XIV returns to Saint-Germain.

20 October: War against Spain declared in Paris.

22–23 October: Luxembourg ordered to evacuate most of French-held territory in Dutch Republic.

12 November: Bonn falls to combined armies of Montecuccoli and prince of Orange.

December: Abortive attempt by Turenne to restrict Louvois's power as war minister.

1674   *14 February*: Kidnaping of Wilhelm von Fürstenberg by imperial soldiers in Cologne ends peace conference.

19 February (O.S.): Treaty of Westminster; Charles II of England makes separate peace with Dutch Republic.

22 April: Bishop of Münster makes separate peace with Dutch Republic.

May: Louis XIV personally leads conquering army into Franche-Comté.

11 May: Elector of Cologne makes separate peace with Dutch Republic.

24 May: German Diet in Regensburg declares *Reichskrieg* against France.

1 July: Elector of Brandenburg formally reenters anti-French coalition.

1675   *January*: Sweden finally enters war by marching an army across the Pomeranian frontier into Brandenburg's territory.

28 June: Swedes decisively defeated by Brandenburg at Fehrbellin.

27 July: Turenne killed in Alsace.

1678–79   Treaties of Nijmegen end so-called Dutch War. Spain is big loser, ceding Franche-Comté to France and about a dozen fortified places in Artois, Hainaut, and Flanders; France's eastern frontier is thus extended and its northern frontier consolidated. France acquires Nancy and Longwy in Lorraine, and the emperor cedes Fribourg to France and accepts French interpretation of its sovereignty in Decapolis of Alsace. The Dutch lose no territory and win reduction of French tariffs to the 1664 level.

1679   Pomponne replaced by Colbert de Croissy as French foreign minister.

1680   Paris bestows title "Louis le Grand" on the king.

The Failure of Louis XIV's Dutch War

ᔕᔐᔕ

I

Louis XIV's Politics: Motives, Men, and Issues

The first historian to attempt to discern a leitmotif in Louis XIV's conduct of war and diplomacy was F. A. Mignet, who received the post of chief archivist at the French foreign ministry as his (the scholar's) share of the spoils after the Revolution of 1830. In his work on Louis XIV's reign, Mignet focused upon the overriding political issue of the early modern European state, which was the pursuit of dynastic aggrandizement. This dynasticism of the Old Regime may be defined as the policy of using the resources of the state to promote the power and prestige of the ruling family, although we must recognize that a man like Louis XIV had great difficulty distinguishing his family's interests from the interests of the French state. Mignet in his voluminous study, *Négociations relatives à la succession d'Espagne sous Louis XIV*, saw the whole fabric of Louis's foreign policy emanating from the king's marriage in 1660 to Marie Thérèse, eldest child of King Philip IV of Spain. According to Mignet, Louis XIV sought to enhance the power of his house, the Bourbon family, by advancing first his wife's, then their son's, and ultimately their grandson's claims to various Spanish territories. Thus dynasticism was the basic determinant of French foreign policy for more than half a century. "One can say that the Spanish Succession was the pivot around which revolved almost all of Louis XIV's reign. It occupied his

[3]

foreign policy and his armies for more than fifty years; it gave grandeur to his reign's beginning and misery to its end."[1]

In the twentieth century, the strength of the dynastic drive is difficult for us to comprehend. But Mignet, though he overstates his case, persuades us that this drive must be understood if we hope to unravel the motives of seventeenth-century statesmen. His thesis has been amplified and reinterpreted by a recent authority, who analyzes the origins of the Dutch War largely in terms of Louis's family interest in the Spanish Netherlands.[2] This is the most satisfying thesis yet adduced to explain the king's policies in the period immediately preceding the Dutch War.

Albert Sorel was a historian of the Third Republic, of an era when French scholars as well as politicians were obsessed with the problem of Alsace and Lorraine, territories west of the Rhine River that had been lost to Germany in 1871. Sorel argued that the quest for natural geographic frontiers, including the Rhine River, had been the basis of French foreign policy for centuries, and that French statesmen during the Old Regime had pursued essentially the same goal as French statesmen of the nineteenth century.[3] Sorel's theory has now been utterly discredited[4] but in any case Sorel thought that Louis XIV had not conscientiously pursued the goal of natural frontiers. As a nationalist of the Third Republic, Sorel felt that establishment of natural boundaries was a compelling and honorable task for French statesmen; this was a truly French, a national undertaking. Louis, according to Sorel, perverted this mission ("Louis XIV le denatura") of the French monarchy, for the king swung away from warfare with a logical national orientation and indulged himself in wars of "magnificence." Louis's excesses thus destroyed the "classic system" of moderation and reason that had been created by Richelieu and Mazarin.[5] Sorel's implication that the great cardinal-ministers always sought national goals, in distinction to Louis's more subjective policies, must be questioned. Who, after all, but Mazarin initiated the king's claim to Spanish lands by arranging the Spanish marriage and attempted to gain the imperial crown for his young master in the Reichs election of 1658? These were personal or dynastic rather than national goals. Moreover, Sorel's ideas about the interests of France and those of Louis XIV were very different, for the king, clearly, could not conceive of national interest in the same sense that nineteenth-century republicans did.

Whereas nineteenth-century historians Mignet and Sorel saw political motives of one sort or another (dynastic ambitions or territorial conquests) behind Louis's foreign policy, twentieth-century scholars have turned to new explanations. The impact of two seminal thinkers, Marx and Freud, has profoundly affected historical scholarship. Although as early as 1776 Adam Smith suggested that the Dutch War was "occasioned"[6] by commercial rivalry between the Dutch and the French, the economic interpretation of Louis XIV's foreign policy has been regularly set forth only since Marxist theory came to influence historians' thinking. This interpretation rapidly gained wide acceptance, however, and in the last fifty years has been used more often than any other to explain the coming of the Dutch War in 1672.[7] Most historians agreed with Sagnac and Saint-Léger when, in their volume of the *Peuples et Civilisations* series, they concluded that "the economic conflict led inevitable to war."[8] An American scholar has pointed out the inadequacies in the economic analysis of Louis's foreign policy in the period leading up to the Dutch War,[9] yet as recently as 1966 Pierre Goubert attributed this war largely to Jean-Baptiste Colbert's mercantilist policies and ambitions.[10] No one, however, who is familiar with the French foreign affairs archives finds this a satisfying analysis.

Colbert's writings from the period preceding the Dutch War leave little doubt that he was prepared to wage war with the Hollanders to fulfill his mercantilist plans for creating French economic hegemony in Europe,[11] but it is an error in perception to see Louis XIV's motives in the words of his finance minister, even one so powerful as Colbert. Colbert did not have the dominating influence on the king that he sought, and that too many historians have credited him with. Louis directed his own foreign policy, and economic considerations are seldom if ever mentioned in his dispatches. The more one gets to know Louis's mind at the time of the Dutch War, the more one doubts that he would have waged war principally for economic reasons. Louis had a lively awareness of himself as first gentleman of the realm; in his mind, to have fought for pecuniary profit would have lowered him to the level of a Dutch merchant. Lavisse's appraisal of the origins of the Dutch War, made more than fifty years ago, shows deeper insight into Louis's war policies than does Goubert's recent assessment: "It appears that not one of Louis's wars, except the expeditions against the Barbary pirates, had an economic motive. Even without the commercial rivalry Louis XIV would have attacked the Dutch. England and Holland made war for commercial reasons but not France."[12] And indeed, though Colbert may have approved of the war against Holland at the outset, he changed his mind when he saw how a prolonged war would undercut his plans for French economic development. The last five years of the Dutch War surely did not stem from Colbert's mercantilism.

Gaston Zeller, who shattered Sorel's thesis that the pursuit of natural geographic frontiers was the principal object of French foreign policy even during the Old Regime, approached Louis's policies from a radically different perspective. In a brief and stimulating review-article written in 1931, Zeller sketched his case for looking at Louis's policies by the light of the king's personality and character. Psychological analysis was used to help unravel Napoleon's motives, Zeller wrote; why not use this same tool to help lay bare the springs of Louis's policies?[13] A fellow scholar, Camille Picavet, objected that "the psychology of one man is not sufficient to explain fifty-four years of continuous diplomatic activity,"[14] but Zeller replied that this was not a cogent objection when the man in question was an absolute monarch, who, moreover, formulated his own policy and oversaw its execution.[15] Zeller of course knew that Louis was neither a dictator nor a despot, that his exercise of power was hedged by a panoply of laws and traditions of the French monarchy. But in matters of war and diplomacy, Louis possessed sole if not unlimited authority to set policy and to act. Picavet was correct to point out that not only men but geography, institutions, and traditions contribute to the mix that determines a state's policies. Yet Zeller was also correct to insist that if we know something about the workings of an absolute ruler's mind, we will be in a better position to understand his government's policies.

According to Zeller, then, Louis XIV's personality is a principal key to understanding French foreign policy during the latter half of the seventeenth century. Louis directed his own policy, and he did so chiefly to satisfy his thirst for *gloire*. Other kings in French history had acted similarly (one need only think of Francis I), but Zeller saw an uncommon taste for war in Louis XIV, and he defined his policy as "intimidating the weak and defying the strong."[16] Although Louis's best biographer, John B. Wolf, has discounted the king's famous deathbed remark—"I have loved war too much"—as "the sort of pious advice that old men have given to children for many, many generations,"[17] Zeller found important meaning in the king's words. It is not simply that Louis loved war, according to Zeller, for most kings during the seventeenth century did, but that Louis himself was aware that he had loved war *too* much.[18] This excess in pursuit of glory on the battlefield made Louis XIV an unusual if not unique French king to Zeller. Although Zeller did not devote a major study to his theory and did not deny that there were other contributing motives behind the king's policies, for a quarter of a century he reiterated his thesis that the mainsprings of Louis's policy had to be sought in the psyche of the king himself. He summed up his position in the opening sentence of his *Histoire des relations internationales de Louis XIV à 1789*: "Louis XIV's personality played such a role in the history of his era, it so decisively shaped the future of France and thus the future of Europe, that one must give it a large place in a study of this kind."[19]

Zeller's overriding interest in Louis XIV's personality as the starting point for understanding his foreign policy was obviously the result of Freud's influence on historical analysis. Before Freud, it would have been inconceivable for a historian to suggest that "the different problems that are posed boil down to a psychological problem."[20] Nonetheless, Louis's contemporaries were aware of the important bearing the king's personality had on European affairs. Bishop Gilbert Burnet had Louis in mind when he remarked that Johan de Witt, the Dutch statesman, "did not consider enough how passions, amours, humors, and opinions wrought on the world, chiefly on princes."[21] At the same time, the English diplomat Sir William Temple hazarded a prophecy, and his extended metaphor leaves no doubt that he was thinking of Louis when he wrote about France: "What the aims of France are . . . I will not pretend to judge; . . . nor perhaps can any one tell any more than a man that leaps into the water in strength and vigour, and with pleasure, can say how far he will swim; which will be, till he is stopped by currents or accidents, or grows weary, or has a mind to do something else."[22] Thus Temple saw the French kingdom as led by a young, vigorous, and aggressive king who would use the French state as an instrument to pursue his personal trials of strength with the other potentates of Europe. The English diplomat perceived that one of the components in Louis's policies was the very pleasure the king derived from exercising his power, and Temple was both intrigued and disquieted by the potentially capricious quality of absolute rule. Although the word psychological had not been coined in the seventeenth century, Louis XIV's contemporaries did not underestimate the importance of the king's mental and emotional makeup in determining French policies and, therefore, Europe's fortunes.

One of the least controversial issues concerning Louis XIV's foreign policy is whether the king was master in his own government. Did he personally control the policy that issued from the royal council? Although Louis may have entrusted domestic affairs almost entirely to his secretaries of state, historians agree that he was careful to guard his prerogatives in foreign affairs. Louis worked hard at his diplomacy, having correspondence read to him in council and directly overseeing the drafting of the most important outgoing dispatches.[23] However, until the death of Hugues de Lionne in the autumn of 1671, the role of foreign minister was substantive. Because of his brilliance, his diligence, and his experience, and because he was a direct "bequest" to Louis from Mazarin, the king's father-surrogate, Lionne usually participated in making policy.[24] But after Lionne's death, Simon Nicolas Arnauld de Pomponne, a member of the famous Jansenist family and an experienced diplomat, was named to head the royal foreign ministry. The Savoyard ambassador to France remarked that "M. de Pomponne . . . is civil, learned, and intelligent, but he is timorous and lacks the expedients and general knowledge of affairs that his predecessor had."[25] Primi Visconti, the Italian adventurer, was another astute observer of Louis XIV's government; he wrote that "Pomponne was soft (*doux*). . . . Pomponne did not have the vigor of Colbert or Louvois in the ministry."[26] Whether Louis wished to assume greater authority in foreign affairs and thus appointed a less forceful person to succeed Lionne, or whether the weakening of the foreign minister's position was simply the inevitable result of the "soft" Pomponne's appointment, is not clear. Louis was often a good judge of men, and he perhaps selected Pomponne to head his foreign ministry because he valued Pomponne's adroitness in composing diplomatic correspondence and because he was carving out a larger role for himself in foreign affairs. Pomponne, the king probably thought, would be ideal, not for formulating policy but for presenting royal policy to Europe in the smoothest and most palatable fashion. Moreover, it was not apparent, when Pomponne was appointed, that his view of the European states' system was quite different from his sovereign's. In any event, Louis named Pomponne to succeed Lionne just before the outbreak of the Dutch War, and the role of foreign minister in shaping French policies declined sharply.

The *conseil d'en haut* was the organ in Louis XIV's government that dealt principally, though not exclusively, with foreign affairs. The king sat in this council with his ministers of state, and often with the important royal generals, to deliberate on affairs of state; after full debate and presentation of diverse opinions, Louis made the ultimate decisions. Although Louis had the last word, the council tended to keep him anchored to the traditional aims and policies of the French monarchy. Many who sat in the council during the first decade of Louis's personal rule had been bequeathed to the king by Mazarin, and in several instances even by Richelieu. This conciliar method of formulating foreign policy was characteristic of the first ten years of Louis's rule and helped to keep his policies within the classic framework established by the two cardinal-ministers. But this pattern changed radically during the first year of the Dutch War, and by the summer of 1673 the *conseil d'en haut* was not really functioning. Colbert was preoccupied, overseeing royal finances and the construction of the new chateau at Versailles, and Michel Le Tellier was convalescing from a stroke he had suffered in December 1672. The rump of the High Council that accompanied Louis's campaign in 1673 consisted only of the king, Louvois, and Pomponne. The latter, however, was distinctly a lesser member of the triumvirate. During the summer of 1673, Louis XIV and Louvois ruled France, and their decisions, made during the campaign, helped shape the course of European history for fifty years.

The Dutch War has not attracted the attention that historians have devoted to the "world wars" of 1688–97 and 1702–13, yet it is in certain respects the most important of Louis XIV's wars. Pierre Goubert remarks that Louis's attack upon the Dutch Republic in 1672 was the "first decisive act of his reign, perhaps his crucial moment."[27] The attack was fateful not only because it began a long and exhausting conflict but because it marked the beginning of the series of great wars that for forty years drained the physical and moral resources of the French state. Thus Robert Mandrou sees the Dutch War as an important turning point in Louis's reign: "*Nec pluribus impar*, Louis XIV dominated Europe for some years at the beginning of his reign. But that hegemony over continental Europe was threatened when the Dutch War was prolonged."[28] It is to oversimplify to divide Louis XIV's reign into two distinct parts, the first notable for internal reform and the second for foreign wars, but perhaps such a dichotomy is useful for understanding the dynamics of Louis's reign.

The War of Devolution (1667–68) had been a test. Louis supported his queen's hereditary claims to parts of the Spanish Netherlands, but he had been willing to satisfy those claims through negotiations rather than by war, and he accepted peace at Aix-la-Chapelle in 1668.[29] The Dutch War was a different matter. Louis anticipated a brief, decisive war, but, as events were to show, he was willing to commit himself and his realm to a full-scale war of attrition against a coalition of powers. Emmanuel Le Roy Ladurie, in his magisterial study of the economy of Languedoc in the seventeenth century, has remarked upon "the causal role of the Dutch War, strangler of commerce, in triggering the decline in the gross national product. The Dutch War, in provoking the fall in French exports, increased the persistent scarcity of money."[30] François Fénelon, who became archbishop of Cambrai and tutor to the duke of Burgundy, Louis XIV's eldest grandson, was the most outspoken contemporary critic of the king's war policies. When, during the War of the League of Augsburg, Fénelon wrote his impassioned, anonymous letter to Louis deploring the condition of the realm and the French people, he singled out the Dutch War as the origin of France's problems: "The frightful troubles that have desolated Europe for more than twenty years, the blood spilt, the scandals, the ravaged provinces, the cities and towns reduced to ashes, all this [was] caused by that war of 1672. . . . It is the true source of all of France's ills."[31] Because of his religious and social convictions, Fénelon was opposed to warfare in general, and he overstated his indictment of the Dutch War. Nonetheless, his famous letter is evidence that the king's contemporaries saw this war as a watershed in his reign.[32] The attack upon the United Provinces in 1672 was Louis's debut in arms, in which he hoped to display the martial qualities that would give eternal luster to his reign.

Historians now agree that it is fatuous to search for a single governing motive behind Louis XIV's conduct of war and diplomacy; his reign was too long and the king too complex a person for so simple an analysis. But the problem of determining what mixture of motives lay behind the king's policies during critical periods of his reign is nevertheless important and largely unresolved. This study approaches this problem by attempting to accomplish two related tasks. The first is to analyze the failure of French policy at the time the so-called Dutch War was evolving into a larger and more generalized conflict. The second is to explain how Louis and his young war minister, Louvois, increasingly monopolized the direction of war and diplomacy, to the exclusion of the other ministers of state and the diplomatic corps in general; to show how, by cutting themselves off from the traditional goals of French foreign policy, Louis and Louvois brought on the reign's first great war of attrition.

This book is a case study of an escalating military adventure, of Louis XIV's groping and stumbling from the Dutch to a European war.

Marquis de Pomponne (1618–1619),
engraving by Robert Nanteuil
(*courtesy of Roger-Viollet*)

∽∽∽

II

The King's Campaign: Maastricht, Trier, and Alsace

When Louis XIV and his allies launched their attack upon the Republic of the United Provinces in the spring of 1672, it appeared to all of Europe that the French king's vengeance upon the Dutch "ingrates" would be swift and total.[1] The apparent diplomatic isolation of the Dutch, Louis's splendid armies, and the combined Anglo-French naval power all gave assurance that the Dutch Republic would be destroyed; only a satellite state, vulnerable to the whims of the French and English monarchs, would remain.[2] Against all odds, the Dutch survived the onslaught. In desperation the Dutchmen opened the sluices and flooded their polders, preferring to give their land back to the rivers than permit the French to conquer it; the rich agricultural land could always be pumped dry and rehabilitated, but the Frenchmen might come to stay. During the last week in June 1672, the States General of the Dutch Republic sent delegates to discuss peace with Louis XIV's ministers at the king's headquarters near Doesburg in Dutch Gelderland.[3] The Frenchmen, either because they were unaware of how the flooded countryside would cripple their military operations or because they expected the Dutchmen's morale to collapse, scorned the Dutch offers and missed an opportunity to gain a profitable peace.[4] Then, within a matter of days, the waters had risen enough to stop the French armies altogether; Amsterdam and The Hague, the key cities of the Dutch Republic, lay secure behind the flooded polders of the provinces of Utrecht and Holland.

The first phase of Louis XIV's Dutch War, which had begun with such *éclat* and promise of total success, thus ended in a dilemma: where could the king's aggressive energies be channeled after his attack upon the Dutch Netherlands had stalled in the flooded fields of Holland? After the French king had been frustrated by the tenacity of the Dutchmen, which he grudgingly admired,[5] a peculiar hiatus in the war of 1672–1678/79 developed. Louis, to ruminate over his frustrating situation and to cast about for new opportunities to indulge his taste for war, returned to Saint-Germain on 1 August, long before the customary campaigning season ended. The striking success of the opening attack on the Dutch in June 1672 had stimulated the king's desire to lead an army, and at the turn of the year 1673, he was open to suggestions about where he might direct the thrust of his next campaign. That there would be another campaign was never in doubt, for the king had no intention of stopping a war that he so thoroughly enjoyed.

During December 1672 and January 1673 the three preeminent French soldiers of the time, the prince of Condé, the vicomte de Turenne, and Sébastien le Prestre de Vauban, sent their recommendations to the court. Louis XIV had land forces totaling approximately 120,000 men, including infantry and cavalry, to defend his realm and to continue the war. Everyone agreed that some troops had to be stationed at the vulnerable gateways into the kingdom: 8,000 in Roussillon on the southern frontier, 5,000–7,000 in Lorraine on the eastern frontier, and 1,000 in Pignerol on the Italian frontier. But the three largest blocks of troops would be deployed to hold the French conquests in the Dutch Netherlands, to cope with the imperial army in Germany, and to face the Spaniards in Flanders. Turenne suggested that the largest of these three armies remain in Holland to continue the war of the preceding year.[6] In a well-known letter to Louvois, Vauban urged that the king use the coming campaign to clear up the "pell-mell" of fortresses and enclaves that, since the Peace of Aix-la-Chapelle (1668), had constituted the frontier between France and the Spanish Netherlands. The fortifications expert was thinking primarily in defensive terms, of a fortress France.[7] Louis XIV was not yet ready for his idea, and Vauban's suggestion was taken up only years later. Condé's recommendations are the most interesting. With more foresight than Turenne, the prince apparently saw in December 1672 that the Dutch War was finished; the flooded polders and logistical difficulties made its pursual impossible. Condé, who was a veteran of the wars in Flanders and had fought on both the French and Spanish sides, saw the Spanish Netherlands as the basic problem. He suggested massing 50,000 French soldiers in Flanders, which, in his words, "would cut this war by the roots."[8]

Late in January 1673 Louis decided to deploy his forces more in accordance with Turenne's suggestions than Condé's, allotting 48,000 men for Holland and 30,000 each for Germany and Flanders.[9] The king's decision to apportion his troops in this way tells us several things about the state of the so-called Dutch War at the turn of the year 1673. Louis had as yet no intention of relaxing his grip upon the Dutch merely because his armies had mired down in the flooded polders; he was deploying his largest army in the Dutch Netherlands, both to occupy the territory conquered in 1672 and to extend the conquests. Nevertheless, the king could no longer focus his attention exclusively upon the Dutch; the war was becoming more generalized and more complex, and Louis was not sure which way it might turn in the coming year's campaign. In January, he was not yet prepared to accept Condé's suggestion and turn the brunt of the war against the Spaniards, but he had not forgotten the Spanish Netherlands, and a sizable army would be maintained in Flanders. Finally, to prevent the Imperials from interfering with his designs on the Netherlands, Louis would count on Turenne, who was about to begin a winter campaign in the empire.[10]

Thus early in 1673 Louis XIV's plans for the coming campaign were still diffuse; he was biding his time, keeping his options open and conforming to his dictum *Je verrai*—"I shall see." Despite the high waters in the Low Countries, everything seemed to conspire for the continued success of Louis's war. A contemporary remarked; "The king has never been better served. He has great ministers who think only of his *gloire* and his best interests. . . . He has a number of great generals who are all submissive and just as obedient as the rest of the realm. Everyone fears him and everyone is working."[11] Who could have foreseen in March 1673 that these advantages did not bring the success they portended and that within six months Louis would be left with more chagrin and frustation than glory?

Why did Louis XIV decide to attack Maastricht, the Dutch fortress that commanded the lower Meuse Valley, as his opening move of the 1673 campaign? First, let us look at the king's description of his decision to lay siege to Maastricht, which, although not written until 1679, tells us much about Louis's thinking during the 1670s:

> I took care . . . that my troops recovered from . . . the campaign [of 1672]. . . . In working for her France, I was serving myself, and it was sweet to see my glory blended with a state as powerful and rich as this realm. But fully to enjoy my good luck I had to make big plans that would succeed on all fronts.
>
> I was involved with the Germans [only Brandenburg and the emperor in early 1673] and with the Dutch. The Spaniards were surely my enemies, but not openly. Therefore I dissimulated with them, wishing that they should be the first to begin war. I had carried my conquests so far in 1672 that I feared not being able to do something in 1673 that could compare with what I had already done; moreover they [i.e. the conquests of 1672] were far from my realm, and I had no sure route by which to protect them. Only Maastricht would do. . . . I created three armies, one under my command, another under the Prince of Condé, and a third led by Marshal Turenne, who was in Germany to observe the army of the emperor and his allies. I sent the Prince of Condé into Holland to keep my enemies occupied and I decided to lead my own army. . . . I decided to attack Maastricht.[12]

A careful reading of these candid sentences from Louis's military memoirs reveals much about Louis the man and his plans for the campaign of 1673. First, in a general sense, the king was determined not to rest complacently as a result of his success in 1672. The campaign of 1673 would be equally spectacular and "big plans" were necessary. Then Louis enumerated several reasons for striking at Maastricht: it was the only Dutch possession vulnerable to attack, because the flooded polders sheltered the unconquered provinces of Holland and Zeeland, and yet worthy of comparison with the conquests of 1672; it was strategically important because it commanded the middle reaches of the Meuse River, whose valley provided the best route from France to the French-occupied territories of the Dutch Netherlands; it was an opportunity for the king to lead a campaign entirely on his own, keeping Condé and Turenne stationed a circumspect distance away from the center of the action.

John B. Wolf, who is a sensitive biographer of the king, picked up Louis's last remark and suggested that "the prospect of commanding an army without the tutelage of these 'great' generals [Condé and Turenne] determined his decision."[13] One feels that Wolf has with this comment cut close to the core of Louis's personality, that he is correct in stressing the role played by the king's inner needs when the decision was made to besiege Maastricht. Indeed, members of the king's government had a lively awareness of the subjective nature of Louis's war plans in spring 1673. One of the most astute of the royal diplomats, Honoré Courtin, wrote to the prince of Condé in May and warned him allusively about Louis's apparent intention to dominate the action of the 1673 campaign: "Your Highness should be careful not to advance by your own actions; this might detract from your *gloire*. If you cross the water [surrounding Amsterdam and The Hague], . . . it could be the shortest route to Chantilly."[14] In other words, Courtin was informing Condé that any military exploit of his that might divert public attention from the king's campaign could well result in the removal of the prince from his command and his exile to his château at Chantilly. Louis's taste for siege warfare in general and his particular desire to attack Maastricht probably stemmed from the king's craving for military glory on the one hand and, on the other, from his lack of ability as a field commander. With a siege, Louis could have Vauban and his engineers defeat the enemy, while the king, as titular chief of the operation, received the honors for it. It was a good solution and, for Louis, had the added advantage of being less bloody than a showdown on the open battlefield; he always liked to avoid squandering his soldiers' lives in pitched battles.

The fortified city of Maastricht had been garrisoned by the Dutch ever since Prince Frederick Henry of Orange captured it from the Spaniards in 1632. In 1648, when Spain recognized the independence of the Dutch Republic, Maastricht was ceded to the republic as part of the Generality Lands, that is, the common territories beyond the seven sovereign provinces of the north. However, the *de jure* sovereignty of the city continued to be shared with the bishop of Liège. Now, in 1673, this bishop was an electoral prince, Max Heinrich of Cologne, who was one of Louis XIV's allies in his war upon the Dutch. The French armies bypassed Maastricht in the onslaught of 1672, but the conquest of the city and its delivery to Cologne had been central points in the offensive alliance that Louis XIV and Max Heinrich had contracted before they attacked the Dutch Republic.[15] Louis, however, had no intention of conducting a costly siege of Maastricht, only to relinquish the prize to his ally, Max Heinrich. The elector would somehow have to be finessed and persuaded to allow the French to retain possession of the fortress, should they conquer it.

In spring 1673, Louis's opportunity presented itself. Franz Egon von Fürstenberg was, with his younger brother Wilhelm Egon, both minister to the elector of Cologne and Louis XIV's hired diplomatic agent.[16] In April 1673 Franz Egon was playing the honest advocate for the elector, and he complained repeatedly to Louvois about the problems that the Dutch garrison in Maastricht created for Cologne. "That thorn [Maastricht] must be removed. . . . The Maastrichters continue . . . not only to demand contributions but to conduct . . . marauding operations in the countryside."[17] Franz Egon seems unwittingly to have walked right into the French snare. Early in May, Louvois wrote craftily to Fürstenberg, informing him that Louis was not planning to go after Maastricht and that Franz Egon should know "very well" why the king preferred other projects, since Elector Max Heinrich wanted the French to seize the city but then deliver it to the elector as bishop of Liège. Louvois concluded by telling Franz Egon that if he wanted Louis even to consider attacking Maastricht, it was up to him to persuade the elector of Cologne to agree that the fortress, if taken, should become a French possession.[18] The denouement of the French stratagem occurred when the French diplomat, Honoré Courtin, met with Franz Egon in Brühl, just outside Cologne; Courtin recounted the conversation to Louis XIV with relish. Franz Egon "finally got around to talking about what really bothered him and admitted an urgent desire to have Maastricht taken. I explained to him the great difficulties involved, and after having emphasized them for some time, . . . I asked him if he thought that Your Majesty should have so many heads broken and expose his sacred person to danger simply to take a fortress that he could not keep. . . . Then he agreed [that] expedients could be found to leave Maastricht in Your Majesty's hands."[19]

When Wilhelm Egon von Fürstenberg visited the French encampment near Maastricht in early June, he signed a new treaty with Louis on behalf of the elector of Cologne. A principal clause of the treaty provided that Maastricht, when taken, would become a French possession.[20] Louis manipulated Elector Max Heinrich remarkably well during the first stages of the Dutch War, but the king's unthinking disregard for his allies' interest would ultimately cancel the dividends earned by diplomatic manipulation. Louis was mistaken in thinking that he could always deceive his allies.

On 1 May 1673, Louis XIV gathered his army, his queen, and two mistresses and left Saint-Germain for the northern frontier. "Never was there a more splendid army,"[21] wrote Pomponne, the foreign minister, who, together with the king and Louvois, made up the royal council for the duration of the 1673 campaign. In mid-May, Louis sent the women to Tournai, in French Flanders, to follow the campaign from a safe distance, and led his army across the frontier into the Spanish Netherlands. During the Old Regime, jurists debated whether harmless passage (*transitus innoxius*) through neutral territory was permissible according to natural law,[22] but Louis XIV took no chances; he persuaded his ally, Charles II of England, to issue a written declaration stipulating that Louis could never be guilty of breaking the Peace of Aix-la-Chapelle because the count of Monterey, governor of the Spanish Netherlands, had violated French territory when he lent aid to the Dutch during the siege of Charleroi in December 1672.[23] Although Monterey sent an emissary to welcome Louis to Spanish territory,[24] the contrived civility of baroque etiquette could not disguise the fact that the French were a threatening force. That, indeed, was precisely the impression the king wished to give. By maneuvering across the Spanish Netherlands, Louis hoped to mask his intentions and prevent the Dutch from reinforcing their garrison in Maastricht. The army, under the king's direct command, moved down the Scheldt River and threatened Ghent. Then, turning eastward during the first week in June, the French marched toward Brussels in yet another feint. Paul Pellisson, who was then the royal historiographer, tells us that after the dreary fare of the campaign trail the fresh sole, salmon, and sturgeon that were bought in Brussels were a special treat and compensated for the cold weather.[25]

From Brussels, Louis moved swiftly east toward Maastricht; the court camped at Vossem (6 June) and then at Kerkum (9 June), while Louis's army invested Maastricht proper and a detachment from Turenne's army of the Rhine swept down on Wijk, the *faubourg* across the Meuse River from the main citadel. This was the type of operation that Louis XIV loved: personal command of a splendid army; his women watching from the sidelines; a slap in the face for the Spaniard; and an elaborate charade to outwit the Dutch. The first six weeks of the 1673 campaign were no more troublesome than a hunting expedition in one of the royal forests, and much more exhilarating for the king.

The French force that engulfed Maastricht was massive, numbering perhaps 40,000 men. Under Vauban's methodical direction the siege progressed rapidly, if perhaps without the *éclat* that Louis XIV might have desired. In his military memoirs the king took most of the credit for the success of the siege, although he was generous enough to mention the lowborn Vauban once: "The general officers and the engineers at first disagreed; but after the enemy had been contained and there was a good view of things generally, Vauban proposed what I thought to be the best approach." [26] In other words, once the infantry and cavalry had swept clear the countryside surrounding the citadel, Vauban's lowly engineers, the sappers and artillerists, proceeded with the siege itself. Vauban's promising young assistant, Paul, and the famous musketeer, d'Artagnan, were killed, although French casualties as a whole were slight. Several errant cannonballs landed among the tents of the French court and generated excitement, but in reality the siege was a gigantic, well-orchestrated spectacle, which Louis took the care to have recorded for posterity by the famous Flemish painter of battle scenes, Adam François van der Meulen.[27]

Charles of England's bastard son, the duke of Monmouth, participated with his friend, John Churchill, and although the dashing young duke became the momentary darling of the Parisians, he was not the kind of person who enjoyed slogging in muddy trenches. Monmouth described trench warfare in his quaint English: "Tis sutch rainy weather that in the trench we are up to the knees in water which is not very comfortabell espetially when wee ar to stay 24 houers in the trench beefor wee ar relived."[28] In fact, even late in June, when the siege was approaching its end, Vauban was worried that the "foot to a foot and a half of water"[29] in the trenches might undermine the earthworks and thereby jeopardize the entire operation. But Vauban's worries were simply those of a meticulous engineer who remained vigilant and fretful right to the end of the project. Within two days, on 30 June at

6:30 a.m., Louis XIV was awakened by his aide-de-camp with the news that the garrison in Maastricht wished to surrender the city. Because the Dutch defenders had not stubbornly resisted beyond the reasonable point prescribed by seventeenth-century rules of warfare, they were allowed to leave the citadel honorably on 2 July and march to 's-Hertogenbosch in the Generality Lands, leaving their wounded behind.[30]

Compared to the other great sieges of the seventeenth century, Louis's siege of Maastricht in 1673 was remarkably brief. When the Dutch had taken Maastricht from the Spaniards in 1632, Frederick Henry, who was no mean military figure, required three months to reduce the fortress. In 1579, the great Parma needed four months to take it from the Dutch rebels. On the day of the capitulation, Louis wrote to the commander of his Atlantic fleet: "I am pleased to inform you that the city of Maastricht has submitted to me only thirteen days after the trenches were opened, and that I have had the satisfaction of conquering in so few days this important fortress, which has in the past held out three full months against the largest armies in Europe."[31] The king was obviously interested in how future historians would judge him, and he had gathered enough historical data so that he could make self-flattering comparisons with victorious generals from the past.

Colbert, the minister who had been left behind to attend to the king's finances and other domestic projects, informed Louis about the reaction in Paris to the French conquest of Maastricht: "Paris has never been so jubilant. On Sunday evening, the bourgeois, on their own initiative, without being ordered, lit bonfires of joy."[32] Colbert's letters show that he was carefully observing the middle classes, whose monies were financing the war. But, more interestingly, the congratulatory letter also reveals Colbert's surprise at the spontaneous celebration generated in Paris by the king's victory at Maastricht; apparently it was already usual for the royal government to promote and orchestrate such events to assure broad public support for the king's policies. Under Louis XIV's guidance, the French state was indeed taking on modern characteristics.

As the news of Maastricht's fall spread, European statesmen began to assess the effect that this French victory would have on the military and diplomatic situation in western Europe. Pieter de Groot, the exiled diplomat from the States party in Holland, thought that Maastricht's fall would demoralize the Dutch and compel them to assent to French demands.[33] The French were more immediately concerned with the effects their victory would produce in Germany, for if the Dutch could be kept isolated and deprived of any aid from the empire, the war in the Low Countries would inevitably end well for the French. According to Louvois, the king expected his victory to serve his interests in the empire: "The besieged in Maastricht have asked for terms, and . . . the king thinks you [Turenne] should spread this news far and wide in Germany, where it can produce only good effects."[34] Robert de Gravel, the French envoy at the Imperial Diet in Regensburg,[35] assured Pomponne that "the capture of one of the strongest and most important fortresses in Europe is glorious for His Majesty and will also serve to maintain some persons in their commitments and thus to sustain His Majesty's interests in Germany."[36] Gravel was prophesying that the French show of strength at Maastricht would keep the various German princes in line, compelling them either to adhere to their alliances with Louis XIV or, at worst, to remain neutral. The policies of the German princes, however, depended heavily upon the policy of the emperor. Thus another French diplomat in Germany, Honoré Courtin, succinctly expressed the most important effect that the fall of Maastricht could produce in Europe: "The capture of Maastricht, if I am not mistaken, will change the resolution of the Viennese court."[37] If Emperor Leopold did not march to assist the Dutch, no one would, and the Dutch would be left at the mercy of Louis XIV.

On 2 July, two days after the garrison in Maastricht had formally capitulated, Louis XIV entered the citadel. This must have been one of the great moments in the life of a king who longed to be a great captain like his grandfather Henry IV. During the next several days, Louis proudly inspected his prize and gave orders to the newly installed French garrison. He then "cast his eyes" on Godefroi, count d'Estrades, for the governorship and was ready to leave Maastricht.[38] By the end of the first week in July, the king and his itinerant court had moved south, up the Meuse River, to a new encampment between Maastricht and Liège. Where would the French juggernaut roll after having reduced Maastricht with such ease? That was the question that preoccupied European statesmen in July 1673.

Louis XIV did not linger at Maastricht because he had already decided upon a bold reorientation of his movements. The king probably had several reasons for beginning an essentially new campaign in midsummer 1673. Once Maastricht had fallen there was little the French could undertake against the Dutch, who were still protected by the flooded polders. Although Louvois ordered Condé to proceed into Holland beyond Utrecht,[39] Condé's reports were pessimistic; heavy spring rains were steadily raising the water level in the Low Countries.[40] One possibility, to help the English establish a beachhead on the coast, was an unpleasant alternative for the French, and would antagonize Sweden;[41] neither the French nor the Swedes wanted the English established in the Low Countries. Furthermore, there was the problem of Germany; what would happen there, and how large an army would the French need to hold their position and their allies? Louis's dilemma as the end of the siege at Maastricht approached was summed up by Louvois in a letter to his father, Le Tellier: "His Majesty is no longer troubled except by what to do with his armies after the siege of Maastricht," and he added that if things remained quiet in Germany and the Spaniards gave Louis no cause to invade the Spanish Netherlands, "His Majesty may be obliged to withdraw all of his armies to this [the western] side of the Rhine."[42]

The French king had so many advantages that he did not know how to use them effectively, and, as often happens in such cases, he squandered them and ultimately wound up short. Louvois's letter also shows us what Louis was thinking as the siege at Maastricht ended. The imminent victory had only sharpened the king's desire for action and he craved further exploits on one front or another; he was eager for war with Spain, if only the count of Monterey, governor of the Spanish Netherlands, would do him the favor of starting it; he was done pursuing the Dutch for the time being because their lands were either occupied by French soldiers or were protected by the water barrier of the flooded polders.

When Monterey, who was held in check by the Spanish government in Madrid, could not meet the challenge of combat in Flanders, Louis decided to lead his army toward the Moselle River and begin maneuvers along the eastern frontier. Although Louis's eagerness for action made his motives for marching southeastward profoundly subjective, his justification for the march was neither capricious nor flippant. In long letters to Condé and Turenne,

Louvois explained what he and the king had planned at a crucial conference at Maastricht on either 30 June or 1 July:[43] 6,000 men would be left to garrison Maastricht; four squadrons of cavalry, under Marshal Humières, would hold Flanders; General Luxembourg would remain with his cavalry in and around Utrecht; Condé would leave Utrecht and move south into Dutch Brabant to secure it for France; and most of the cavalry that Turenne had lent for the siege would be returned to strengthen his army in Germany. As for Louis himself, he would march into Lorraine by way of Luxembourg, station most of his cavalry in the electorate of Trier, have a pontoon bridge built across the Rhine at Philippsburg,[44] and then retire to Nancy, where his infantry could improve the fortifications. Louvois explained to Turenne that the king considered the Spaniards and the Dutch basically impotent, but that he would not push the Dutch so hard that they would have to cede the fortified coastal towns demanded by the English, "which His Majesty would find quite contrary to his interests." Louis thus calculated that Charles II of England would soon reduce his demands at the peace conference and that the Dutch, "seeing no relief for their troubles," would have to accept peace on French terms.[45]

Louis's plans look sound enough, if perhaps he was a bit complacent. Safeguarding the conquest of Lorraine and providing support for Turenne in Germany, which, it must be stressed, Louvois cited as the principal reasons for the march southeastward, were obvious necessities when the emperor was the most imminent threat to Louis's expansionistic policy. Yet neither Louis nor Louvois seems to have perceived that their plans of 1 July were strategically weak; Louis's armies would be strung thinly over vast distances, from the North Sea to the Franche-Comté of Burgundy, while another force had to be kept in Roussillon to block the Spaniards' entryway to the Midi through the passes of the Eastern Pyrenees. Moreover, Louis made the mistake of thinking that Charles II could be manipulated as easily as the elector of Cologne and kept as an ally while one of his chief objectives of the war, a foothold on the Dutch coast, was denied him.[46] By 1674, Louis XIV, who liked to think he could always buy allies, stood almost alone, as stripped of his allies as the Dutch had been of theirs two years before.

Preceded by Louvois, who went ahead to reconnoiter the valley of the Moselle, Louis set out southward from the vicinity of

Maastricht on 12 July.[47] Following a roundabout route because of rough terrain and bad weather, Louis and his immediate entourage moved across countryside that is elegiac now with soldiers' graves of later, larger wars but was then merely idyllic, with alternating pastures, vineyards, and forests; the open land of the northern European plain gave way to the Ardennes, and then to the picturesque ruggedness of the Moselle watershed. The French king's destination was Thionville, on the Moselle River below Metz and just above the electorate of Trier.

Louis's decision to change the theater of war in order to pursue an active and personal military policy was one of the major developments of the Dutch War. Instead of provocatively leading an army to the eastern frontier (French kings traditionally traveled to the frontiers of the realm only for momentous occasions), Louis might have left an army in eastern France to support Turenne in Germany and might have returned to Saint-Germain to try to obtain a satisfactory settlement from the Dutch through diplomacy. Thus he could have sufficiently chastened the Dutch "herring-mongers" and still have provided himself a strategic position for a future attack upon the Spanish Netherlands. The Spanish Netherlands, unlike Holland, was a logical strategic objective for the French state. It was weak and accessible, as Turenne had demonstrated in 1667, and it would have served French interests to push back the northern frontier, making Paris less vulnerable. But this was not Louis XIV's style in 1673; he had to achieve his *gloire* not through the arguments of distant diplomats but by himself on horseback. Nothing characterizes the youthful Louis better than this restless activism; not content to wait patiently for results, he wanted to grasp them immediately. And when the king turned from Maastricht and marched southeastward toward Alsace and the empire, he was opening a new phase in the Dutch War.

Robert de Gravel, the French diplomat most experienced in German affairs, disagreed with the king's decision. He wrote to Louis from his post at the Imperial Diet in Regensburg to make his case, suggesting that Louis should not press toward the Moselle until Vienna's reaction to the fall of Maastricht became known. Gravel argued that this French victory should help persuade the emperor not to send an army across Germany to assist the Dutch, and that if Louis would pause, instead of pushing down the Moselle Valley, he "could prevent the rumors that the Imperials will certainly stir up about this new advance and gain some time, which we very much need these days."[48] Gravel had no scruples about using armed force to support diplomacy, and he sometimes favored military intimidation to keep the German princes in line with French policy, yet he was uneasy about Louis's plan to march an army toward the electorate of Trier. When Gravel's dispatch was read to him, the king must have been baffled or amused by the diplomat's rather cryptic comment about the French having need for time, for a breathing space. After his conquest of Maastricht, Louis saw no need to let the situation develop passively; he wanted to press on with his campaign. Gravel, on the other hand, felt that, after the moral and strategic victory at Maastricht, Louis should not advance, but rather negotiate a favorable peace from the Dutch before alarming the Germans by marching a threatening force into the valley of the Moselle. Gravel, unlike Louis XIV and Louvois, did not underestimate the difficulties that the Germans might cause for the king's policies. By the end of the campaign, Gravel's arguments would be wholly vindicated.

In the royal government, each of Louis's four secretaries of state, in addition to their duties defined by function (war, marine, foreign affairs, royal household), had jurisdiction over a number of provinces within the realm. Louis's aggressive new policy on the eastern frontier was signaled at this time, when Alsace and Lorraine were formally transferred from the jurisdiction of the secretary for foreign affairs to the secretary for war, who of course was Louvois.[49]

During the first week of July 1673, Louvois left the king and the royal army and proceeded to Nancy, the capital of Lorraine. After making a brief tour of inspection of the province, Louvois rejoined the king at Thionville on 22 July, and on the following day orders were sent out, over the war minister's signature, that began a new phase in the Dutch War. The chevalier de Fourilles, who commanded the largest body of cavalry in Louis's army, was ordered to lead his men into the archbishopric of Trier and bivouac them throughout the countryside; he was to intercept commerce on the Moselle River, the economic lifeline of the archbishopric, to provide supplies for his men. Although Fourilles was not to attack the city of Trier and was admonished to maintain tight disciplinary rein on his troops, the orders dispatched by Louvois on 23 July were for a veritable military occupation of an electorate of the empire whose government had not taken up arms against France.[50]

Why did Louis XIV decide to engage himself hostilely with the empire by moving against Trier when he had not concluded his war in the Low Countries? Four days after Fourilles's marching orders were sent out, the king, almost as an afterthought, it appears, ordered Pomponne to draft instructions for a special envoy to the elector of Mainz.[51] The venerable Elector Johann Philipp von Schönborn, the "German Solomon," had died in the winter of 1673.[52] Nonetheless, the new elector, Lothar Friedrich von Metternich, was also the archchancellor of the empire and one of the important neutral princes in Germany, and Louis was sending an envoy to Mainz to explain his actions against Trier after his soldiers had begun to occupy the electorate. The king thought he could well afford to act first and provide explanations later. Louis's envoy, the marquis d'Arcy, was instructed to inform the elector of Mainz that the French occupation of Trier was justified might have left an army in eastern France to support Turenne in Germany and might have returned to Saint-Germain to try to obtain a satisfactory settlement from Dutch through diplomacy. Thus he could have sufficiently chastened the Dutch "herring-troops garrisoned in Koblenz and Ehrenbreitstein, two fortresses that belonged to the elector of Trier and commanded the strategic confluence of the Rhine and Moselle rivers, which, to Louis XIV, meant that Emperor Leopold was preparing for war by securing allies on the vulnerable eastern flank of France. Louis therefore decided "to defend himself against the danger presented by the elector's territories by stationing some troops in the Archbishopric of Trier."[54]

The marquis d'Arcy was thus to go to the elector of Mainz and explain the French invasion of Trier as a necessary defensive action. And Louis was apparently acting in good faith when he sent this explanation, for he had no intention of conquering German territory in 1673; the occupation of Trier was not a simple act of French imperialism or pugnacity. Although Emperor Leopold had indeed sent troops to garrison Trier's Rhenish fortresses and had promised to assist the Dutch,[55] Louis's decision to occupy Trier was a rash act; it was a risk that far outweighed the threat presented by the elector of Trier to Louis's lands or enterprises. Perhaps the king incurred this risk because he was relying too heavily upon the advice of one minister, Louvois, whose interests as war minister would be served by continuing an aggressive policy. But Louis XIV was too strong willed to be led blindly by any minister; a minister's proposals had to strike a deep chord within the king before they were approved. Louis ordered the invasion of Trier because his position and his upbringing had instilled in him two very strong drives: the need to meet fully the responsibilities and the demands of his office, and the desire to protect what rightfully belonged to him as king. He invaded Trier because he had a compelling need to fulfill the traditional kingly role of protecting the realm against foreign aggression. Any threat to his possessions, no matter how remote, was very real to Louis. He would assure the sacrosanctity of his territories even if this required violating the sovereignty of a prince of the empire. The king felt his case was so strong that his representative at the Imperial Diet in Regensburg, Robert de Gravel, could "justify with ease the precautions"[56] he had to take.

Louis's plans during the latter part of July 1673 are thus fairly clear. He was sending a large part of the army that had been under his personal command into the electorate of Trier, while he, Louvois, and Vauban toured the defenses of the eastern frontier and awaited developments in Cologne, Vienna, the empire, and Brussels. Louis was perhaps hoping that the Dutch would accept his harsh terms at the Cologne peace conference.[57] This would compel Emperor Leopold, who would lose Dutch financial support and would no longer have a credible *casus belli*, to remain innocuously in his own hereditary lands. Yet the king was not greatly concerned about what happened in the negotiations at Cologne. He was prepared for action and he would be content to see the outbreak of war, whether it was with Spain, with the emperor, or with both of them in alliance with the Dutch. Louis viewed a further trial by arms as a stimulating prospect.

In Brandenburg, which had made peace with France at Vossem only two months earlier, the French invasion of Trier provoked surprise and alarm—the former because, after the laborious negotiations that had led to the Peace of Vossem, Frederick William was taken aback to see Louis XIV so recklessly provoke another elector of the empire; the latter because Louis's aggression into Germany would give the emperor an opportunity "to bring the entire empire onto his side,"[58] which was in neither France's nor

Brandenburg's best interests. Frederick William had no desire to see Emperor Leopold act as protective patron to the German princes.

But it was not only the Germans who were scandalized by the march of French cavalry into the electorate of Trier. Even Louis's ambassadors and agents in Germany, who had to face the consequences of the king's provocative policies among the aroused Germans, were moved to protest. Abbé de Gravel, Robert's brother, was the French resident in Mainz, but in midsummer of 1673 he was preparing to depart for a meeting of the Franconian and Saxon Circles at Mühlhausen, where he would lobby against their cooperation with the emperor. The abbé wrote to Pomponne: "The Trier affair is beginning to cause a great deal of commotion here; it will doubtless cause even more where I am going."[59] Robert de Gravel, who had more stature in the French diplomatic corps than his brother, dared to write directly to the king. He began his dispatch by perfunctorily agreeing with Louis's right to station French troops in the electorate of Trier, but then filled many pages with sharp criticism of the king's action. The question, Gravel argued, was not whether the elector of Trier deserved to be treated harshly—doubtless he did—but that, as one of the "principal members" of the empire, this "particular prince" would be seen as an example by the rest of the German princes; if the king of France abused the elector of Trier, he might well do the same to any prince of the empire.[60] Thus Gravel insisted that Louis's punitive measures were more likely to provoke than coerce the German princes. But more importantly, Gravel was also trying to teach the king a lesson in reason-of-state politics, which Gravel himself had learned from Cardinal Mazarin and twenty years of arduous experience as a diplomat. He was suggesting to Louis that even if the elector of Trier had connived with the emperor to thwart French plans, the king should not react hastily and punish a single prince when the disposition of the entire empire was at stake. Gravel concluded his dispatch with quiet advice that the king should moderate his imperious tone in dealing with the Germans: "Some persons here [i.e. at the diet], even those who are not opposed to us, find it a little harsh that the phrase 'it is ordered' is being used in the empire even when there is no declared war."[61]

Robert de Gravel's subtle arguments were lost on Louis and Louvois because their minds were fully occupied with military concerns. Thus, at the very center of the royal government, there was a lapse in concentration upon an area of affairs, the disposition of the German princes, that demanded the sharpest focus if a successful policy were to be pursued.

While the Gravel brothers used studied diplomatic words in criticizing royal policy vis-à-vis Trier, Wilhelm von Fürstenberg, a native-born German, sent Pomponne a personal and emotional condemnation of French policy in Germany. Wilhelm had been sent to placate the elector of Mainz while the abbé de Gravel was busy at the meeting of the imperial Circles in Mühlhausen. From his vantage point in Mainz, which, at the confluence of the Rhine and Main Rivers, was a political as well as a strategic center of the empire, Fürstenberg wrote heatedly to Pomponne:

> I assure you that it would have been very easy to have foiled all of the emperor's plans and even to have swung most of the empire onto our side if His Majesty had only withdrawn his troops from Germany immediately after the peace with the elector of Brandenburg. . . . I am obliged to inform you . . . that all Germans are worried because they think that France wishes to establish a sort of empire over all other nations and monarchies. . . . Although most of them think that I am more loyal to His Majesty than his own subjects are, they cannot conceal their thoughts from me when their minds become a little heated with wine or when I mention something that shows I am not without some love and affection for my fatherland.[62]

Wilhelm intended to make two points, one political and one personal, in his letter to Pomponne: French policy in the empire was taking a reckless turn away from the careful courting of the Germans that Fürstenberg had seen practiced by both Mazarin and Lionne; and against great odds, Fürstenberg was doing the best he could to serve Louis XIV. Wilhelm's self-proclaimed patriotism seems out of character for a seventeenth-century mercenary diplomat and was doubtless intended as a gambit to raise the price of his services by stressing the awkwardness of his position as a German who served the French king.

Wilhelm's crafty letter also helps us to understand the growing split in Louis XIV's government between the diplomatic corps, on one hand, and the king and his war minister on the other. The day before Fürstenberg wrote to Pomponne, he had addressed a dry, perfunctory dispatch to the king.[63] Why did Wilhelm write so differently when he corresponded with Pomponne? Perhaps it was merely a routine difference in style that he employed when writing to a minister, rather than the king; but perhaps it was because Wilhelm knew Pomponne well enough, as a man and a diplomat, to surmise that the foreign minister would be sympathetic to his criticisms of royal policy in Germany. Both Fürstenberg and Pomponne had been friends and protégés of the late Hugues de Lionne, Pomponne's predecessor at the foreign ministry; and though Georges Pagès exaggerated that "Lionne did nothing in Germany without consulting him [Fürstenberg]"[64] the statement is generally reliable. Thus it would seem that when Fürstenberg wrote to Pomponne he was calculating, and correctly, that if the king was ignoring his advice about Germany, he was likewise ignoring Pomponne's advice. Yet Wilhelm continued to think that his best hope of turning Louis back to a moderate policy in the empire—thus easing the difficulty of his own position, of serving two masters—was through Pomponne, who after all was still the king's foreign minister.

Even Turenne, whose advanced position in Germany the royal army was ostensibly supporting, had serious reservations about the invasion of the electorate: "Concerning the elector of Trier, I believe that we should do nothing to give the empire valid reason to complain. This is simply my own opinion, and everything could be justified as necessary for the [king's] march."[65] In any event, those men—French and German, diplomats and soldiers—who knew Germany and the German people the best agreed: occupation of the electorate of Trier would damage French interests in Germany by providing anti-French advocates with good material for their briefs against Louis. The contest for control of German public opinion had begun.

Two days after Fourilles was ordered to invade Trier, news arrived at the French king's headquarters that, for Louvois, vindicated the decision for the action. On 17 July Jacques de Grémonville, the French special envoy in Vienna, had written to Louis XIV that the swift conquest of Maastricht had not intimidated Leopold's government, as the French had anticipated. The influence in the Imperial Council of the more or less Francophile Lobkowitz was rapidly waning and that of Montecuccoli, Hocher, and Schwarzenberg, who were the advocates of a strong posture toward France, was on the rise. Moreover, plans had already been laid for a rendezvous of the imperial army in western Bohemia.[66] On the day that Grémonville's dispatch arrived in French headquarters at Thionville (25 July), Louvois wrote to his father, Le Tellier, that a courier had just arrived with news of the emperor's plans: his army would begin to march this month and would rendezvous in Bohemia on 10 August. These revelations, according to Louvois, "made His Majesty pleased with the decision he took to come here [the eastern frontier], and have humiliated those [Pomponne and Fürstenberg] who objected to that decision."[67]

Louvois's letter is especially interesting because in it he was doing more than briefing Le Tellier on the international situation; he was also revealing the conflicts of opinion within Louis XIV's high council. The proud son was in effect telling his father that he, Louvois, and not Pomponne, was functioning as the king's closest adviser on foreign affairs. Louvois's jibe at Pomponne and Fürstenberg shows us, however, that the young war minister was unaware that what was occurring in Vienna did not justify the decision he and the king had made to invade the electorate of Trier.

Emperor Leopold and his councilors had formulated a restrained and rather shrewd policy. Although they had begun to mobilize the imperial army and were publicizing this fact, they had no intention of marching the army out of Bohemia and into Germany proper until the circumstances were propitious for such a move. In July, Emperor Leopold had retired with a group of select councilors (significantly, Lobkowitz, the Francophile, did not accompany them) to the pilgrimage town of Maria-Zell, where the emperor prayed for the soul of his recently deceased wife, Margaret Theresa, the younger sister of Louis XIV's queen. Characteristically, while Louis XIV drafted grandiose plans in his mistress's quarters, Leopold made modest plans during a religious retreat. In secret conferences, the emperor and his advisors decided to proceed firmly but cautiously. Their decision was recorded in a memorandum drafted at the time by Chancellor Hocher. While a minimum of imperial troops would remain in Hungary to keep the unruly Hungarians and the Turks at bay, the bulk of Leopold's army would be marched to Eger in far western Bohemia, close to the German frontier.

In this way a defensive position will be maintained and the emperor does not have to fear that the French army might invade his lands and inflict damages. This will also give the States [General of the Dutch Republic] enough breathing space so that Turenne with the French allies cannot jump on their neck. In the meantime, the emperor's commitment will not be so extended that it cannot be withdrawn. In five or six weeks we will see what has happened at sea [i.e. if the Dutch continued to hold off the Anglo-French fleet], how things are going in the Empire, and how successful the Turks and Hungarian rebels might be.[68]

Thus Leopold planned to proceed step by step, beginning with a careful mobilization of his forces in Bohemia and keeping his options open. Leopold tended to be dilatory and indecisive, but his policy of restraint in 1673 proved to be more effective than Louis XIV's restless activism. Paradoxically, the emperor's weaknesses served him well, as long as he had councilors like the Franc-Comtois, Franz Paul von Lisola, who could compel him to make tough decisions when they had to be made.

During the two months that followed Leopold's conferences at Maria-Zell, events in Europe meshed into the strategy worked out by the Imperials. Louis XIV's provocative policy toward Germany, the success of the Dutch navy in fending off the Anglo-French fleet in the North Sea, and the relative quiescence of the Turks and Hungarians all conspired to support Leopold's military plans. The emperor's commander in chief, Count Raimund Montecuccoli, was able to lead the imperial army out of Bohemia and into Germany with little risk or trouble. The French invasion of the electorate of Trier played into Leopold's hands, for this untimely action drew the German princes to his side and provided him complete justification for sending an army back into Germany. Leopold could argue that he was simply honoring his election oath by coming to the aid of a distressed prince of the empire. In mid-August, Elector Lothar Friedrich of Mainz warned Wilhelm von Fürstenberg that the invasion of the electorate of Trier "would not only alarm Germany and increase her mistrust of the king [of France], but, moreover, it would furnish the emperor with a perfect pretext for going to the aid of the elector of Trier."[69] No matter how strongly Louis XIV protested that Leopold's commitments to the Dutch, the presence of his troops in Koblenz, and his plans to return an army to Germany justified the advance of French troops into the electorate of Trier,[70] the irreducible fact in the minds of the German princes and people was that Louis had invaded the Holy Roman Empire of the German Nation. Neither Robert de Gravel's arguments in the Imperial Diet nor the increased subsidies he handed out to French clients could alter that fact, and the stage was set for a stunning reversal of French fortunes in the autumn of 1673.

For 150 years, from the reign of Francis I until 1672, French statesmen had assiduously cultivated friendly relations with the German princes; this policy had been the cornerstone of Valois and Bourbon opposition to Hapsburg hegemony in Germany. Not until 1673 did a French king break that tradition, when Louis XIV deluded himself by thinking he could antagonize the princes of the empire, who were small individually but collectively important. Condé had warned Louvois that "the strength of the empire is awesome when she is united,"[71] but apparently neither Louvois nor the king was willing to heed that warning.

On 30 July the French court moved upstream along the Moselle River, from Thionville to Nancy, the capital of Lorraine. The entire province of Lorraine had been occupied by a royal army in 1670 when Louis had grown impatient and found it no longer possible to deal peaceably with the contentious and independent-minded Duke Charles IV.[72]

While Louis temporarily headquartered in Nancy, Louvois and his protégé, Vauban, traveled eastward to inspect the fortifications in Alsace. This province had been a French dependency since the Treaty of Münster (1648), but its relationship to the French crown had not been definitively established.[73] In January 1673, Louis sent the prince of Condé to Alsace to assess the French position there, and Louvois wrote to the prince that the king wanted him "to be utterly honest about Breisach and Philippsburg so that your trip will put him at ease once and for all about these two fortresses."[74] When Emperor Leopold had begun openly to aid the Dutch late in 1672, Louis XIV became concerned about his eastern frontier; Breisach and Philippsburg were the easternmost French fortresses. Moreover, the proudly independent towns of Alsace—the famous Decapolis—had not welcomed French rule after the Peace of Westphalia, and Condé reported that it was time that Louis imposed his full sovereignty on the province. The prince wrote to Louvois from Breisach on the upper Rhine: "I must say that the king's authority is disappearing altogether in Alsace. Far from submitting to the king as they should ... according to the Treaty of Münster, the ten imperial cities are almost enemies. I believe that the king should take the time to straighten things out with Colmar and Haguenau."[75]

Condé had never been in Alsace before January 1673 and perhaps he was not as sensitive as he might had been to the traditions of independence that had developed in the Alsatian cities over several centuries. But he was correct in remarking that the situation was deteriorating in Alsace, particularly while the French governor of the province was Duke Charles-Armand de Mazarin. This nephew-in-law of Cardinal Mazarin encouraged a sense of independence in Alsace by presenting himself as a sort of royal vassal, functioning as an intermediary power between the king and the province.[76] Obviously, such a feudal concept could not square with the monarchy of Louis XIV.

Condé returned to court from Alsace late in the winter of 1673, but nothing was done to implement his suggestions about disciplining the Decapolis. Louvois did not forget those unruly Alsatian cities, however, and during the summer of 1673 he sent another French soldier, Philippe, duke of Navailles, to Alsace to appraise the situation. Navailles discovered that the citizens of Colmar, the leading city of the Decapolis, "were affecting a great independence. Their city was well stocked with munitions and foodstuffs, and they appeared little disposed to receive orders from the king or to submit to them if they came."[77]

The last week in July, Louvois personally escorted Navailles to the royal headquarters in Nancy and had the duke give Louis a detailed description of the situation in Alsace. Then, early in August, the war minister himself went to Alsace. Not surprisingly, when Louvois returned to Nancy in mid-August, he, like Condé and Navailles before him, stressed the need for Louis XIV to clarify the relationship between the French crown and the Alsatian cities, which had been left ambiguous by the Treaty of Münster in 1648. Louvois wrote to his father about the king's reaction to his report on Alsace: "He appeared to be satisfied with my proposals to remedy the miserable condition of everything in that area. . . . Eight days from tomorrow the king will depart to make a two-week tour of the Breisach region, and will use the pretext of his passage to force the ten cities to receive [French] garrisons."[78] Louvois had the schedule calculated to the day; on 24 August Louis departed Nancy for Alsace.

Preceded by his troops, Louis followed a tributary of the Moselle from Nancy to Saint Dié in the foothills of the Vosges, and then marched over the mountains into the lush vineyards of the Ill Valley. Louis was boastful and scornful in his account of the expedition:

> I crossed the mountains with my troops. . . . As I had, unquestionably, the right to oversee the cities [of Alsace], I could put troops in them anytime that I pleased. Some of them had not been very obedient, particularly Colmar, which considered itself important and appeared too proud to have anything to do with a man like me. I calculated that it was necessary to make use of a stratagem to save the lives of some of my officers and soldiers. I sent a message to Colmar that I wished to enter and I had my regiment of French and Swiss Guards go in on August 28. They arranged themselves in battle formation, and the inhabitants were told that I wished to raze their walls and take their cannons to Breisach. They were very surprised, and everything that I had ordered was carried out. Sélestat also submitted, and during the several days that I was at Breisach all of the other cities followed suit. After I had put everything in order in Alsace, I returned to Nancy [on 8 September].[79]

This passage provides a sharp vignette of the king's mentality. Always worried about his troops, Louis was certainly not a bloodthirsty or even a particularly combative man, but he was obsessed with military glory. He therefore had his war minister arrange a triumphal march that gave him victories without pitched battles and bloodshed, and emerged in his memoirs as a clever, conquering hero.[80] Louis was trying hard to be a great captain, yet his braggadocio reveals that he could never be one. The king's abilities were those of a *roi bureaucrate* and not a *roi commandant*.

In any event, the walls of Colmar and Sélestat, the two largest of the ten Alsatian cities, were demolished. As a modern French historian remarked:

> That military occupation, which inaugurated Louvois' taking possession of the province, marked the end of an era. . . . The grand policy of Richelieu, Mazarin, and Lionne of alliance with the Rhenish states was finished. The conception of Alsace as an entryway to the Germanies that maintained certain ties with the empire was destroyed. One relationship had to exist between the prince and the subjects of Alsace, that of obedience.[81]

On the eve of Louis's march into Alsace, Robert de Gravel, who had been a protégé of Mazarin and Lionne, wrote to Pomponne and advocated that the old policy of treating the Decapolis diplomatically and strictly within the limits set by the Treaty of Münster be continued: "I am concerned only with His Majesty's interests. And it would be preferable to promote them by using methods that could not reasonably be contested than by using others that could be disputed and would be hard to defend."[82] Perhaps Gravel's judgment on this matter had been prejudiced because he had personally to face Colmar's bitter complaints in the Imperial Diet, but in any case Louis had decided the fate of the Alsatian cities before Gravel presented his case.[83]

As we have noted, the king had been considering his policy toward Alsace even before Condé traveled there to assess the situation in January 1673. Not only Condé, but every other military expert who visited the province agreed that something had to be done about the increasing weakness of the French position there. It would seem that Louis was obliged to attempt to put an end to the confusing and potentially dangerous situation in Alsace. The ambiguous relationship established by the Treaty of Münster between the Decapolis and the French crown had to be clarified, for if the absolute dynastic state did not demand neat linear boundaries, as the modern state does, it required undivided sovereignty; the quasi-feudal status of the ten Alsatian cities was anachronistic by the late seventeenth century. Even at the time the Treaty of Münster was being negotiated, the imperial diplomat, Isaak von Volmar, had remarked about Alsace: "The strongest will prevail."[84] Condé, Navailles, and Louvois were not unreasonable when they advised the king to clarify and solidify his military position in the strategic eastern province.

But how could Louis XIV so cavalierly reject the argument of Robert de Gravel that the royal interests would be best served by handling Alsace cautiously and diplomatically? First, at the time of the Dutch War Louis was much more inclined to listen to the advice of his generals than to that of his diplomats; in 1673 the king was not about to be restrained by Gravel's sophisticated discussions about public opinion in the empire. Second, Louis's conception of the war was changing. As the summer progressed, the king thought more about the Hapsburgs and less about the Dutch; by mid-August he had almost reconciled himself to war with the emperor, if not with the empire at large. Louis had not wanted war with Leopold when he attacked the Dutch in 1672, but events and the emperor's stubborn refusal to let the French have a free hand with the Dutch had pushed Paris and Vienna inexorably toward war. On 12 August Louis wrote to his special envoy in Vienna about the latter's desultory negotiations with the imperial ministers: "If I am permitting you to listen to them [the emperor's proposals] without rejecting them . . . it is only to feed a diversion, which, in the present situation, will delay the emperor's plans and will be useful for my affairs."[85]

The movement toward peace between the Austrian Hapsburgs and the Bourbons that had begun with the secret partition treaty of 1668 and had been furthered by Leopold's secret treaty of neutrality with Louis XIV in 1671 was coming to an end. Perhaps neither ruler expected the peace to last, although the French envoy in Vienna, Grémonville, had worked hard for ten years to maintain an enduring détente. In any event, as renewed war between the Bourbons and Hapsburgs in Germany became imminent, the French felt that Alsace had to be secured.

In August 1673 Louis was preoccupied with the problem of securing his eastern frontier, and the march into Alsace was only part of a larger plan of action. The king's other thoughts were still fixed upon the electorate of Trier, where the countryside but not the capital city had been occupied by French troops. Louvois wrote to Condé and briskly outlined Louis's plan for dealing with the elector of Trier: the king had heard, according to Louvois, that Emperor Leopold would send his army into the empire only *after* he was assured that Monterey, the governor of the Spanish Netherlands, would move at the same time to garrison Trier. Louis felt that Monterey had neither the wherewithal nor the permission from Madrid to do so; "nevertheless [Louis] thinks that it is advisable to occupy the city of Trier. . . . He has just ordered the Chevalier de Fourilles and M. de Bissy to invest it with 3,000 horse; immediately thereafter M. de Rochefort will march with ten battalions of infantry and six cannons to storm the city."[86]

It is strange to read that Louis discounted Monterey's ability to march from the Spanish Netherlands and garrison Trier, yet judged it expedient that he storm the city himself. Surely the king well knew that to attack the capital city of an imperial electorate would only sharpen German resentment of French arms.

Interestingly, both Louvois and Louis began to justify the

planned seizure of Trier on the very grounds that Louis had discounted—that is, he was compelled to get into Trier before the Spaniards did. This was Louvois's explanation to Le Tellier on 22 August and Louis's to Robert de Gravel on 26 August.[87] Louis's letter to Gravel contains some curious passages. After recounting why he was obliged to occupy the electorate of Trier, and charging that all the turmoil in the empire was the emperor's responsibility, Louis continued:

If the entry of my armies into that archbishopric [Trier] has already caused a big uproar in the empire, the capital, which will soon be in my hands, will doubtless provoke a much larger one.

While my troops had orders simply to reside in that territory and to live there with the greatest discipline, the chevalier de Fourilles, who commands them, learned that a corps of Spanish infantry had arrived from Luxemburg with orders to throw itself into Trier. He considered it vital for my interests to prevent this and he therefore invested the fortress. So that he will not be exposed to the peril of falling into the enemy's hands, I have decided to send my troops in.[88]

This dispatch from the king to Robert de Gravel contains many blatant falsehoods. First, Louis's casual mention that Fourilles had taken it upon himself, with no direct royal orders, to attack the city of Trier is incredible. First, not only would Fourilles never have done such a thing, but Louvois on 19 August had sent him the *orders* to invest the fortress.[89] Second, Louis's explanation that he was sending an army to assure the safety of the chevalier de Fourilles is preposterous. Gravel must have been puzzled indeed to read that the king was willing to antagonize the entire empire for the sake of a single cavalry commander. Third, although the king explained to Gravel that Fourilles had sent the news about the Spaniards' marching toward Trier, Louvois's orders to Fourilles of 19 August imply that the news came from a different (though unspecified) source: "The king has decided to force Trier to accept a French garrison because His Majesty heard that the count of Monterey plans to put some Spaniards in there."[90] The only information that either Louis or Louvois received about Spanish plans to garrison Trier were two innocuous dispatches from Fourilles that simply mentioned there were rumors to the effect that Spanish cavalry had marched from Flanders to Luxemburg.[91] At the beginning of August, Louvois warned the governor of Charleroi (in

Flanders) to be on the watch for any Dutch or Spanish troops moving toward the electorate of Trier, and the governor never had occasion to give alarm.[92]

Thus, it seems that Louis and Louvois had decided that the city of Trier had to be taken, and trumped up the justification for investing it.[93] When Louis ordered the city besieged, he threw off his mask of benign boarder on the elector of Trier's lands and served notice that any friend of the emperor was an enemy of the king of France.

The decision to attack Trier revealed the division of opinion within Louis's high council. The Savoyard ambassador, who accompanied Louis throughout the campaign of 1673, reported that "M. de Pomponne was opposed to attacking Trier for fear that it would antagonize the entire Empire and turn it against France. This, together with the emperor, would be very troublesome for France, but M. de Louvois, who proposed the attack, prevailed."[94] Pomponne, as foreign minister, also had the responsibility of drafting the fabricated justification for attacking Trier that was sent to Gravel at Regensburg. Pomponne, who was well-known for his "great probity,"[95] apparently objected to writing these bald lies for the king, particularly since he was opposed to the policy. In any case, the next letter from the court to Gravel, which repeated the spurious justification for storming Trier, was written by Louvois and not Pomponne.[96]

The marquis of Rochefort approached Trier with his infantry and siege train on 28 August, and the great Vauban stopped briefly to help him lay the plan of attack. As the French surrounded the fortress, Rochefort reported scornfully that "the bourgeois are very worried about their clocks,"[97] which the marquis saw as symbols of middle-class pettiness. The bombardment began three days later, but despite its meager garrison the city did not succumb as quickly as the French anticipated. Louvois had expected such rapid progress in the siege that he wrote to Rochefort suggesting that his cavalry could be sent to Germany to reinforce Turenne's army, which had begun its critical maneuvers with the imperial army.[98] The intendant of the French army at Trier, who was functioning more or less as Louvois's personal emissary, replied to the war minister, explaining that if cavalry were sent to Turenne from the besieging force at Trier, the siege would have to be lifted because "the circumvallation of the fortress is very extensive and cannot be guarded except with the cavalry."[99] The king and his war minister did not have enough troops at their disposal to succeed in all the diverse and widely scattered projects they had initiated. Louvois had also misjudged the resistance that Trier could muster and had not allocated enough men to make a swift job of the siege.

Before the city sent a drummer to beat a *chamade* of surrender on 7 September, Louis XIV became acutely impatient with the entire affair. He wrote to Louvois that "the siege at Trier is not progressing as one might wish, and this upsets me a great deal. I do not wish to be shown up in this affair and I will do everything necessary to take Trier. But I believe that it would be appropriate to chastise the inhabitants when the city is taken so that a bad example will not be set for those whom I attack in the future."[100] This letter gives us an interesting glimpse of Louis XIV's mentality. Although there is no evidence that the defenders of Trier held out beyond the point considered honorable by the etiquette of seventeenth-century warfare, the king wanted them chastised. Somehow, the usual rules did not apply when the Sun King's vanity was threatened.

Elector Max Heinrich fled to his fortress of Ehrenbreitstein for sanctuary. But the French retained Trier only until the campaign of 1675, when Duke Charles of Lorraine, Louis XIV's *bête noir*, recaptured it for the allies.

Not only did Pomponne, the foreign minister, disagree with Louis's decision to attack Trier, so did the king's closest observers of the situation in Germany, Robert de Gravel and Turenne. Gravel had been under mounting pressures in Regensburg during the summer of 1673, and as his king's policies became more provocative, he was repeatedly shouted down by pro-imperial representatives in the Diet. Antagonisms had become so sharp by August that Gravel's French domestics were assaulted and beaten in Regensburg's taverns. Gravel did not have to present his objections to the attack on Trier to the king in writing; he provided more eloquent and concrete testimony. Gravel had worked long and hard to maintain French influence in Germany, and when the news arrived in Regensburg that Louis was besieging the city of Trier, he was stricken with a coronary heart attack (*"apoplexie"*).[101] The king, who was returning from his conquest of Alsace, did not take the time to write to Gravel, but Pomponne, who shared Gravel's disapproval of Louis's belligerent policies, wrote sympathetically to his beleaguered colleague:

> As for me, Sir, not only because of my concern for His Majesty's interests but because of my personal regard for you, I will be as happy with your complete recovery as I have been upset by your illness. Doubtless, you are going to need all of your strength in the present situation.[102]

Was not Pomponne subtly suggesting to Gravel that the two of them were part of a common but futile effort to moderate Louis's policies? The two diplomats were witnessing the destruction of a policy that they had seen develop during the two decades they had served together in the French foreign service.

Turenne had been anxious about French relations with Trier since mid-July because he felt that he might require reinforcements in Germany. When the marshal heard rumors (false, as it turned out) that Louis XIV and the elector of Trier had resolved their differences, he expressed relief and satisfaction. If this were true, then the king's army would not be immobilized on the Moselle River but would be available to support Turenne in central Germany, should the need arise. Thus when Turenne was informed by Louvois of the imminent attack upon Trier, he replied with a short, icy sentence that expressed, unmistakably, the marshal's disapproval of the attack: "I have seen the king's decision about Trier."[103]

Turenne saw clearly what was happening along the Moselle. The army that had been intended to support him in Germany was fully occupied in Trier; and the king was using troops with abandon while Turenne was left wanting. Before the end of the 1673 campaign, Louis and Turenne would pay for this misuse of the royal armies, and the French would be thrust out of Germany altogether.

Several strategic objectives underlay Louis XIV's extended campaign of 1673. He wanted to continue to press the war against the Dutch, and Maastricht was a prize worth winning; its conquest was a heavy blow to the Dutch and improved the French military posture. As Turenne acknowledged, "the capture of Maastricht makes the king's business incomparably more easy because we can now reach the Rhine without trouble."[104] The invasion and occupation of the electorate of Trier did not serve the Dutch War *per se*, but, in Louis's mind, were necessary to protect his eastern frontier should the emperor march an army into Germany. Given Leopold's apparent willingness to send an army toward the Rhine to assist the Dutch, Louis's concern about his vulnerable eastern flank is comprehensible, even though the seizure of Trier was a highly provocative reaction. Finally, Louis's march into Alsace was not an unreasonable way to stabilize a potentially dangerous situation in the king's easternmost province. The campaigns against Maastricht, Trier, and Alsace could be justified on objective, strategic grounds, although one must remark that Louis was too solicitous of his own interests and insensitive to those of the Germans. Honoré Courtin, the diplomat who was a frequent critic of the king's policies, pointed out that "everything the king has done with regard to the elector of Trier . . . and the cities of Colmar and Sélestat, although justifiable for the welfare of his interests, has aggravated the Germans."[105]

Yet, in following the campaign of 1673, one is struck by a more personal and subjective motive behind the king's actions. This was Louis's compulsion to achieve his *gloire*, to fulfill a driving need to prove himself worthy as a king and a man—to himself, to his contemporaries, and to posterity. This subjective aspect of the king's motivation during the campaign of 1673 can perhaps best be seen in his relationships to women. Louis was thirty-four years of age in the summer of 1673, and he was involved with three women: his queen, Marie Thérèse, who had never held any attraction for Louis; a mistress, Mlle. de la Vallière, whose attraction for the king had faded; and a second mistress, the marquise de Montespan, to whom the king looked exclusively for satisfaction of his sexual needs.[106]

These women were "the three queens" to the dazzled French peasants who saw them pass by in a coach. All three women accompanied Louis XIV on the campaign of 1673—an incredible entourage to accompany a king from Saint-Germain, for no European king, before or after Louis XIV, ever trundled three women on a four-month military campaign that ranged over hundreds of miles. Louis's determination to have a full female gallery for his martial exploits seems curiously out of place in the late seventeenth century, and it is reminiscent of the chivalric tournaments described by Froissart in the fourteenth century.

The king's desire to have the queen and La Vallière accompany him can be seen as generous, cruel, or merely insensitive (probably the last), but it was principally for Montespan that Louis wanted to play the conquering hero. A great beauty, from an old and distinguished family, possessing a better intelligence than the king, and remarkably fertile, she had borne Louis children in 1669, 1670, and 1672, and she was pregnant again in the spring of 1673. The Savoyard ambassador remarked that her "powder ignites quickly."[107] Complications in Montespan's latest pregnancy prompted the king to delay his departure from Saint-Germain for Flanders. Originally scheduled 15 April, his march was postponed to 25 April and then to 1 May.[108] This was highly unusual for the king, who loved precision and punctuality in his military operations. Undoubtedly, Louis wanted his mistress to see him in the lists against all challengers during the campaign of 1673.

When Louis, with his army and court, arrived in Flanders, the king sent the women to Tournai before he crossed the frontier into the Spanish Netherlands. From Tournai the women could watch Louis taunt the Spaniards and then march on Maastricht. On 16 June 1673, during the height of the siege, the marquise de Montespan bore Louis XIV his fourth child by her, Louise-Françoise de Bourbon. The king was concerned about the health of his mistress and their child and he wrote regularly to Tournai from his camp at Maastricht. Franz Paul von Lisola, who had established temporary headquarters in Brussels, informed Chancellor Hocher in Vienna: "We have intercepted four letters to mme. de Montespan written in the king's hand. They are filled with countless blandishments . . . that fully reveal the abjectness of this prince and the nature of his ruling passion. But the most loathsome thing is that the letters contain detailed descriptions of the siege, as if they were intended for one of his generals."[109]

We do not have to agree with Lisola that sending love letters to one's mistress who has just given birth is a mark of "abjectness," nor do we have to condemn Louis's "ruling passion," which seems healthy enough, but Lisola's last sentence is more revealing of the king's personality. It was boorish of Louis to send Montespan a detailed account of a rather routine engineering project, and Lisola quickly spotted the vainglory in the king's chivalric courting of his mistress. The Savoyard ambassador reported that Louis was spending more and more time with Montespan as the court moved from Maastricht into Lorraine. She remained with the king throughout the 1673 campaign, and councils of war were sometimes held in her chambers.[110]

In his *Mémoires*, written for the instruction of the dauphin, Louis admonished his son to keep mistresses out of politics, to "keep the affections of a lover separate from the decisions of a sovereign."[111] Historians of Louis's reign have since assumed that the king adhered to his own advice and refused to allow his mistresses to influence affairs of state. At one level this was true; none of Louis's women headed a faction at court, controlled a minister of state, or possessed political patronage. Perhaps, however, a superb and demanding mistress like Montespan exercised a more subtle influence upon the king's policies. Perhaps Louis's war policy during the 1670s was governed not only by considerations of reason-of-state but also by the king's need to demonstrate his virility to Montespan, and to himself. Given the deep-rooted sense of insecurity that Louis's most sensitive biographer has detected in him,[112] it seems likely that he had a strong need to be seen as a conqueror by Montespan.

Louis's campaign after the siege of Maastricht was improvised. The king had not planned the 1673 campaign beyond the siege because the conquest of this heretofore almost impregnable fortress was to be the most dramatic event of the year. But when victory came so easily and quickly at Maastricht, Louis found himself, in the middle of the summer and the campaigning season, with time on his hands and an unslaked thirst for adventure. Thus he decided, in collaboration with Louvois, his war minister, but against the considered opinions of his best diplomatists, to begin an essentially new campaign. He marched his army southeastward into Lorraine, Alsace, and Trier before the emperor's army offered a clear and present danger to France. These "defensive" moves gave Emperor Leopold the chance to march his army back into Germany, more or less with the blessing of the German princes.

Paradoxically, Louis's move to fortify the eastern frontier weakened his position in Germany and the Rhineland. The king's campaign left Turenne isolated, with a decaying army in mid-Germany; French forces were spread too thin to provide him adequate manpower or logistical support when he needed them.[113] If Louis had not insisted on monopolizing the war effort with his own triumphal marches, if he had not needed to prove his manliness on the battlefield, if he had listened to his experienced and reliable advisors, such as Pomponne, Turenne, and Robert de Gravel, he might have avoided turning a limited and potentially profitable war into a general European war of attrition, into a war that hurt France and, consequently, weakened France's ruler, Louis XIV.

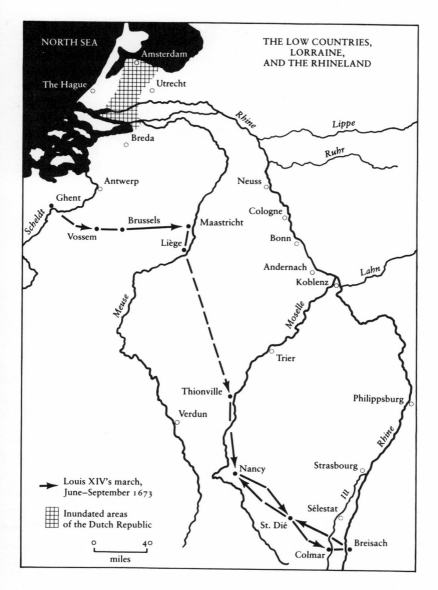

Louis XIV's Campaign, May–October 1673

∽∽∽

III

Ordeal in Germany:
A Shadow on Turenne's Glory

While Louis XIV spent the winter of 1673 at Saint-Germain, preparing for his forthcoming campaign, the vicomte de Turenne was encamped with his army in central Germany, still coping with a remnant from the first year of the Dutch War. After the French king and his allies had attacked the United Provinces in 1672, Elector Frederick William II of Brandenburg and Emperor Leopold I entered the war on the Dutch side.[1] They joined forces with the unpredictable and feisty Duke Charles IV of Lorraine (whose duchy had been seized by the French in 1670) with the aim of stopping Louis XIV in the Netherlands and checking the king's desire for conquest. Their intention was to attack Louis where he was most vulnerable, along his distended lines of communication and logistics on the lower Rhine, between France and the Dutch Republic.

Before the allies could march against the French, however, the emperor ordered the commander of the imperial army, Count Raimund Montecuccoli, to go slow.[2] These orders from Vienna added sluggishness to the other weaknesses of a campaign conducted by querulous allies. In addition to Leopold's usual indecisiveness, two things prevented him from fully committing his army to a war against France in 1672: the nagging presence of the Turks and Hungarians on his eastern flank, and a secret treaty of neutrality he had signed with France in November 1671.[3] The

[48]

emperor's intervention in 1672 had been forced upon him by the possibility that the hard-driving elector of Brandenburg might gain effective leadership in the empire by leading the German resistance to Louis XIV's aggressive policies. Leopold did not relish seeing the growth of French power and influence, but Frederick William presented a more imminent threat than Louis XIV to his authority in Germany. Leopold agreed to support Frederick William as much to keep a rein on him as to wage serious war with Louis XIV.[4] During February 1673, Turenne led a brilliant campaign against the Lorrainers, Brandenburgers, and Imperials, pursuing them throughout Westphalia and Münster. Frederick William's Rhenish territories were devastated by both the allied and the French armies,[5] and by late February, Frederick William no longer wished to engage in an unprofitable war in alliance with a reluctant emperor; unlike Louis XIV, Frederick William never indulged in war for its own sake. He wrote to Emperor Leopold, explaining that the only way to save Brandenburg's Rhenish territories from total destruction was through a "good armistice" with France.[6]

Duke Philip William of Neuburg, who had signed treaties of amity with both Louis XIV and Frederick William, began trying to reconcile France and Brandenburg as soon as they began hostilities in the summer of 1672. The duke's patently embarrassed position, caught between two larger powers, moved him to try to mediate a peace between his two patrons, the king of France and the elector of Brandenburg.

By March 1673 Turenne's army was bivouacked in Frederick William's Rhenish territories and the States General of the Dutch Republic was far in arrears in the subsidies it had promised the elector to support his army. Elector Frederick thus decided to fulfill his threat to the emperor by making peace with Louis XIV. He gave Dietrich von Stratmann, the duke of Neuburg's vice-chancellor, permission to begin negotiations with France in order "to damp down the fires of war"—with an armistice at least, a peace treaty at best.[7] Stratmann immediately left Germany for the French court, and on 10 April 1673, he and Pomponne signed a preliminary treaty at Saint-Germain-en-Laye. Stratmann returned forthwith to Germany and brought the provisional treaty to Elector Frederick William in Berlin. Then, in mid-May, the elector dispatched his secretary of state, Franz von Meinders, with full powers to conclude a definitive treaty with Louis XIV.[8] Meinders

Vicomte de Turenne (1611–1675),
engraving by Robert Nanteuil
(courtesy of the Art Institute of Chicago)

found the French king, with his court and his army, encamped near Vossem, just east of Brussels, on their way to lay siege to Maastricht. Between 6 June and 21 June, Meinders conferred with Louvois and Pomponne, the two ministers of state who had accompanied Louis XIV on campaign. On 21 June 1673, in Louis XIV's camp outside the besieged fortress of Maastricht, Meinders and Pomponne signed a final treaty that was substantially the same as that of 10 April. The treaty restored to Elector Frederick William nearly all of his occupied Rhenish territories, provided him with an indemnity of 800,000-livre, and guaranteed protection of his rights as set down in the treaties of Westphalia.[9] The elector's fickleness—a treaty with France, war with France, and a new treaty with France—paid off. Louvois wrote to Turenne that "the ratifications of the treaty with Brandenburg having been exchanged, His Majesty wants you to proclaim to your troops that there is peace between His Majesty's subjects and those of the elector of Brandenburg."[10] Frederick William was out of the war for the time being.[11]

During April and May 1673, while the diplomats haggled over the wording of the Peace of Vossem and French armies converged upon Maastricht, Louis XIV and his counselors debated what should be done with Turenne's army, which was still in Germany. After Turenne had driven the Brandenburgers eastward across the Weser River in his winter campaign, he took up quarters in Soest, in the county of Mark, which was one of Brandenburg's Rhenish states. As the summer of 1673 wore on, the deployment and discipline of Turenne's army became major determinants of French diplomatic and military fortunes in Europe, with consequences for years to come. Success or failure in managing the German princes—in maintaining the precise balance of fear, respect, and loyalty—was critically important for the French, for all of Louis XIV's wars, including the so-called Dutch War, were fought largely on German soil. What the king decided to do with Turenne's army after he had made peace with Brandenburg was to affect the relations between France and Germany for decades—though, of course, neither Louis nor his counselors foresaw this in the spring of 1673.

Louis XIV's only military objective in the empire during the years 1672–73 was to prevent any German prince from attempting to intervene in Louis's war in the Netherlands. Thus, even before negotiations began with the elector of Brandenburg, Louis had committed himself to withdrawing his forces from the empire, provided·Frederick William and Leopold did likewise. As early as mid-March 1673, Pomponne had written (over Louis's signature) to abbé de Gravel, the French envoy in the electorate of Mainz, and ordered him to try to convince the elector of Mainz to help arrange a German peace based upon a mutual withdrawal of French and imperial troops from the empire.[12] A month later Louvois wrote to Turenne about the same problem. The war minister informed the marshal that the recently signed treaty was very advantageous for Brandenburg, that quick ratification by the elector was expected, and therefore that French troops would soon have to march out of Frederick William's Rhenish territories, the county of Mark and the duchy of Cleves. To leave Brandenburg's territories—this was obvious and imperative; but how about Germany in general—should Turenne remain there at all? Louvois wanted Turenne's advice on that delicate matter. The king's opinion, according to Louvois, was that if Leopold kept his imperial soldiers in Bohemia, Turenne would have to withdraw into "Liège or Brabant. But if the emperor maintains his troops within the empire [i.e. Germany proper], His Majesty would be within his rights to do the same thing."[13]

Turenne, as circumspect in his advice as in his maneuvers with the army, answered Louvois's letter on 29 April from his headquarters in Soest: "It is apparent that if the elector of Brandenburg accepts the king's offer [of peace] the emperor's army will in fact retire into Bohemia. This being the case, it is certain that all I can do is to march against the Dutch in Brabant or Liège."[14] Louis XIV, Louvois, and Turenne thus seem to have had a lively awareness of the German situation as it was developing in early 1673. If the emperor's army withdrew from Germany proper and into Bohemia, which had been a hereditary possession of the Austrian Hapsburgs since the Thirty Years' War, the French army also would be obliged to withdraw from Germany; otherwise, Louis XIV would bring upon himself the onus of pursuing an expansionistic policy in the empire.

Indeed, Louis had no plans to conquer German territory and no desire to wage war with anyone in Germany, including the emperor. The king had called a special meeting of his ministers on 14 March to discuss the German situation. Louvois wrote letters to

Turenne both before and after the council meeting, and his message was the same: the king wants an end to the turmoil in Germany so that he can more effectively wage war in the Netherlands, and the only purpose in warring with the elector of Brandenburg was to persuade him to stop meddling in affairs outside the empire that were beyond his jurisdiction.[15] Louvois's letters to Turenne must be accepted as truthful. Louis XIV did not want to get involved in the empire; but could the king have his wish of waging a major war in the Netherlands without provoking protest from the empire? This indeed was Louis's worry.

Even before Turenne's letter of 29 April reached Louvois at Saint-Germain, Louis XIV had written to Robert de Gravel at the Imperial Diet concerning the situation in Germany. The position of the French government had shifted slightly but significantly in the two weeks since Louvois had affirmed that the French army would have to be withdrawn from the empire as soon as the emperor retired into Bohemia. Insofar as the dispatches written for the king by his ministers of state accurately reflect Louis's mind (a valid assumption),[16] Louis's attitude had stiffened, becoming uncompromising and legalistic. He ordered his representative at the Diet to "ask for a categorical response from the imperial princes whether or not they plan to allow the emperor or any other prince . . . to violate the treaties of Westphalia. . . . If they are willing to fight to enforce . . . the treaties, I would then promise them to remove my armies from Germany."[17] Louis was using the old ploy of presenting the king of France as the benevolent protector of the German princes against the threat of Hapsburg dominion in Germany; but he was adding new conditions for the French withdrawal of forces from Germany. Louis insisted that the neutral German states must serve as armed guarantors of the Hapsburg withdrawal before he would reciprocate. Characteristically, Louis wanted to leave nothing to chance; he had to have iron-clad contracts to protect his position and his honor.

Shortly after adopting this stiffer position, Louis XIV received news from Grémonville in Vienna that appeared to justify his cautious, unyielding posture in Germany. Grémonville informed the French court that Leopold had already dispatched orders to withdraw the imperial army into Bohemia,[18] but within six days the envoy sent another dispatch with forbidding news: Leopold's chief of staff, the count of Montecuccoli, was planning for war, and the emperor was conferring closely with him and Lisola, the Francophobe. Montecuccoli and Lisola were working openly to discredit Prince Lobkowitz, who was Grémonville's principal contact in Leopold's government and a steadfast opponent of war.[19]

Thus the news that came to the French court, which had already moved from Saint-Germain to the northern frontier in preparation for the summer campaign, was ominous. True, the Imperials apparently would soon march out of Germany, but the clear-cut solution of an immediate mutual withdrawal of the French and imperial armies, which an overcautious Louis XIV had already qualified in his letter to Robert de Gravel, had become further clouded by developments in Vienna. Persons who advised Leopold were arguing vigorously that the imperial retreat should be only temporary, that soon the emperor must return to the old battleground between Hapsburg and Bourbon in Germany, that he had to face Louis XIV's challenge to the European system of states in general and, specifically, his threat to Leopold's position as moral leader of the German-speaking world. How would Louis react to this mixed news from Vienna, where the divided counsels and vacillating character of Emperor Leopold seemed to be solidifying and finding new strength?

Grémonville's dispatch of 27 April reached Louis and his army at Lille, in French Flanders, in mid-May, as the French were preparing to maneuver across the Spanish Netherlands toward the Dutch citadel of Maastricht. The newly acquired firmness, even bellicosity, of the Viennese court threw Louis and his councilors slightly off balance; Louis, after all, did not want war with Emperor Leopold. Pomponne quickly answered Grémonville, telling him that Louis was indeed concerned about Leopold's new determination, but the king thought the emperor's plan to raise an army of 22,000 men was overly optimistic.[20] Moreover, Brandenburg's recent withdrawal from the war should have enough shock effect to convince Leopold to honor his neutrality treaty (November 1671) with Louis and leave the Dutch to the mercies of the French. "The settlement with the elector of Brandenburg was still unknown [in Vienna]. . . . It appears that they [Austrians] will change their tune when they hear about it."[21]

The French king's posture, however, was no longer conciliatory. If Leopold would not follow Elector Frederick William's lead and leave Louis free to consummate his plans in the Netherlands,

Turenne would be readied to cope with the Imperials on German territory. If the emperor continued to prepare an army to enter Germany, Louis would have Turenne maneuver south and west toward the bishopric of Würzburg, on the Main River, as soon as he got word that Brandenburg had ratified the peace treaty.[22] Thus by mid-May 1673, Louis XIV had determined to maintain a royal army deep within Germany while Emperor Leopold carefully withdrew his army into his hereditary lands—a course of action that was to prove one of the most fateful of the entire Dutch War.

During the month of May, couriers from east of the Rhine carried rumors and bits of news into the French court as Louis, with his retinue of queen, ministers, and mistresses, moved leisurely from Arras to Lille and then down a tributary of the Scheldt to Courtrai. The Imperials were *not* retiring into Bohemia but were in Thuringia, awaiting reinforcements;[23] the Imperials were *indeed* withdrawing into Bohemia, but were sending several regiments with the Lorrainers to join the Spaniards in the Low Countries;[24] the Imperials *were* withdrawing from Germany, but a substantial body of troops would be sent toward the upper Rhine and Alsace, where the frontiers of France could be approached via Franche-Comté;[25] a regiment of imperial troops *was* holed up in Friedberg, where it could easily enter the electorate of Trier and occupy the fortress at Koblenz, which dominated the confluence of the Rhine and Moselle Rivers.[26] This illusive regiment nagged at Louvois and Turenne throughout the month of May and no doubt was one of the factors that lay behind Louis XIV's crucial decision of late May 1673.

Fearing that Leopold was girding himself for serious war but with no hard information at hand, save that the main body of imperial troops had orders from Vienna to retire into Bohemia, Louis implemented the plan he had been ruminating on for several weeks: Turenne's army would push into the heart of Germany. On 22 and 23 May, a host of couriers carried the news from the king's headquarters at Courtrai in Flanders to French ambassadors, envoys, and generals throughout Europe. Louvois sent Turenne his new marching orders: "His Majesty wants you . . . to convince the emperor that we can march as far as Bohemia in order to force him to abandon his alliance with the Dutch, and to instill fear in the imperial princes, and to encourage them . . . to compel the emperor to give the declaration [i.e. a written guarantee not to aid the Dutch] that His Majesty wants before he withdraws his troops from Germany." Turenne was told to spare the lands belonging to princes allied to France, "but with regard to the abbey of Fulda and other neighboring lands that belong to princes engaged with the emperor you should show much less consideration. You should also show very little for those belonging to the elector of Trier."[27] The phrases, "show much less consideration" and "very little," have an ominous ring to them, for a seventeenth-century army showing even "great consideration" was calamitous to the territory through which it marched. Thus, Louvois was inviting Turenne to devastate a wide swath of central Germany.

Louvois's orders to Turenne also provide a sharp vignette of Louis XIV's frame of mind in 1673. Although the imperial abbey of Fulda obviously supported the emperor, the "other neighboring lands" belonged mostly to uncommitted princes, such as the counts of Nassau and Hesse-Darmstadt and the bishop of Würzburg. The careless lumping of unspecified "neighboring lands" into the category of enemies shows that the king was in no mood to tolerate or respect neutrality at this time. Indeed, although the elector of Trier was formally allied to Emperor Leopold, he had engaged in no overt hostilities against France.[28] Unless one assumes that Louis was already thinking seriously about invading Trier,[29] his orders not to spare the lands of that elector show a peculiar petulance. Louis was indulging himself by punishing those princes who had not accepted his gold or knuckled under to his threats. Moreover, this sort of punitive measure would put pressure upon the emperor —and provide him with complete justification—to reenter the war against France as protector of one of the great imperial princes. All this occurred, remarkably, at a time when Louis genuinely desired détente with the emperor. The French king's impulse to bully the Germans was harmful to his own interests; with no clear guideline for policy, Louis unwittingly snared himself in a welter of contradictory policies that would take a heavy toll on French fortunes by the end of the year.

On the same day, 22 May, that Louvois dispatched Turenne's orders to advance his army, Louis sent instructions to Robert de Gravel in Regensburg. Gravel was ordered to inform the Diet that Louis XIV regretted that he had to maintain Turenne's army in the empire, but that his only objective was to ensure the peace and well-being of the empire. Gravel was also to declare that Louis truly wished to withdraw the royal army from Germany and that his only condition for effecting the withdrawal was "that the emperor state in writing that he will give no further aid to the States General . . . and that he will agree that the entire empire shall be the guarantor of his word."[30] Gravel duly addressed the diet with these explanations and justifications, and soon Grémonville, Gravel's colleague in Vienna, informed him of the reception his address received in the emperor's capital: "Your last declaration has been printed in a public gazette and entitled a manifesto inaugurating the king's designs on the empire."[31]

The accusations that were bruited in Vienna were untrue; they were merely imperial propaganda. In May 1673, Louis XIV had no desire to extend his conquests into imperial territory. However, the presence of an army of some 20,000 men, even with no intention of conquest, could not be justified after the imperial army had withdrawn into Bohemia.

After Turenne's army marched out of Brandenburg's territories and deeper into Germany, the first reports that came to the French court were mixed. Abbé de Gravel reported from Mainz that Elector Lothar Friedrich von Metternich was troubled; that, as the Imperials had withdrawn into Bohemia, he had no way to answer the steady hail of complaints from the small princes along the Lahn River about French cavalry on their lands. The elector was convinced that the situation "would do Your Majesty's interests no good."[32] On the other hand, Turenne reported that Grémonville's dispatches from Vienna continued to describe Leopold's strenuous efforts to raise an effective army to send westward toward the Rhine. Moreover, the imperial regiment that had been left in Friedberg had accepted the elector of Trier's invitation and marched to garrison Koblenz.[33] Turenne explained that the presence of imperial troops in this strategically located fortress provided a justification for the presence of his army in Germany, but "it would also be very dangerous . . . for the king's army to be in the Circles [i.e. the empire] while the emperor's army is in his hereditary lands. German affairs seem very easy to manage when neither the emperor nor the princes are armed but they quickly take on a different complexion when they have troops on foot. So it appears to me that this is an interval that the emperor wishes to make the best of."[34]

Turenne was surely aware that there was a contradiction in

his letter: his army was needed in Germany, yet its continued presence there created great danger. But the marshal, in his laconic though not unsubtle manner, let the contradiction stand as the best testimony to the complex reality of his position in Germany. Turenne was astute enough not to underestimate Emperor Leopold. Though Leopold was notoriously dilatory, the French general saw that there might be a purpose in the emperor's slowness to act. While the French army under Turenne's command wasted away with disease and inactivity in a hostile land, Leopold recruited and equipped a formidable army within his hereditary lands. The different circumstances of the French and imperial armies during the summer of 1673 would count heavily when Turenne and Montecuccoli faced each other for high stakes in the fall of the year.

In Germany, the reaction to Louis's decision to advance Turenne's army was swift and unequivocal. The French client states, as well as the neutral princes, were taken aback by the news. Franz Egon von Fürstenberg, the more nervous and impulsive of the Fürstenberg brothers, wrote to Pomponne: "For the love of God (but keep this just between the two of us) dissuade the king from this decision or else we will have the entire empire against us."[35] Franz Egon, a fidgety type, became frightened that his sharp protest might jeopardize his position with the French court and recanted in his next letter to Pomponne; but he had not changed his mind. His brother Wilhelm Egon, the more able and levelheaded of the two, sent Pomponne a calm and cogently reasoned protest against Turenne's imminent advance. Wilhelm said that he had visited the duke of Neuburg (a French client) and discovered that the duke agreed with the elector of Cologne that Louis had a right to know the emperor's intentions in Germany, but that Neuburg was extremely worried lest Turenne's march into Franconia would have an effect precisely opposite to what Louis expected.[36] Thus the duke of Neuburg, who was no enemy of the French, was prophesying that Turenne's presence in Germany would damage rather than aid Louis's interests there. The duke and the elector of Cologne had jointly urged Fürstenberg to try to persuade Louis to rescind his marching orders to Turenne, and Wilhelm Egon made it clear to Pomponne that he was in full sympathy with those German princes when he closed his letter with the prediction that the emperor would profit "twenty times more" from Turenne's march into Franconia than he had from his alliance with the elector of Brandenburg.[37]

Louis XIV thought that he could intimidate the imperial princes with Turenne's army, thereby forcing them to side with him, whereas Louis's German clients felt that force would only antagonize and alienate the princes. This was of course a rather fine judgment, but the prophecies of the Fürstenberg brothers and the duke of Neuburg proved to be remarkably accurate.

Robert de Gravel had worked in Germany most of his career and was the best reader of German opinion among the French. He had no fear of openly stating his views to Louis, and when he received the news of Turenne's imminent advance, he immediately drafted a dispatch to the king, spelling out half a dozen reasons why it was a mistake to advance Turenne's army.[38] Gravel based all his arguments upon his fears that Turenne's march "would not only create an uproar in this assembly [the Diet] and in most of the empire, but the emperor and his allies would also reap advantages from it that could prove to be costly."[39]

When Gravel wrote this dispatch to Louis XIV on the morning of 7 June, he was in total agreement with the Fürstenberg brothers. However, by the afternoon or evening of the same day, Gravel almost reversed himself. French ambassadors customarily included a brief letter to the foreign minister in the diplomatic pouch that carried their weekly dispatch to the king, and between the writing of his dispatch to Louis and his letter to Pomponne, Gravel had received a letter from Grémonville, the French special envoy in Vienna. Grémonville was spreading the news that the general of Emperor Leopold's armies, Montecuccoli, hoped to have 30,000 troops on the march by mid-July, and that the Imperials had not blanched at Brandenburg's withdrawal from the war because they fully expected Elector Frederick William to rejoin the anti-French coalition when the time was ripe.[40] Thus on 7 June Gravel wrote to Pomponne that Grémonville's letter "gives me excellent arguments in support of His Majesty's decision not to recall his troops from Germany until the emperor and the princes have given him any assurances that he demands."[41]

Indeed, Gravel did not deny in his letter to Pomponne that Turenne's march would cause an uproar in the Diet, and he may have written it in the fear that in his dispatch to the king he had too severely criticized the decision to advance Turenne. Nonetheless, Vienna's apparent determination to send a large army back into Germany took some of the pressure off Gravel, who was faced with the difficult task of justifying his royal master's policies to the representatives of the German princes in Regensburg.

By mid-June 1673, Louis's ministers, generals, and diplomats were generally agreed that the presence of Turenne's army in the empire was necessary while Emperor Leopold threatened to march an army back across Germany toward the Rhine. Even Pomponne, Louis's moderate foreign minister, may have been convinced that the French had to maintain an army in Germany until Leopold had given his word not to renew hostilities.[42] The only French diplomats who unequivocally opposed Turenne's advance into Franconia were the Fürstenberg brothers, whose views were colored by their roles as double agents, serving both the elector of Cologne and the king of France.

The Fürstenbergs were keenly aware that if the German nation became thoroughly aroused against France, Cologne, as Louis XIV's principal German ally, would pay a heavy price, and the Fürstenbergs' basis of power and influence in the empire would be undercut. Their motives for opposing Turenne's advance were simply those of self-preservation. Nonetheless, the Fürstenbergs were sensitive barometers of the political climate in Germany, and it had been wise of the late foreign minister, Lionne, to confer closely with Wilhelm Egon while formulating French policy toward Germany. When Wilhelm wrote to Pomponne at the end of May that "at present, the situation has changed drastically and what was once advisable [i.e. a tough policy in Germany] no longer seems opportune,"[43] his admonition might well have been heeded.

Although the French were intent on keeping Turenne in Germany, they were not insensitive to the problems created by his army. Louvois insisted repeatedly to Turenne that the strictest discipline had to be maintained among his troops.[44] Finally, Louis took the unusual step of writing to Turenne personally, urging him that "for the sake of my interests it is of cardinal importance that you maintain tight discipline with your troops."[45] Turenne did not have to be prompted. He answered the king and the war minister by informing them that he had just hung three soldiers for pillaging a chateau.[46]

The French had no deliberate scorched-earth policy in 1673.[47] Louvois wanted a royal army that would perform in Germany with surgical skill and precision, fulfilling its task of protecting French interests without opening festering sores by pillage and rape. However, even with the "new army" created by Louvois and his father, Michel Le Tellier, this was no more than wishful thinking.[48] No seventeenth-century army operated with the clean hands that Louvois demanded. Turenne summarized the dilemma for the war minister: "So far as it depends upon me, I will do everything in my power to reconcile two such contrary things, to remain in Germany until we have the emperor's assurance [not to reenter Germany] and to keep the empire content while we devour their country."[49]

During the early summer of 1673, a propaganda battle raged over who was responsible for disrupting the peace of the empire—Leopold, for his threat to send a large army back into Germany, or Louis XIV, for maintaining an army in Germany to prevent this. Both the French and the Imperials adduced legal arguments in their propaganda. Robert de Gravel, at Regensburg, was instructed to emphasize to the diet that France, as a guarantor of the treaties of Westphalia, had the right to deploy an army in Germany to prevent any prince of the empire from aiding Louis's enemies.[50] On the other hand, as French diplomats in Germany reminded Louis, Emperor Leopold was obligated by his oath of election to protect Germany from all foreign intrusion.[51] The possible validity of the French legal claim was not what mattered; Leopold's argument was clearly more compelling to the German princes. The emperor's claim to be the leader of the German-speaking world was not entirely without foundation, despite his weak political position. Turenne himself remarked that the Germans could be moved when the name of the emperor was invoked.[52] Even before the modern nation-state emerged in the western world, Germany was alien territory for an army of the French king.

During the spring and summer of 1673, the presence of Turenne's army in Germany gave the Imperials an immediate propaganda advantage. However, the substantive damage to French interests would come in the fall of the year, when Montecuccoli and Turenne would engage in critical maneuvers along the Main River. By the end of June, a French news-gathering agent in Frankfurt could report that "commerce is ruined throughout Germany, . . . and the most important families are being hurt more by this war . . . than they were during the thirty-three years of the last war in Germany."[53] The agent surely exaggerated the situation. But the advancing French army did not simply intrude upon the German peasants; it also disrupted the affairs of the influential classes in German society.

Turenne's success depended upon a modicum of support from the local gentry and burghers, from the persons who controlled both public opinion and the flow of goods. With the German bourgeoisie thoroughly alienated, Turenne's logistical problems became almost insuperable, for a hostile countryside can quickly cripple an army that depends upon local contributions.

Before May 1673, the onus for the war in Germany had fallen largely upon the Imperials and Brandenburgers, whose march westward toward the Rhine had brought Turenne into Germany. But when Brandenburg made peace at Vossem and Leopold withdrew his army into Bohemia, the situation was reversed. The Germans began to show that hatred of the French whose provocation was one of the cardinal errors made by Louis XIV in the course of the Dutch War.[54] If Louis had planned a war of conquest in Germany, he would of necessity have antagonized and alienated the German nation. But because he had no plans of conquest, his provocation of the Germans was largely gratuitous; it was the result of misconceived policy.

How can this error in judgment be accounted for? First, the French were ebullient when the decision was made to advance Turenne's army. Turenne had beaten the Brandenburgers and Imperials, Elector Frederick William was withdrawing from the war, and the emperor's army was in full retreat. Louis XIV was about to march on Maastricht with a splendid army. Everything was going well for the French, and they were in no mood to worry much about German sensibilities. Turenne himself thought that his army could be used to keep Germany in line: "I do not doubt that [advancing his army] will have a profound effect upon the Franconian and Swabian Circles and, after the fear of being pillaged, the only one that will make them hold firm."[55] Turenne, who usually did not indulge himself by writing in this manner, continued scornfully to Louvois: "The Germans are a cowardly people but because they are just as vainglorious as the Spaniards they want no one to notice it. They are more self-interested, however, and are thus easier to cope with."[56]

This sort of cavalierly drawn national character analysis hurt the French cause during the campaign of 1673, for the Germans proved themselves proud and obstinate beyond Turenne's calculations. However, that Turenne would write in such a manner shows the overconfidence that marked the French attitude in the spring of 1673.

Louis XIV, in deciding to advance Turenne's army, displayed several of his deepest-seated personality traits. A cautious man, he liked to provide for all contingencies. Nothing was to be left to chance when it concerned his affairs, because chance infringed upon the autonomy of the king. The intervention of Leopold and Frederick William had surprised the French in 1672, and Louis was not willing to risk a second interruption of his war in the Netherlands. A certain cautiousness also marked the king's decision to maintain a royal army in Germany even after the Imperials had withdrawn; yet this cautious policy was sure to arouse the suspicion and anger of the German princes. While clumsily attending to his interests, Louis generated outrage among the Germans—whom he had no wish to alienate and whose enmity would not be in his long-run interests. Thus the die was cast for Turenne's disastrous fall campaign of 1673 when Louis chose to maintain a royal army in Germany, after peace had been concluded with Brandenburg and the Imperials had discreetly retired into Bohemia.

Many persons have written about Turenne's second campaign of 1673. Before the French Revolution, Philippe Grimoard, who also edited a collection of Turenne's letters, compiled a detailed though dry and unanalytical chronicle of this campaign.[57] To Napoleon I, the campaign was a black mark on Turenne's career; it was "a shadow on his glory; it was the great captain's greatest mistake."[58] Camille Picavet, in his biographical study of Turenne's last years, described this campaign and focused upon the enmity that grew between Turenne and Louvois as French strategy began to unravel.[59] Yet from the standpoint of military history, the most important question of the campaign has not been studied: how did the imperial army outmaneuver and elude Turenne and then join forces with the Dutch army, after which the allied armies seized Bonn, the capital city of Louis XIV's closest ally, Elector Max Heinrich of Cologne? To understand the weakness of the French military posture and the consequent loss of Bonn, Turenne's campaign must be seen in relation to the king's campaign, which was progressing concurrently with Turenne's and which was more important to the king.

In Germany, toward the end of May, Turenne received the news from Louvois that Elector Frederick William of Brandenburg had ratified the Treaty of Vossem and thus concluded peace with France. As soon as Turenne received the war minister's orders of 22 May, he gathered his troops and marched them out of Brandenburg's Rhenish territories and southward toward the Main River. The marshal was fully aware of his awkward position in an empire that was nominally neutral, and when he was forced to requisition cattle from the countryside to feed his army he wrote to Louvois, carefully explaining his actions: "I have given orders to obtain cows for the infantry, and because it is proper to justify the presence of the royal army in the empire that compels us to requisition these cows I am sending you a copy of the requisition orders; I have also sent a copy to m. de Gravel in Regensburg."[60] Turenne was maneuvering in Germany under orders from Louvois and he wanted the war minister to know the precise conditions with which his army had to cope. Robert de Gravel had the task of justifying the presence of Turenne's army in Germany to the Imperial Diet, which continued its desultory sessions at Regensburg in lower Bavaria.

Turenne left the county of Mark in the latter part of June and, following a course parallel to but some 60 miles east of the Rhine River, traveled slowly southward, beyond the elector of Brandenburg's territories. In mid-July he occupied the imperial free city of Wetzlar, on the Lahn River some 35 miles north of Frankfurt-am-Main, and established new headquarters. Persode de Maizery, the French news-gathering agent in Frankfurt, described the distress and alarm caused by Turenne's approach to the Main: "I am speaking . . . about the fear aroused in the electors of Trier and Mainz and other princes along the Main River. They fear that the royal army will seize a passage over the river and bivouac itself in the area, which would entirely ruin commerce."[61] Turenne admitted to Louvois that some "disorders" were unavoidable, even though he was exerting the strictest discipline to control pillaging by his troops.[62]

Turenne was not an arrogant soldier, but after his brilliant winter campaign in Westphalia he was confident of his position in Germany. The marshal's confidence was bolstered when Maastricht capitulated to the French at the end of June. "You will see," he assured Robert de Gravel in Regensburg, "what a new complexion that will put on things and with what ease the king's armies can now maneuver wherever they wish."[63] Nonetheless, Turenne was willing to face the reality that his presence in Germany would not necessarily prevent Emperor Leopold from sending another army to confront the French on German soil; yet this realization did not disquiet him. From his headquarters at Wetzlar, north of Frankfurt, he wrote to Louvois that "when I learn that the emperor's army is assembled and ready to leave Bohemia, . . . I will advance up the Main. . . . I do not know the size of [the emperor's] army, but the king will be warned in time. The king knows how many companies I have here, and I believe that he will understand that it would be in his interest to see to it that I am not much inferior so that we can force a battle, for which the entire army is most eager."[64]

What a superb attitude for Turenne to assume—that he would require an army only approximately the same size as Montecuccoli's to force a battle and achieve victory. The results of the campaign would show that Turenne's confidence was misguided, that he misjudged the imperial army, as well as his own army's capacity to function in a hostile German countryside. Montecuccoli's skill and the difficult terrain of Franconia would soon make Turenne wish he had not grown quite so confident in the midsummer of 1673. Also, it is possible that Turenne's overconfidence reflected a need to write haughtily and disdainfully to Louvois, who the previous year had implied that Turenne might lack the nerve necessary for combat.[65]

Behind the superb facade, however, Turenne was telling the young war minister to make sure that he had correctly calculated the size of the respective armies and that Turenne was not left wanting for troops. From Thionville on the Moselle, Louvois reassured Turenne on this point: "You can be sure that His Majesty has eighty-six squadrons in this vicinity . . . of which he will send you as many as you need when the size of the emperor's army is known more precisely."[66] Both the marshal and the war minister were confident they could fulfill their mission of stopping the imperial army and maintaining French prestige in Germany. Both were deluded.

Turenne's self-assurance, which remained steady throughout

May, June, and July, began to waver in early August; for the first time, a vague uneasiness appeared in his correspondence. When he heard that the Franconian and Saxon Circles would meet during the latter part of August to discuss the security of the empire, Turenne suggested to Louvois that a French representative be sent to the meeting to justify the French position, for "a foreign army in Germany when the emperor's is in his own territory affects everyone; . . . naturally any German will favor the emperor against the French. And this unanimous agreement, which appears insignificant in the beginning, sometimes turns into a great deal at the end."[67] Turenne was becoming worried lest French provocation bring the usually contentious Germans together and weld them into a force with which to be reckoned. The French marshal's attitude was manifestly different from what it had been in May, when the decision was made to maintain his army within Germany.

Turenne, however, was uneasy not only because he noticed anti-French sentiment welling up among the Germans. By early August Turenne perceived that, despite Louvois's promises of almost unlimited support, Louis XIV was absorbed in his own campaign in Lorraine, Trier, and Alsace, and that providing support for Turenne's army in Franconia was a secondary objective of the king. Turenne wrote to Louvois on 5 August and suggested that 1,000 infantry and four or five squadrons of cavalry be dispatched from Maastricht to garrison one of the many strong points in Germany east of the Rhine and north of the Main Rivers. This would have given the French continued control over the lower Rhine after Turenne moved his army to the south bank of the Main. Turenne foresaw that, should a showdown occur between himself and the imperial army within the empire (all of Europe was expecting it), he could not singlehandedly hold Germany both north and south of the Main. "If I advance into Swabia against the emperor's army, I will leave the country between the Main and the Rhine entirely unprotected. . . . If the king sees things heating up in Germany, some troops there will certainly be required."[68]

Louvois's response to Turenne's suggestion shows the direction the French campaign of 1673 was taking, and one of the principal reasons why it ended so calamitously: "His Majesty cannot now detach from the garrison at Maastricht the thousand men and five squadrons that you propose because there are now only five squadrons there and he has already taken two battalions to garrison Trier."[69] Thus, the king's projects had absorbed the troops that Turenne needed in Germany.

Louis's determination personally to dominate the action of the 1673 campaign made him distribute his soldiers in a manner that violated basic strategic considerations. Louvois, although he may have seen the weaknesses in Louis's plans, was too preoccupied in currying the king's favor to argue with him, too much the sycophant to tell Louis that his pursuit of *gloire* was weakening the French posture in Europe. Everything depended upon stopping the Imperials in central Germany, but Louis could not supply Turenne with the manpower necessary to accomplish that task with certainty.

From Cologne, Honoré Courtin's quick eye caught the importance of Turenne's maneuvers for maintaining the French political position on the Continent. He sketched his opinions in a letter to Pomponne at the end of the first week in August, saying "nothing is more important than to make the king's army [in Germany] appear so large and powerful that no one can doubt that m. de Turenne will be able to dominate the campaign. . . . This is the true and only means of holding the Germans, disabusing the Dutch of their hope of Spanish help, forcing them to accept a peace agreeable to His Majesty, and finishing the war with all the eminence and brilliance befitting the enterprises of the world's greatest king."[70] Courtin was his usual self—not above flattering the king in the hope that it might advance his career, but, as always, maintaining the capacity to place the purely military aspect of affairs within the larger context of French interests. Moreover, Courtin was eager to conclude a peace settlement at Cologne in order to achieve a personal success and thereby further his career in the royal diplomatic service.[71] Courtin knew that he could negotiate only from a position of strength, which meant that the Imperials would have to be cut off before they approached the Rhine and disrupted French operations.

Louis recognized that Turenne's mission in Germany was vitally important—if only to permit the king to continue his maneuvers in Lorraine and Alsace. During August and September, no fewer than four contingents of reinforcements were sent into Germany across the French-held bridges on the Rhine at Philippsburg and Andernach.[72] But the king was too late. Only one of these contingents reached Turenne before the marshal began his fateful maneuvers with Montecuccoli near Würzburg during the first two weeks in September.

Early in the month, while the king and Louvois were headquartered in Nancy and planning the siege of Trier, the war minister wrote Turenne a long letter in which he presented his views on the relative strength of the armies in Germany. Louvois calculated that Turenne had a 4,000-man advantage in cavalry, although he acknowledged that Montecuccoli had a slight edge in infantry. He also informed Turenne that seven squadrons of cavalry had been sent from Trier via Philippsburg to strengthen his army.[73] Turenne received Louvois's letter on 15 September at Ochsenfurt, on the Main River some 15 miles southeast of Würzburg, and began his reply by noting that the seven squadrons would be most welcome "because with the entire countryside opposed to me additional troops will be necessary to procure food."[74] Turenne then noted that it would be pointless to quibble about the details of Louvois's calculations and simply remarked that the war minister's estimates were grossly inaccurate with regard to both infantry and cavalry. He suggested that Louvois had not adequately considered the difference between an army on paper and one in the field maneuvering under adverse conditions,[75] which indeed Louvois seems not to have done.

Disease and desertion were decimating Turenne's army, which had been continuously on campaign since January. Trying to apportion a dwindling supply of royal soldiers, Louvois chose to ignore this crucial fact, for in his letter to Turenne of 9 September he advocated a defensive posture for the marshal's army on the grounds that the imperial army, after its long march from Bohemia into Franconia, would be weaker than the French.[76]

Louvois's analysis is a striking example of how his lack of experience in the field distorted his strategic judgment. In theory, a defensively stationed army should have an advantage in logistics and morale over an opposing force that has marched a long distance to the battle. However, this theoretical axiom was not relevant to the military situation in Germany in the autumn of 1673.[77] The imperial army had not deteriorated significantly during its slow march through friendly territory, whereas Turenne's army had been substantially weakened by its prolonged sojourn in Germany, where the populace was increasingly hostile toward the French intruders. Not since the Thirty Years' War had so many handbills appeared in Germany, but in 1673 the epigrams were no longer religious; they were political and they did not pit German against German but German against Frenchman. Louis XIV's policies had begun to generate, however faintly, a sort of German nationalism:

> *Rouse your spirits, brave Imperial soldiers;*
> *Matching steel against iron, strike at the Frenchmen,*
> *Who bring death and disrupt the German peace.*
> *Now is the time to do brave deeds.*[78]

Turenne remained headquartered in the free imperial city of Wetzlar on the Lahn from mid-July to mid-August and then proceeded south to the Main River, just upstream from Frankfurt. Despite the efforts of the Imperials to prevent news from leaking out of Bohemia, abbé de Gravel had agents sending reports from Eger, the rendezvous for the imperial army in western Bohemia.[79] By the end of August, Turenne heard from Gravel that Montecuccoli was prepared to march back into Germany and that he would lead his army into Franconia.[80] Upon receiving this news, Turenne crossed the Main River to the southern side on the elector of Mainz's bridge at Aschaffenburg and led his army eastward up the valley of the Main. The French marshal's intention was to seek out the imperial army and destroy it.

The university city of Würzburg is on a southern loop of the Main, where the vineyard-covered banks rise abruptly from the river. During the beginning of September 1673, Turenne and Montecuccoli prepared for battle near Würzburg. From Regensburg, Robert de Gravel wrote to Louis XIV that everything in Germany depended on the imminent confrontation between the French and the imperial armies.[81] The English ambassadors at Cologne wrote to Lord Arlington that "it is at present the great Crisis of our Negotiation, God grant it [be] prosperous."[82]

Louvois, agitated by thoughts of the impending battle, wrote Turenne a curious letter. During the 1672 campaign French courtiers had circulated rumors that Turenne's reluctance to rush into battle was due to cowardice rather than the true professional's circumspection. On 9 September Louvois wrote to Turenne: "to prevent similar things this year you have only to describe fully to His Majesty what you are prepared to do, or, if you judge that it would be in his best interest to do nothing, to inform him precisely what has prevented you from doing something."[83] When Louvois wrote in this tenor in the same letter in which he "explained" Turenne's numerical superiority over Montecuccoli, he seemed to want to intimidate Marshal Turenne, who retorted with his famous remark that he did not think it in the king's best interests to give such specific orders even to the most incapable man in France —implicitly, of course, much less to the vicomte de Turenne.[84] Turenne's answer was simply an angry reaction to Louvois's attempt to bully him, for Louvois had sent him no specific orders; Turenne's only orders were to prevent the Imperials from approaching the Rhine River or giving aid to the Dutch. A rift had nonetheless developed between Louvois and Turenne, and the denouement would occur when Turenne returned to court late that year.

The decisive battle, however, for which Europe had been waiting was never fought. During the first two weeks of September, two of the best strategists of modern times did a minuet of march and countermarch on the middle reaches of the Main River. A contemporary remarked that "Monsieur le Prince [de Condé] is the best in the world for one day, and Monsieur de Turenne is the best for a campaign";[85] but in Montecuccoli, Turenne would more than meet his match. By mid-September Turenne had progressed upstream past Würzburg and was separated from the imperial army by only a two hours' march.

Turenne wrote Louvois an anguished report on 15 September; he wanted to give battle, but, given the rugged terrain, his logistical difficulties, and the decaying state of his army, the issue could not be joined unless Montecuccoli also wanted to fight. "If you do not believe me, please look at a map,"[86] Turenne advised the war minister. Montecuccoli, however, had no intention of fighting. He was too shrewd to do what his opponent wanted him to do, and moreover, he had plans of his own.

On 17 September, two days after Turenne sent his report to Louvois, the bishop of Würzburg, whom Turenne had considered a friendly neutral, gave his bridgehead on the Main to Montecuccoli. This altered the strategic setting immediately and radically. Turenne explained the situation in a second report to Louvois, telling the war minister that because Montecuccoli now controlled Würzburg, "the key to all of Franconia," and most of the strategic bridges on the Main, the French army would have to retreat.[87]

With the bridges and thus the river under his control, Monte-cuccoli led his army downstream toward Frankfurt at his leisure. There is no doubt, however, that Turenne wanted to engage in battle. An Englishman in his army described the situation at the end of September: "If we can gette the Imperiallists at an ad-vantage we shall certainly fight them, and doubtles they have the same intentions; so that nowe two of the greatest generalls in Christendom employ all that their long experience has tought them, for the interest and good of their great masters, and the preserving of their own honor, knowing the great consiquence the losse of a Battle would be to either side."[88]

The Englishman was correct in his observations, except on one vital point: Montecuccoli did not wish to meet Turenne head-on and offer battle. He was not obliged to do so in order to accom-plish his mission, which was to disrupt French operations along the Rhine River, undercut French influence in Germany, and em-barrass the French position in the Netherlands.

Can Turenne be faulted for letting Montecuccoli elude him? If the French marshal had had overwhelming numerical superiority, he might have forced a battle in mid-September, when the armies were only two hours' apart, but it is probable that he had no superiority whatever. Louis XIV and Louvois might have assured him the necessary manpower, but they had their own campaign under way, which precluded establishing a superior French force in Franconia; those seven squadrons sent from Trier arrived too late to help Turenne when he was maneuvering near Würzburg.

If Turenne had not trusted the bishop of Würzburg but had seized and held his bridge, Montecuccoli's maneuvers might well have aborted. Turenne did not seize the bridge for three good reasons: (1) he thought it unwise to coerce a neutral imperial prince while his French army was making the French very un-popular in Germany; (2) the abbé de Gravel, who had visited the bishop of Würzburg in August, reported that the bishop appeared to be a peace-loving man who did not wish to take sides in the Franco–imperial conflict; and (3) Turenne simply did not have a sufficient number of soldiers to garrison Würzburg and to hold the bridgehead.

That Montecuccoli maneuvered with consummate skill, mak-ing the best use of the topography, his men, and a sympathetic populace, cannot be doubted. How Turenne, with his limited resources, could have stopped him, without risking a military debacle of the first order, is impossible to say. Turenne's mistakes were not in his maneuvers; probably no one could have done better. The young marquis de Chamlay, who was under Turenne's command but who wrote directly to Louvois, did not fault the marshal's leadership.[89] The marshal's error in judgment had occurred during the spring and summer, when he repeatedly expressed every confidence that he could deal with Montecuccoli by himself with relative ease. If he had received reinforcements earlier, he might have done just that. Undoubtedly, however, Turenne had underestimated Montecuccoli's capacity to conduct a campaign of elusive maneuvering over difficult terrain. Indeed, Montecuccoli may have been "the best in the world" for such a campaign, and only relative to this great imperial soldier's brilliance was Turenne's glory tarnished.

After Montecuccoli eluded Turenne near Würzburg, he had control over the entire area of Germany east of the Rhine and north of the Main—unless Turenne could make a forced march downriver, cross the Main on the elector of Mainz's bridge at Aschaffenburg, and intercept the imperial army somewhere east of Frankfurt. Louvois, who knew there was no French force of consequence east of the lower Rhine, had repeatedly impressed upon Turenne the necessity of holding the bridge at Aschaffenburg.[90] If, as Louvois envisaged it, Turenne's army was to be the only French presence in Germany, a bridge over the Main was the *sine qua non* of a successful campaign; otherwise, Turenne would be cut off south of the Main and the lower Rhine would be open to the imperial army; the electorate of Cologne, Louis's close ally, would be vulnerable; and the Imperials could easily move into the Low Countries to support the Dutch.

Although Montecuccoli crossed the Main and forced Turenne to fall back downstream, Turenne still held the elector of Mainz's chateau at Aschaffenburg, defended by 550 men and two cannons.[91] It was a small garrison, but all that Turenne's meager supply of men would allow. Explaining his dilemma in a letter of 28 September, he was pessimistic about holding the Aschaffenburg bridgehead because it was difficult to defend and because he was obliged to bivouac the mass of his army some 35 miles away on the Tauber River, the Tauber Valley being his only tenable logistical base when Montecuccoli and the imperial army had "every place in Franconia at their disposal."[92]

Although, during the first week in October, Turenne increased the garrison at Aschaffenburg to 1,200 men,[93] he informed Louvois on 16 October that he was returning the château at Aschaffenburg to the elector of Mainz on the elector's guarantee that he would not deliver the bridge to the Imperials.[94] Turenne made this critical decision for two reasons. First, Montecuccoli, who controlled all the bridges over the Main and was favored with a cooperative populace, which minimized his logistical problems, could mass his forces at Aschaffenburg more quickly than Turenne; therefore the French position at Aschaffenburg was no longer tenable. According to Lord Arlington's correspondent in Turenne's army, the bridge could not be held "above 24 hours if an army with cannon comes before it."[95] Second, Turenne did not know Montecuccoli's intentions precisely. If the elector of Mainz surrendered his Rhine bridge to the imperial general, Montecuccoli might plunge directly westward into Trier and Lorraine, threatening France itself. Thus Turenne struck a bargain with the elector of Mainz that at least would help assure the safety of the French frontier. The elector destroyed his bridge on the Rhine and Turenne returned the strategic bridge at Aschaffenburg to the elector.[96]

Elector Lothar von Metternich genuinely wished to remain neutral at this point in the war because he could not judge the outcome of the campaign;[97] and Turenne found it prudent to cooperate with him, even if this opened the lower Rhine to Montecuccoli's army. Turenne's first priority was to hold the line of the Rhine and secure the eastern frontier of France, and Louis XIV's Rhenish allies, Cologne and Münster, would have to fend for themselves in the face of the imperial forces. The intendant in Turenne's army, Camus de Beaulieu, reported to Louvois (his real master) that "M. de Turenne is very content. . . . The march since Aschaffenburg has made it impossible for the enemy to initiate anything in Alsace, Lorraine, Franche-Comté, or Trier."[98] This did not provide much consolation to the war minister when the entire lower Rhine lay exposed to the imperial army. But Beaulieu's remarks tell us two things, that Turenne saw the protection of the French frontier as his principal responsibility, and that Beaulieu, Louvois's man in Turenne's army, had no criticism to make of the marshal's maneuvers.

After forfeiting Aschaffenburg, Turenne moved the bulk of his army westward to a position directly south of Frankfurt. Persode de Maizery, the French agent in Frankfurt, kept the marshal informed of Montecuccoli's activities. The city magistrates entertained the imperial general and his staff at dinner, but they feared French reprisals too much to turn the city's bridge on the Main over to the Imperials.[99] Montecuccoli therefore began to build a floating bridge across the river, using barges for support. Turenne no doubt found it hard to believe that Montecuccoli, having carefully avoided a pitched battle near Würzburg, would recross the Main to face the French south of Frankfurt, but he waited several days to be certain. Turenne reported to Louvois in his most laconic prose: "Although it has been four days since I have taken the honor to write to you, I do not have much to add to my previous letters because events are working out as I informed you they would."[100] Turenne's deliberate, cool style was more than simply a professional soldier's mannerism; it told Louvois that Turenne was in no way responsible for the ominous situation that confronted the French in Germany. After all, Turenne had advised Louvois in August that a blocking force should be stationed in Germany north of the Main River to safeguard French interests.[101]

The abandonment of the Aschaffenburg bridgehead meant that Turenne would have to backtrack all the way through Heidelberg, to the bridge on the upper Rhine at Philippsburg, before he could march his army to the lower Rhine on the western side of the river. When, in late October, Louvois heard that Turenne had forfeited the bridge at Aschaffenburg, he no doubt immediately grasped the seriousness of the situation: the whole of the lower Rhine lay virtually unprotected, and the possibility was very real that Montecuccoli could join forces with the prince of Orange and undertake offensive action against Louis's allies, Münster and Cologne, or even against France itself. Louvois's sarcastic and scornful response to Turenne's bleak news reveals the war minister's consternation: "You can imagine that the king is waiting with some disquietude for your first letters in order that he might know your plans. The prince of Orange has not been able to pull himself out of the mud."[102] Louvois might have shown more respect and less contempt for the young prince, for within one month of Louvois's belittling letter the prince's exploits would embarrass Louvois enough to jeopardize his position on Louis's high council.

On 21 October, Turenne learned that Montecuccoli had broken up his half-built bridge near Frankfurt (it had been a feint) and was moving his army down the Main toward its confluence with the Rhine at Mainz.[103] Thus, during the last week in October, Turenne turned south and marched his army toward the bridge on the Rhine at Philippsburg. Abbé de Gravel, who spent much of the day and night observing the imperial army from a church spire high over Mainz, kept the French marshal informed of Montecuccoli's new engineering project—a floating bridge across the Rhine just downstream from Mainz.[104]

Fearing that Montecuccoli might penetrate eastern France after completing his new bridge, Turenne led his army on a forced march toward Philippsburg and arrived there on 26 October. He had given up all hope of preventing Montecuccoli from ravaging the electorate of Cologne—if that was the imperial commander's objective—and simply counted upon intercepting the imperial army west of the Rhine.[105] A member of Turenne's English contingent (young John Churchill, the future duke of Marlborough, was apparently an officer among the Englishmen who served under Turenne)[106] sent Lord Arlington a description of Turenne's weary army as it approached the bridge on the Rhine at Philippsburg:

> Since my last to your Lordp. of the 22 of this month, we have been on the march heither. The Elector Palatin made us two bridges over the Necker att Lauenback, near Hidelberg; monsieur de Turenne had his dinner brought to the bridge, and was there two days to see the army pass. He made all horses and cowes taken by the soldiers to be return'd to their owners. . . . This day all our army will have past the Rhin on the bridge at Philisbourg. The armys [Turenne's and Montecuccoli's] are nowe att that distance, and the winter comes on so fast 'tis believed this will goe suddenly into winter Quarters.[107]

In keeping with his character, Turenne remained the professional, overseeing the river crossings and trying to maintain discipline among his troops. One wonders, however, what thoughts ran through the aging marshal's head as he sat, ate, and watched his army trudge across the two bridges—and out of his second campaign of 1673, a campaign that had been nothing but forced marches and frustration. If Turenne harbored no bitterness toward his king for the delinquent promises on behalf of his campaign, he must have considered wreaking vengeance on that overbearing bureaucratic upstart, the marquis of Louvois.

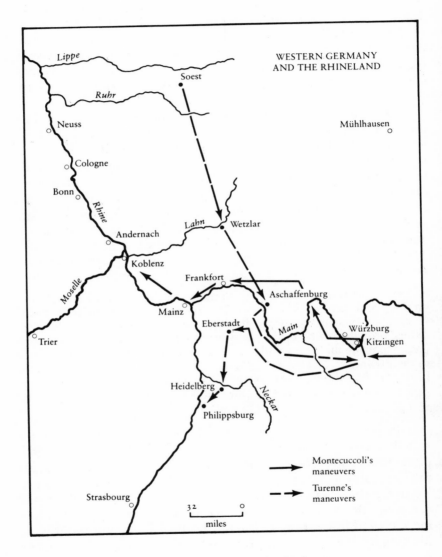

Turenne's Campaign, June–November 1673

IV

The Cologne Conference:
Honoré Courtin's Disenchantment

When Louis XIV attacked the Dutch in the spring of 1672 and threatened to annihilate their republic, Sweden was caught in an embarrassing position of her own making. The Swedish economy was wholly dependent upon the Dutch—upon their investments, their financial expertise, and their massive merchant fleet that plied the Baltic.[1] Although the Swedes occasionally resented their dependence upon the Dutch, sheer necessity dictated their interest in preserving the Dutch Republic. Thus in 1668 Sweden had entered the Triple Alliance in order to stop Louis's first attack upon the Low Countries during the War of Devolution, and had joined in the renewal of this alliance in January 1670.[2] But despite these commitments to help keep the French out of the Netherlands, the impecunious Swedes found the prospect of French subsidies too tempting to resist, and in April 1672 they signed the Treaty of Stockholm with France. By this instrument the Swedes bound themselves to send an army to support Louis XIV if any prince of the empire should dare, for any reason, to mount an attack against the French armies.[3] Trapped in this web of contradictory treaties and interests, Sweden had strong motives to try to arrange a peace settlement between the French and the Dutch. By autumn 1672, Swedish diplomats were feverishly at work at Saint-Germain, London, and The Hague, attempting to convince the three principal belligerent powers to agree to peace negotiations. Early in

Honoré Courtin (1626–1703),
engraving by Robert Nanteuil
(courtesy of the Bibliothèque Nationale)

October, Louis XIV gave in to Swedish demands and agreed to send plenipotentiaries to a conference at which the Swedes would try to mediate a peace between the Dutch and their French and English antagonists.[4]

Though rumors of an impending peace conference were circulated throughout Europe before the end of 1672, the conference did not convene in the free imperial city of Cologne until June 1673. While the 1673 campaign continued, the diplomats tried desperately to get serious negotiations started, but they failed. The peace conference ended fruitlessly in February 1674, when the abduction of Wilhelm von Fürstenberg in Cologne by imperial soldiers gave Louis XIV an excuse to recall his diplomats.

The Cologne Conference has been stigmatized by a recent authority as unfertile ground for the historian: "There was never the slightest chance of agreement. . . . A detailed account of the negotiations would be as barren as they were."[5] A contemporary seventeenth-century historian and diplomat, the informed and often penetrating Abraham de Wicquefort, had no kinder words for the Cologne Conference. Louis XIV, he wrote, had intended to send Godefroi, count d'Estrade, who had served as French ambassador in London and The Hague, as the head of the royal negotiating team. "But this cagey minister complained to the king that he would be sorely chagrined, if after . . . so much success he were flung into a negotiation which there was no intention of making succeed, and that would cost him the reputation he had acquired in preceding assignments; and he implored the king to relieve him of the embassy if he did not intend to make peace. This was why the duke of Chaulnes replaced him as the head of the embassy."[6]

These disparaging judgments would seem to indicate that the Cologne Conference was a mere bagatelle, hardly worthy of the historian's time and effort. Although the conference was abortive, the negotiations that were held in Cologne during 1673–74 are important because they tell us much about Louis XIV's policies during the Dutch War and because they reveal an interesting interplay of personality and politics.

Why, in fall 1672, did Louis XIV, "in the midst," as he said, "of all the advantages my arms have won,"[7] agree to a peace conference? It was not because Louis sought peace, for the king agreed to let Sweden mediate a conference only in order to manipulate the Swedes. The Swedes had shown themselves loath to honor the Treaty of Stockholm and assist the French in Germany while Louis XIV was threatening to destroy the Dutch Republic. Louis was counting heavily on Swedish assistance in his conflict with the emperor and the elector of Brandenburg, and by "proving" his moderation in consenting to a peace conference he hoped to entice Sweden into the war on his side. When, in October 1672, Louis accepted the Swedish offer to mediate, he wrote to his ambassador in Stockholm that he had done so "to provide more tangible proof of my confidence in Sweden and of my disposition for peace."[8] A month later, Louis was even willing to grant a cease-fire in order to convince the king of Sweden "of the sincerity of my intentions for peace."[9] In early February 1673, Louis XIV stated his position with remarkable candor and bluntness for his new ambassador in Stockholm, the Marquis Isaac de Feuquières: "To calm the suspicions of Sweden is my *only* goal in this affair. I have *no* desire to make peace."[10] During the winter of 1672–73 Louis thought he could defeat the Dutch and that, with one more campaign, he could deliver the *coup de grâce* to the Dutch Republic.

Yet, by the end of February 1673, Louis seemed to be changing his attitude, if only slightly. He wrote to his ambassador in London that "whether we continue the war or end it with a treaty, nothing is so important as to show all Europe that we want peace."[11] Then, several weeks later, Louvois wrote to the commander of the French army in the Dutch Netherlands: "The king is not thinking of taking Holland [the province] by force at the present nor of conquering Friesland and Groningen."[12] By 1 April, Louvois could flatly declare that "the king has decided to give the Dutch peace if they accept his conditions but to continue the war if they prove stubborn."[13]

Thus there was a perceptible change in Louis XIV's thinking about the Dutch between early February and April of 1673. In February, he had been unrelenting in his pursuit of the war in the United Provinces, but by April he was considering some kind of settlement. Certainly in April, Louis was not yet prepared for hard negotiations in which he might have to forfeit some of his Dutch conquests of the preceding year, but he was at least ready to use a peace conference as a forum to dictate his terms to the Hollanders. Precisely one year after he had invaded the Dutch Republic, Louis XIV was contemplating ending the Dutch War without fulfilling his objective of destroying the republic and creating a satellite state in the Low Countries.

Why, at the end of March 1673, did Louis XIV change his posture toward the Dutch, stepping back from his earlier determination to carry the war into the heartlands of the Dutch Republic? First, the war in the United Provinces was becoming a burden. After the Dutch flooded their countryside in summer 1672, stopping the royal armies, the French hoped that they could still overcome the water barrier in one way or another. Perhaps waterborne operations could be carried out; perhaps the polders would freeze during the winter and the French could march across the ice toward Amsterdam and The Hague; perhaps 1673 would be a drier year and the flood waters would recede enough to permit the French to push beyond Utrecht into the heartlands of the republic.

By early spring 1673, all of these possibilities had come to naught. Luxembourg's attempt to march his cavalry on a thin coat of ice across the polders foundered when a warm front had swept into the Netherlands.[14] Although there had been an isolated success in approaching the unconquered Dutch provinces by water, the French were not equipped to mount a general waterborne assault. Finally, by the end of March it was apparent that the flood waters would be even higher in 1673 than in the preceding year.[15] The flood waters not only crippled French offensive operations, but also turned French headquarters at Utrecht into an isolated and beleaguered outpost, difficult and expensive to supply with men and materiel. Utrecht was a long and watery way from the French logistical bases in metropolitan France. Luxembourg, the royal commander in occupied Utrecht, wrote to Louvois in mid-March that he could not depart on an inspection tour of his fortifications until he found out "about certain boats that are supposedly being prepared in Amsterdam."[16] In other words, Luxembourg was worried that he might have to go on the defensive against a Dutch sortie from Amsterdam.

Louvois's response shows the irritation that was developing at Versailles as it became apparent that Louis XIV's war of *éclat* had been squelched by the flooded polders: "If Dutch finances were as well off as the king's, they would ruin themselves experimenting; it seems that six months never pass without their concocting something else. I am convinced that the boats they are now making will be of no more use to them than their other machines have been."[17] Louvois's blustering was an attempt to conceal his anxiety that the genius of the Dutch bourgeois experimenters would frustrate French plans for a decisive victory. Increasingly, the war in the Dutch Netherlands was a frustration, and there was little hope that it would finish in the dazzling fashion it had begun a year earlier.

In addition to the mounting difficulties of the war in the Low Countries, Louis XIV was no doubt persuaded to begin negotiations because, at the end of March 1673, the international situation took a sudden turn that could only help the French extract favorable terms from the Dutch. A settlement between France and Brandenburg, who was the only active ally of the Dutch in spring 1673,[18] was imminent. On the last day of March, Louvois, writing from Saint-Germain, remarked that "a representative of the elector of Brandenburg arrived here yesterday with powers to make a settlement with the king."[19] Louis XIV was therefore surely thinking that when he made peace with Elector Frederick William, the isolation of the Dutch would make them easy prey at the bargaining table. The duke of Vitry, Louis's special envoy in Bavaria, summed up the French attitude: "The accommodation with the elector of Brandenburg makes it absolutely necessary for the Dutch to make peace, since it shatters any hope they had of receiving aid from Germany."[20]

Thus by spring 1673, with the royal army in the Netherlands bogged down and the diplomatic situation ripening, Louis XIV was prepared to consider dictating a peace settlement to the Dutch at a formal conference. As Louvois explained to the officer who was charged with disseminating French propaganda in Utrecht and Holland, the settlement would be a good one: "The misery to which the Dutch will be reduced by the prince of Condé on the one side and by the king on the other will provide you with an opportunity to distribute many pamphlets. . . . Being reduced to a condition in which they cannot survive without making peace, they will have to pay twice as dearly for it as they would have last year."[21] To be sure, Louvois was exaggerating the strength of the French position; he was trying to make himself feel better about having urged the king to spurn the Dutch offers at Doesburg in June of 1672. In any event, Louis XIV's strategy in late spring 1673 was to keep pressure on the Dutch until the wealthy merchants had had enough of the war that was disrupting their commerce and biting into their pocketbooks. They would then force the bellicose young prince of Orange to make peace on Louis's terms. But the French ruler was underestimating the tenacity of the Dutchmen and their prince.

Conforming to the usual practice of the Old Regime, Louis sent a high-ranking nobleman, Duke Philipe de Chaulnes, as titular head of the negotiating team that would meet the Dutch in Cologne. Honoré Courtin, a career diplomat from a family of the lesser robe nobility, went to Cologne as principal negotiator. A contemporary who saw Courtin negotiate at Breda in 1666 said of him: "He was always gay and inspired gaiety in others. He was considered a highly intelligent and experienced man, and it appeared to me that he was the soul of the negotiations."22 Courtin was a vain, high-strung man with a finely developed sense of the absurd—though he was utterly serious about his peacemaking mission in spring 1673. Paul de Barrillon was taken from the intendancy of Turenne's army, which was often a stepping stone to high office in the bureaucracy of the Old Regime, and sent to Cologne as backup negotiator to Courtin. Barrillon thus began a distinguished career as a royal diplomat with a thankless assignment at the doomed-to-fail peace conference.

Peace conferences during the Old Regime were as much social as diplomatic events. Courtin, a *bon vivant*, began the festivities early, as he and Chaulnes moved northward down the Meuse River, having left Paris on 30 April. As they proceeded by stages down river, Courtin reported to Pomponne, who as foreign minister was Courtin's immediate superior, on the progress of their trip. Pomponne had gone to the Low Countries early in May with the king's army, and he replied with good humor and high spirits: "The gaiety, Sirs, with which your voyage has begun . . . is a good augury for all Europe. The joy that accompanies you seems to be a foretaste of the fruits that your negotiations must bring. . . . However, we here are in the midst of a train with a very different air than that of peace; never was there a more beautiful army nor one better maintained to act with the greatest glory and success."23

The exhilaration of a spring campaign had infected even the cool and nonbellicose Pomponne, although he hints in his prose that peace was a long way off; indeed, too distant for a man who was a diplomat and not a warrior. In any event, the foreign minister and his diplomats were on cordial terms at this point, and

Courtin would have his chance at making peace for Louis XIV.

Courtin and Chaulnes arrived late in May at the elector of Cologne's town, Brühl, a short distance outside the free imperial city of Cologne. There they awaited the neutralization of the emperor's garrison stationed in Cologne, for the marquis of Grana's regiment was to take an oath of fidelity, binding it exclusively to the municipal government for the duration of the peace conference.[24] While waiting in Brühl, the French plenipotentiaries were entertained by the Fürstenberg brothers, Wilhelm Egon and Franz Egon, at their country house. Courtin was pleased to report to Pomponne that Barrillon, the new diplomat, had arrived from Turenne's army in Germany and that he gained much honor in a drinking bout in "the finest room of the château—viz. the wine cellar. We drank to His Majesty's health from glasses that were his gifts and of which he knows the depth, and we hope that he will thus know how well he was served on this occasion."[25] Heavy drinking was a necessary part of diplomacy in early modern Germany.

Courtin also wrote to Condé from the château at Brühl, informing the prince that he was writing in the same room where "Cardinal Mazarin meditated his return to France."[26] Here Courtin was thinking of what he saw as his own historic moment: he would go to Cologne and make peace, as Mazarin (who had patronized Courtin) had returned and pacified France to end the Fronde.

The three French diplomats entered Cologne on 6 June and the following day they reported to Pomponne on their entry: "We arrived yesterday in this city incognito, although to the roar of cannons, the magistrates not being able to dispense rendering this honor to our station."[27] A baroque passion for intrigue and drama provided an absurd moment as the loud welcome revealed the diplomats' identities.

The English plenipotentiaries, Joseph Williamson and Leoline Jenkins, were delayed by contrary winds over the Channel and arrived in Cologne one week after the Frenchmen. After being assured by the "messieurs de la ville" that rumors of plague in the city were false, they began their lessons in politics and etiquette with Courtin. He informed the Englishmen that it was permissible for them to visit the Dutch, "in Regard their King did still in his passports call them Tres-cheres and grand amis, and that this Kind of Visit was practis'd at Münster and Breda"; that the French and English should allow the Dutchmen to make the first move, because "a Month, or two, or three at furthest (within which time a good account of Maestricht was to be expected), would ripen things very much"; and that Lisola was "the Person most likely (when he arrived) to attempt something in Order to raise Jealousies and to disconcert us, it being suitable to his Talent and Manner of Proceeding."[28] The English plenipotentiaries were no fools, particularly Williamson, but because both of them were serving on their first diplomatic mission, they readily accepted the tutelage of the knowledgeable and experienced Honoré Courtin.

The delegation of Swedish mediators, headed by Count Tott, won the conference's first honors by entering Cologne "in such complete incognito that they occupied their lodgings without anyone knowing it."[29]

Louvois ordered the French commanders in the Netherlands to treat the Dutch plenipotentiaries "as ambassadors despite the contempt that we have for the people of that nation,"[30] so that Hieronymous van Beverningk, the hard-drinking but shrewd head of the Dutch delegation, and his colleagues passed through French-occupied territory to arrive in Cologne three hours after the English delegation. By mid-June the peace conference was about to begin "in a city not only today the most celebrated in Germany but even in all Europe."[31]

As they shuttled between the French, Dutch, and English delegations, the Swedish mediators encountered immediate obstacles to the negotiations. The French were bound by their instructions not to present demands but to await offers from the Dutch.[32] The Dutch, in turn, demanded to know Louis XIV's justification for attacking their republic and insisted that they could not make concrete offers without risking the grisly fate of the De Witt brothers, whose alleged softness had cost them their lives in August 1672.[33] England's demand for certain towns on the Dutch coast was simply unrealistic, too extravagant to consider.[34]

The Swedes attempted to break the deadlock by arranging a plenary conference at a Carmelite monastery in Cologne. On 28 and 29 June the French and English delegations (the Dutch did not appear) met with the Swedes, who proposed that some of the smaller matters of contention be taken up in detail in order to start the negotiations and that, in the meantime, a general cease-fire be arranged to provide an atmosphere more suitable for negotiating.[35] Neither the French nor the English diplomats liked these suggestions, however, and Tott therefore decided to try another approach. He departed Cologne for Maastricht, which, thanks to Louis XIV's besieging army, had eclipsed Cologne to become for the moment the most celebrated city in Europe. Count Tott's purpose in traveling to Maastricht was to meet the French king in person and attempt to persuade him to make concessions that would allow the Swedes to activate the stalled negotiations in Cologne.[36]

Before Tott left for Maastricht on 30 June, Courtin, a seasoned diplomat, had perceived the drift of affairs and decided that Maastricht, at least for the moment, was the center of diplomacy. Courtin asked Louvois, his friend and regular correspondent, to obtain permission for him to come to the siege because "m. de Barrillon is so proud of his last campaign that I must conduct a small one of three or four days in order to stand beside him."[37] Despite this disarming plea, Courtin's request was denied. He thereupon wrote to Louvois in curious words—unusual even for the mischievous Courtin (whose impish brilliance was captured by Nanteuil in an engraved portrait):

> You'll see what's going to happen. I am going to make a peace that will surprise you, and you'll be in some fix when you're left with all those cannons you love so much. And when you have to disband the larger part of those troops you march so well you'll be not a little mortified. Our dispatches . . . are not so good as you might wish if you had nothing better to do than to listen to the fallacious arguments that ambassadors often use; but, since that's not your problem, we will continue to do the best we can, and the king will be carefully and faithfully served.[38]

This brief paragraph is filled with information, suggestions, and subtlety, and it could be analyzed and reanalyzed at length; however, we will make just a few remarks. After only one week at Cologne, Courtin decided that he had been sent on a hollow mission: his royal master apparently was not much interested in the peace conference or its possible results. Courtin was proud of his trade as a diplomat and took the success or failure of his mission as a point of honor. Also, Courtin's desire to witness the siege of Maastricht was not rooted in a sense of chivalric competition with his colleague Barrillon; Courtin, like the Swede Tott, doubtless hoped that he could influence the course of high politics by visiting

Louis XIV at his encampment near Maastricht. Apparently, Tott and Courtin were correct: the center of action in June 1673 was Maastricht. The French king's attention was riveted on his siege, and the negotiations in Cologne were relegated to the periphery of his vision of affairs.

Tott arrived at the French camp on 4 July and was permitted only one talk with Louis. The king received his proposals for a cease-fire and a reduction of French demands courteously but coldly. Elated over his recent conquest of Maastricht, Louis was in no mood to moderate his stiff terms at Cologne or to give the Dutchmen respite by granting them a cease-fire.[39] Tott countered by telling the king some hard facts: Sweden accepted the humiliation of the Dutch Republic, but she would not accept its annihilation. The Swedes vitally needed the Dutch trade, and King Charles XI of Sweden equated the Dutch Republic's survival with that of his own state. Although Sweden wanted Louis to soften his demands upon the Dutch, the English demands, particularly for cautionary towns on the Dutch coast, were the most objectionable, Tott said. The Dutch ambassadors had insisted that they might as well be asked to agree to the destruction of their republic, for that was what the English demands amounted to. Tott informed Louis that he not only agreed with the Dutch but that the Swedish king would never accept the English demands. It was important to all the "Northern powers," Tott remarked, that no single state control the coasts of both England and the Low Countries.[40]

Louis, taken aback by Tott's vehemence, admitted to his ambassador in England, Colbert de Croissy, that he did not know "how to take this speech, but that it certainly smacked of a protest designed to justify Swedish plans to help the Dutch."[41] In a dispatch to his plenipotentiaries at Cologne, Louis expressed his worries more explicitly, saying that he was baffled by Tott's speech and was not sure whether Tott was acting upon orders from Stockholm. "If you believe that he acted upon orders, ... and that Sweden might not only not oppose plans to aid the Dutch but that she may even abate them, you must above all avoid giving the Swedish mediators the least suspicion that I might have any misgivings concerning the alliance, the friendship, or the treaty [of Stockholm, April 1672] that I have with that crown."[42]

The French king was confused and shaken by Tott's visit to his camp, but his worries about Sweden's intentions were unfounded. The Swedes had no thought of joining an anti-French coalition because they were even less prepared to fight France than to join her, as the Treaty of Stockholm required.[43] Only later, when the Swedes entered the war on the French side, would Louis XIV learn how feeble once-mighty Sweden had become.

Colbert de Croissy, in London, was also sent detailed instructions about how to handle Count Tott's complaints. Louis ordered him not to press Charles II openly in urging him to drop his demands for the Dutch coastal towns; rather, Croissy was to give Charles a full description of Tott's visit to the French court, including "all the details."[44] Thus Croissy would amply demonstrate to the English king that his demands were preventing a settlement and the responsibility for the deadlocked negotiations would be placed upon him. Louis could not risk alienating Charles by directly asking him to abandon one of his principal goals of the war; instead, he would let Tott speak for him through Croissy. Louis had no more interest than the Swedish king in seeing the English implanted on the Continental side of the North Sea, and he was perhaps hoping that a timely concession from Charles on this point would bring the desired peace settlement.

One week after Count Tott returned to Cologne from Maastricht, the principal Dutch negotiators, Van Beverningk and Van Haren, departed for The Hague. The ostensible purpose of their trip home was to get additional instructions from the States General on how to cope with the harsh terms of the English and French.[45] This, however, was not the true purpose of their trip. Dutch statesmen were engaged in a critical waiting game that depended upon delaying the negotiations in Cologne; they wanted to see if Emperor Leopold would aid them by sending an army of relief toward the Rhine. When the Dutch learned from Tott that Louis XIV was in no mood to moderate his demands, they decided to delay the peace negotiations on the chance that help would come from Vienna before their military position worsened. The result of this delicately timed maneuver by the Dutch might well determine the fate of the Dutch Republic, for if Emperor Leopold, who was notoriously dilatory,[46] chose not to act or merely procrastinated for long, the Dutch would be compelled to accept peace terms that would leave their country at Louis's mercy in the future.

With the Dutchmen gone, the situation in Cologne became

more relaxed and the other diplomats had time for recreation. Franz Egon von Fürstenberg, who was bishop of Strasbourg (derisively called Bishop Bacchus by his enemies), not only entertained high society in Cologne with three-hour sermons in the baroque mode, he also threw parties in his sumptuous Italianate palace. Courtin, writing to Pomponne on a Tuesday, noted that because Franz Egon was giving a "fête" that night, it would surely be a "mardi gras." Two days later, Chaulnes, Barrillon, and Courtin attended a *Wirtschaft* at Fürstenberg's palace, for which the three Frenchmen dressed respectively as a sultan, a grand vizier, and a Venetian merchant. Joseph Williamson showed his prowess at the costume balls as the most unflagging dancer in Cologne society, relishing his vacation from what was then a very provincial London. Count Tott took advantage of the break in the negotiations to visit his mistress in Aix-la-Chapelle.[47]

The relaxed mood that prevailed in Cologne after the Dutch diplomats departed apparently convinced Jenkins and Williamson that everything was progressing smoothly. The Englishmen were so naively optimistic that a settlement was imminent that they wrote to Lord Arlington and asked for instructions on how to receive the Dutch coastal towns that the English were demanding as security for the peace settlement.[48]

Courtin, who was both the principal French negotiator and the author of the dispatches that were sent from the French delegation to the French court, was not so sanguine about the prospects for a quick peace. In a long memorandum that Courtin sent to Louis XIV on 18 July, he frankly explained that no headway had been made in the negotiations, that the Swedish mediators were trying hard to effect a settlement that would please Louis and yet assure the survival of the Dutch Republic, and that Louis would have to adopt a more flexible negotiating posture before any progress would be possible.[49]

Courtin also wrote to Pomponne, and in this dispatch he was more blunt and specific in his recommendations: "We believe, Sir, that you will understand that we must receive further instructions, or at least that His Majesty must allow the Swedish ambassadors to talk to the Dutchmen about the possibility of an exchange of fortresses."[50] This "exchange of fortresses" concerned the proposition that the French would give up some of their conquered territory in the Dutch Republic in exchange for comparable territory in the Spanish Netherlands. In this way Louis XIV would be compensated for his war efforts at the expense of the Spaniards, the Dutch Republic would be preserved intact, and the French and the Dutch could make peace. Courtin therefore went to the root of the problem and suggested that it was futile for the French to pursue the war in the Dutch Netherlands proper.

During most of July 1673, the French, English, and Swedish diplomats in Cologne waited for the Dutchmen to return from The Hague in the hope that they would bring new concessions from the States General. By the end of July, however, everyone recognized that the Dutch were in no hurry to return to Cologne and accede to the joint demands of the French and their English allies. Then a new trial of nerves developed. The French and English diplomats began waiting for each other to lower their demands so that the Dutch would begin to negotiate seriously.

Charles II, eager for peace because of the disquieting prospect of having an anti-French, antiwar Parliament meeting in the autumn, began to crack first. By the end of July, Colbert de Croissy was spreading the word that Charles was preparing to sacrifice his demand for cautionary coastal towns, the demand that the Dutch found most objectionable.[51] On 5 August the French plenipotentiaries wrote to Pomponne that their English counterparts could not believe that the French diplomats did not have more freedom to maneuver in the bargaining.[52] Courtin was putting pressure on Pomponne to give him more latitude in the negotiations, but the English were near the breaking point. In their next dispatch to Pomponne (8 August) the French diplomats described Williamson's peculiar behavior. He lurked near the Frenchmen's lodgings and waited for the courier from the French court; upon his arrival, Williamson would immediately call on the French in hope of hearing that Louis XIV had made concessions that would expedite the negotiations.[53] Courtin was telling Louis and Pomponne how desperate their English allies were to begin substantive talks.

Courtin was furious with the apparent intractability of his superiors. The English diplomats in Cologne wrote to Arlington on 7 August that "M. Courtin did not stick to break out into very extravagant Expressions against their ministers, who have kept them in the dark all this while."[54] The pressure of a failing peace conference had loosened Courtin's sharp tongue.

Although Courtin cursed the French ministers, Louis was

responsible for the continued rigidity of the French negotiating posture; the king was viscerally opposed to bargaining away territory that he and his army had won the preceding year. But with the military situation in Germany becoming increasingly delicate, Louis yielded. In dispatches posted on 4 and 10 August, the king reduced his demands on the Dutch. He informed his diplomats in Cologne that he was prepared to drop his demand for several towns in Dutch Brabant, on the estuary of the Scheldt and Meuse rivers, in exchange for the fortified towns that lay between the Waal and Meuse rivers in Dutch Gelderland.[55] Louis considered this proposal a major concession and his dispatches show he thought peace was imminent during early and mid-August: "As for me, the treaty is very close to conclusion."[56] "Your next letters will evidently inform me of the Dutch ambassadors' return to Cologne, and if the news that I have received from The Hague is accurate they will return with instructions to satisfy me."[57]

Pomponne also wrote enthusiastically about the possibility of a rapid settlement: "It appears, Sirs, that the new instructions you will receive . . . will smooth the road that leads toward peace in Europe. Until now, in my opinion, there has not been much appearance of peace; but truly, neither the march of the emperor's army nor the declaration of war by Spain will prevent . . . the Dutch from making a settlement soon."[58] Louis and Pomponne had apparently received wildly inaccurate information from their correspondents at The Hague, for they were far wide of the mark when they wrote these unjustifiably optimistic letters.

When the French plenipotentiaries in Cologne received Louis's and Pomponne's dispatches of 4 and 10 August, they answered Louis by describing the English plenipotentiaries' shocked reaction to the French proposals: "They sat for a long time with closed mouths, staring at each other in astonishment. We could get nothing out of him [Williamson] but some intermittent words, which only served to impress us the more with his inner turmoil."[59] The French diplomats also noted that the Swedes reacted so similarly to the Englishmen that they could have sworn the English had spoken to them before the French did. The plenipotentiaries' answer to Pomponne's optimistic letter shows, unmistakably, Courtin's gathering bitterness and his acid tongue: "You can judge, Sir, in reading the letter we have had the honor to write to His Majesty, if the new instructions we received permit us to hope that we can soon make peace. If you believe that, as it appears by your letter of the 10th, we have the misfortune to have a different opinion."[60]

The day before this letter was posted from Cologne, word arrived from Lord Arlington that the English ambassadors could agree to "the total Expunction of that Article of Places, in case . . . the Peace cannot otherwise take Effect."[61] Charles II was apprehensive about the approaching session of Parliament; he needed a settlement of affairs abroad to save his position at home (conversely, he had earlier engaged in the war to strengthen his rule in England). When the Englishmen in Cologne gave their French colleagues the unexpected news that Charles was willing to drop his demand for Dutch coastal towns, the allied diplomats agreed pressure had to be applied to Louis XIV from three directions to compel him to moderate his terms and make peace possible: from England via Croissy; from William Lockhart, the English ambassador with the French court; and especially from Cologne through Courtin's dispatches to Pomponne and Louis.[62]

Croissy had been broadly hinting to Louis and suggesting to Pomponne that the French terms at Cologne should be modified to achieve a rapid settlement. Otherwise, according to Croissy, the anti-French, antiwar mood that was burgeoning in England would force Charles II to quit the French alliance. "The king [Charles] . . . to tell the truth, is carrying a heavy load in favoring France against the inclination of all his people and with only the support of the duke of York and Lord Arlington."[63] Croissy, who became the hard-headed foreign minister of the 1680s, was urging, with the other French ambassadors, moderation in autumn 1673.

When, on 17 August, Louis XIV heard from Croissy that Charles II had dropped his demand for cautionary towns, Louis immediately wrote to his ambassadors in Cologne, withdrawing his demand for territory in Dutch Gelderland.[64] The French apparently wanted peace also, for Louis's demands for Dutch territory now consisted of only the fortified towns that controlled the Meuse River and dominated the Generality Lands, especially Maastricht. Louis, Louvois, and probably Pomponne felt that these terms were reasonable and just, and that, together with the retraction by Charles II of his demand for cautionary towns on the Dutch coast, they would quickly effect a peace settlement. The three members of the high council who were on campaign wrote at least five letters between 15 and 20 August that indicate they thought peace with the Dutch was imminent and that only extreme obstinacy and unreason on the part of the Dutch would prevent it.[65] Louis's dispatch, posted from Nancy on 17 August, reached Cologne in only two and one-half days via a special courier route that Louis had established between his temporary headquarters in Lorraine and Cologne, which testifies to his seriousness about making peace in mid-August. When Louis's proposals of 17 August arrived in Cologne, the English ambassadors praised their reasonableness. The Swedes were also pleased, although they thought that the French demands were still too high to effect an immediate settlement.[66]

The French proposals, which arrived in Cologne during the night of 19/20 August, were indeed too harsh—and too late. On 14 August Van Beverningk and Van Haren returned to Cologne from The Hague, carrying the official Dutch replies to the English and French demands.[67] When the Dutchmen submitted them to the Swedish mediators, the Swedes were shaken by the vehemence with which the Dutch rejected the English and French demands, and they needed several days to work up the courage to face the English and French delegations. The Dutch response to the French was so sharply worded that the Swedes apologized to the Frenchmen before they read it to them, which they felt was necessary in order to defuse the rhetoric. The Swedes claimed they had told the Dutchmen that if they were looking for a pretext to break off the negotiations, they could surely find a more plausible reason than insisting that *all* the Dutch towns in French hands had either to be returned to the Dutch or given to the Spaniards in an exchange. The Dutch reply to the English, the Swedes said, was even more provocative, "a sort of manifesto," rejecting all but the most trifling of the English demands.[68]

What had happened during their month at The Hague that made the Dutchmen so truculent, while most of their country was still covered either with water or French soldiers? While the negotiators in Cologne had passively awaited the return of the Dutch plenipotentiaries, other diplomats had been feverishly busy. In May, Franz Paul von Lisola, the imperial ambassador at The Hague, who had been the bugbear of French diplomats for twenty years, was ordered to go to Cologne as the emperor's envoy at the peace conference. However, Lisola had become convinced (before his imperial master) that Louis XIV could be dealt with only by force of arms. Thus, rather than proceeding directly to Cologne, he remained in the Low Countries, where he felt he could be more useful. During spring and early summer 1673, Lisola shuttled back and forth between Brussels and The Hague to sound out the positions of Monterey, governor of the Spanish Netherlands, and Prince William III of Orange, who had been steadily consolidating his power in the Dutch Republic since the murder of the De Witt brothers and the demise of the States Party in August 1672. Lisola soon discovered that Monterey and Orange completely agreed with him about Louis XIV; the link that needed strengthening in the chain of anti-French protagonists was his own master, Emperor Leopold.[69] Thus in June, with the encouragement and blessing of Lisola, the Dutch sent Coenraad van Heemskerck as a special emissary to plead the Dutch case at the Viennese court. Heemskerck returned to The Hague from Vienna in mid-July with encouraging news: Emperor Leopold would be willing to send an army to assist the Dutch if he could count on subsidies to support such an enterprise.[70] At the end of July, while the Dutch plenipotentiaries were still at The Hague, Heemskerck was again sent to Vienna, with a definite offer of Dutch gold to finance the imperial army.[71]

In short, when the Dutchmen returned to Cologne in mid-August, an anti-French coalition, consisting of the emperor, the Spaniards, and the Dutch, was in the making. Although the treaties that would officially weld together this grand alliance had not yet been signed, by mid-August the Dutch were confident that they were about to receive powerful allies, and thus they could spurn the demands of both the French and the English kings.

Louis XIV had not been thinking of peace in February when he bowed to Swedish pressure and agreed to send plenipotentiaries to a peace conference. By mid-August, when Louis first began to show interest in serious negotiations, the Dutch had decided to wage a full-scale war of attrition. When Louis held the advantage in the war, he had no desire for substantive peace talks; and after the Dutch became certain that they would not have to face the French alone, they wanted to pursue the war to its bitter end. The Dutchmen, whom the French had contemned for their bourgeois qualities, were proving to be, under the leadership of the prince of Orange, stubbornly resourceful in defending themselves.

The proof that Lisola's task was completed as chief liaison for the emerging anti-French coalition appeared when the imperial diplomat arrived in Cologne on 20 August. This Franc-Comtois who served the emperor set to work in Cologne to convince Louis XIV's allies to abandon the French cause. The French diplomats in Cologne described Lisola's frantic activities as he pursued his work of confounding French foreign policy:

We could write an entire book on Lisola's everyday activities: sometimes he is asking the bishop of Strasbourg [Franz Egon von Fürstenberg] to arrange an accommodation between the elector of Cologne, the emperor and the States [General]; sometimes he claims to have news that Spanish troops have invaded Roussillon; another day he is assuring the Danish envoy that the emperor and the King of Spain will make peace in Paris or London rather than here. All in all, he is showing the true colors of Lisola—restless, full of intrigue, and treacherous in all the rumors he spreads.[72]

When Lisola suggested that Louis XIV's enemies would carry the war into Paris, it is clear that his diplomatic triumph had gone to his head; his suggestion was too farfetched to be effective propaganda. But triumph it surely was when, on 28 August, the two houses of Hapsburg, Spanish and Austrian, were reunited in alliance, and two days later the Hapsburgs allied with the States General of the Dutch Republic and the duke of Lorraine to form a coalition whose ambitious aim was to undo the Peace of Aix-la-Chapelle (1668) and push the French back to the frontiers established by the Peace of the Pyrenees (1659).[73] The coalition of 30 August 1673 would never accomplish that aim, but it did engage Louis in a trying war of attrition that would compel him to pay dearly for every square mile of territory he acquired in the peace settlements at Nijmegen in 1678/79.

When Louis received news of the Dutchmen's truculence upon their return to Cologne, he was inclined to dismiss it as a facade they used to disguise the weakness of their position. He reasoned that the Dutch plenipotentiaries had not exhausted their powers, and he intended to stand firm upon his proposals of 17 August.[74] At Cologne, the French, English, and Swedish ambassadors were somewhat baffled by the intractability of the Dutch, but they did not dismiss the stance as a bluff. The diplomats found the deadlock in the negotiations very real and felt that further war was probably the only solution.

Courtin was weary and discouraged when he wrote to Louis

that "if His Majesty judges it appropriate . . . to entrust us with further and more detailed instructions, it would perhaps not be impossible for us to utilize them to obtain the satisfaction that His Majesty desires."[75] By the end of August 1673, Courtin was increasingly pessimistic, because peace was eluding him at Cologne and because he feared that France was facing isolation. He wrote the king to inform him that the elector of Cologne and the bishop of Münster were rapidly tiring of the war, and then, with his usual phrase that indicated he had turned from hard news to personal opinion, he continued: "To tell things as they really are (*mais à dire les choses comme elles sont*), we will be lucky to maintain alliances that are already now so weak."[76]

While on march through Alsace during the latter part of August, the French court received news (false, it turned out) of an Anglo-French naval victory over the Dutch fleet. As late as 4 September, when Louis XIV was en route back to Nancy from Breisach on the Rhine, Louvois wrote to Condé that "the king hopes to find news in Nancy that will inform him if the Dutch have changed their minds after their bad luck in the naval battle."[77] This was hoping against hope, however, and reveals how Louis had lost touch with the mainstream of European affairs as he became increasingly engrossed in his military campaign. News of the imposing anti-French coalition spread quickly across Europe during the first week of September, and on 7 September Louvois wrote to the intendant of the French army in the Netherlands, Louis Robert, and ordered him to begin procuring supplies for continued war.[78]

On 10 September, Louis agreed to a proposal to exchange most of his Dutch conquests for territory in the Spanish Netherlands. For the first time, Louis stated precisely what he wanted from the Spaniards, without insisting that the Dutch first specify what lands they were willing to sacrifice to Spain in return. This was perhaps a final attempt to negotiate a settlement with the Dutch, but Louis had another, more important, motive in making this concession; he was still courting the Swedes, still hoping to draw them into Germany to neutralize Emperor Leopold. Louis wrote that "if . . . the Spaniards and the Dutch refuse to profit from this new overture, Sweden will be convinced that I have neglected nothing to gain peace and that the house of Austria is making use of Dutch stubbornness to touch off a general European war."[79]

It seems likely that Louis had not entirely given up negotiating with the Dutch before their treaty of 30 August with Leopold and the Spaniards had been ratified. Probably, however, his concessions of 10 September were aimed more at the Swedes than at the Dutch. Although the French were becoming nervous with the thought that Sweden would not aid them in Germany, they still hoped that Swedish intervention would be the panacea for their troubles with Emperor Leopold. This was a persistent delusion of Louis and Pomponne.[80]

When Courtin received Louis's dispatch of 10 September, he was outraged over his superiors' refusal to take either him or the peace conference seriously. Not daring to vent his rage to Louis, or to Pomponne, whose correspondence might be read in the high council, and whom he did not trust at this point, Courtin unleashed his pent-up anger on Louvois, who was his friend despite their very different views of foreign policy. He began his letter to Louvois by noting that Louis's dispatch of 10 September was the "extreme unction" of the negotiations, then enlarged on his clinical metaphor of the peace conference: "I consider it so sick that if you were to send us some emetic not a drop would come back up. But you hold that emetic so dear, and it is of so little importance to you . . . if peace is made, which would destroy the chance to add still new conquests to those that His Majesty has already made, that I do not expect to receive any emetic in any case."[81]

Louvois's response to Courtin's angry letter was suave, diplomatic, and even more interesting than the diplomat's anguished outburst:

> You have painted me a hideous portrait of . . . the war, which I regard not as an advantage but as a necessary evil that is impossible to avoid unless we make a peace like that of 1668 [Aix-la-Chapelle]. The king is a long way from doing anything like that. He believes that his enemies joined in coalition . . . would still require several years to retake what His Majesty has conquered. And although it may be true that funds are scarce and become more so daily . . . His Majesty has the wherewithal to go further than all of his enemies joined together.[82]

There is sharp dramatic irony in the phrasing of this letter, for the eventual settlement of the Dutch War at Nijmegen in 1678 was precisely "a peace like that of 1668"—that is, an anti-French coalition compelled Louis XIV to negotiate a compromise agreement. Louvois's description of the king's belligerence catches the spirit of Louis's motto, *Nec pluribus impar*. The king seems to have been exhilarated by the challenge of confronting a coalition by himself. As the English diplomat Sir William Temple had earlier perceived, Louis saw foreign affairs as an arena for testing his strength. And the king's abhorrence of the Peace of Aix-la-Chapelle (1668) is remarkable, for it was not unfavorable for France; in proportion to the effort expended, the gain was considerable. Louis abhorred it not because it was unprofitable or contrary to French interests but because, at this time in his career, he could not tolerate being thwarted by anyone or anything, not even a coalition of states determined to preserve their existence within the context of the European states system. Louis would learn to take foreign affairs less personally.

At the end of September Louis reduced his demands considerably. He made further territorial concessions, including an offer to relinquish Maastricht to the bishop of Liège (that is, the elector of Cologne), and he reduced his demand for reparations from 8 million to 6 million livres.[83] By 26 September Louis's negotiating posture was moderate by anyone's standards, but there was one catch: he was no longer considering a peaceful settlement. Since mid-September Louis knew that De Ruyter had held off the combined Anglo-French fleet at the battle of Texel (Kijkduin, 21 August) and that the prince of Orange had made his first successful counterattack of the war by recapturing Naarden (12 September). Convinced that the Dutch, with their newly acquired allies and recent naval and land victories, were now bent on continued war, Louis's proposals of 26 September were only bait to lure Sweden into the war by demonstrating his reasonableness to the Swedish mediators at Cologne. Early in October, Louvois wrote frankly to Courtin that "the king in no way wished to make peace by ordering M. de Pomponne to send you the dispatch of the 26th of last month. His Majesty only pretended to desire peace in order to put pressure on Sweden to fulfill her treaty obligation and join France in war."[84] When Louis ordered Pomponne to send the proposals of 26 September, he was gambling that they would not be accepted, and he was right—though he did not accomplish his aim of drawing the Swedes into the war until 1674, when they proved themselves of little value as allies.

If Louis had truly desired peace early in summer 1673, he would have taken the advice of his ambassadors at Cologne and moderated his demands soon after the peace conference convened in June. Wicquefort wrote to De Groot from The Hague on 18 September that, one month before, the "grandes villes" of the Dutch Republic had wanted a prompt peace and had been willing to sacrifice a great deal to obtain it. By September, however, the Dutch bourgeoisie was willing to go along with the prince of Orange and fight it out.[85] Louis XIV did not want peace badly enough to bargain seriously for a compromise settlement during 1673. For Louis, the Cologne Conference never had more than two purposes: to dictate a peace to the Dutch or to lure Sweden into the war. With the Dutch unwilling to be intimidated and the Swedes unwilling to be gulled, Louis was left with the dubious accomplishment of having driven the two houses of Hapsburg together in alliance with the Dutch.

Wicquefort continued his letter to De Groot by recalling that Huges de Lionne, the former French foreign minister, had once told him that the principal objective of French foreign policy was to prevent the reunion of the two houses of Hapsburg, and that if they did in fact reunite, France could not successfully oppose them.[86] Lionne had simply been reiterating the divide-and-conquer policy of Richelieu and Mazarin. When, in 1673, Louis XIV ignored the classic policy formulated by these three master diplomats, he involved himself in a major war of attrition that made heavy demands on the resources of the French monarchy before a compromise peace was achieved in 1678–79.

As the end of 1673 approached, Courtin warned Louvois about the possible consequences of continued war: "I will always maintain that it is better, both for the king and the state, to be content with a little in order to get out of this unfortunate mess [the Dutch War] . . . than to continue for one city more or less in a war that could bring great upheavals (*revolutions*) upon us. And you, sir, are more vulnerable than anyone because you have had such a large part in it."[87] Courtin seemingly did not know very well the mind and the heart of his sovereign, who had earlier written that "reputation cannot be preserved without adding to it every day. . . . Glory . . . is not a mistress who can be neglected, nor is one ever worthy of her first favors if he is not always wishing for new ones."[88]

Perhaps one should also be suspicious of Courtin's criticisms and prophecies of doom—for he had a vested professional interest in seeing the Cologne peace conference succeed, and he was the kind of slightly neurotic personality who tends to project his own problems onto a situation, forecasting a general debacle because his interests are suffering. In fact, Courtin's jeremiads concerning the immediate future were wrong; the upheavals did not come (though revolts did), and Louvois did not lose his office for the part he played in the Dutch War. However, Louvois's position was threatened, and eventually the Revolution, which was at least in part a consequence of the bankruptcy brought on by Louis XIV's war policies, also came.

When Courtin discovered that Louis XIV did not intend to use the peace conference to settle the war, he expressed explicitly his anger to Louvois, but took out his frustrations and anxieties less openly on Pomponne. Courtin had been a prominent candidate for the office of foreign minister after Lionne died in September 1671, and the disappointment of having been passed over in favor of Pomponne undoubtedly contributed to Courtin's rather paranoiac attitude toward Pomponne, although they were long-time friends and colleagues in the French diplomatic corps.[89] The frustrations of the stalemated peace talks in Cologne worked upon the high-strung and ambitious Courtin until he broke down during autumn and early winter 1673.

When, in late September, Courtin saw that "his" negotiations were failing, he first concluded that Pomponne was bypassing the Cologne Conference and conducting the substantive negotiations through the marquis de Feuquières, who was Pomponne's relative and protégé and the French ambassador in Stockholm. Courtin was willing to concede that it was perfectly proper for Pomponne to promote the career of a member of his family; no politician, particularly during the Old Regime, could argue with that. But Courtin was torn by anxiety that his own career might suffer. He thus decided to write to Pomponne and present a fabricated plea that Count Tott, the head of the Swedish delegation in Cologne, was worried about the correspondence between the French court and Stockholm and wanted to know if anything important was happening. Courtin tried to conceal his anxieties by noting that he did not intend "to gain new opportunities to negotiate," but it must have been obvious to Pomponne that it was Courtin, not Tott, who was anxious. Courtin closed his letter to Pomponne on a strong note of self-pity, complaining of the financial plight his peregrinations as ambassador had inflicted upon him: "Those are the ambassador's fruits."[90]

Pomponne replied calmly to Courtin that Feuquières's task in Sweden was to convince the Swedes to uphold their end of the Treaty of Stockholm, and only that. Concerning Courtin's financial difficulties, Pomponne answered soberly and sympathetically: "You can certainly believe that I am very much moved by the loss that you have incurred, and may it please God that I can do something to make your embassies produce more bountiful fruit, which you so richly merit."[91] Pomponne duly wrote to Colbert on 30 September, informing the finance minister that Courtin was owed back pay, as well as remuneration for his embassy at Cologne, and that the king desired that he be paid.[92] However, Courtin wrote to Louvois on 3 October and thanked him for the letter of exchange for 6,000 écus that he had received from M. Sadoc (a financier with whom Louvois had frequent contact).[93] This is another indication that Pomponne was indeed a "second class" minister in 1673; whereas he could not apply the necessary pressure to have his ambassadors paid promptly, Louvois controlled the levers of power sufficiently well to obtain money when he needed it. In this sense Louvois was a better politician than Pomponne, although he lacked the requisite qualities of character and personality to be a statesman of Pomponne's caliber.

A month after Courtin's unfounded suspicion surfaced that Pomponne was dealing behind his back with Feuquières in Sweden, he decided that Pomponne was bypassing the Cologne Conference by negotiating directly with Austria through Grémonville in Vienna. Courtin immediately assailed Pomponne about Grémonville's negotiations, telling him that persons in Cologne were entirely in the dark concerning events in Vienna, "but if we are to remain here [in Cologne] we must be informed of what has been proposed."[94] Pomponne, once again, calmly replied to Courtin that the negotiations in Vienna had been simply "to divert the Imperials and to gain time. Thus those negotiations, neither on the part of the imperial ministers, who doubtless had the same idea, nor on his part [Grémonville's] had any substance whatever."[95] Despite Pomponne's reasonable and conciliatory letters, Courtin was convincing himself there was a conspiracy afoot to rob him of the honor of concluding peace. To be removed from the court was an agonizing experience for a royal servant with ambitions.

The Cologne Conference did not end, as Courtin feared it

would, because the war was settled through direct negotiations between the great powers. Superficially at least, the conference collapsed over the problem of the duchy of Lorraine, which Louis had occupied in 1670. Early in October 1673, the Dutch plenipotentiaries at Cologne formally notified the Swedish mediators that because their treaties with Spain, the emperor, and the duke of Lorraine had been ratified, they were no longer at liberty to continue negotiations unilaterally; representatives of their allies would have to be admitted to the negotiations in Cologne.[96] Although Louis XIV was willing to see Spain and the emperor represented at the peace talks, Lorraine was a wholly different matter; it was not a sovereign state, either friendly or hostile, in Louis's opinion.

In the *Mémoires* Louis wrote for the instruction of his son, he expressed his feelings that Lorraine was a part of the ancestral patrimony of the French kingdom, which it was his duty to reunite with the realm. Moreover, Lorraine provided an indispensable gateway into Alsace and the Netherlands. For historical and strategic reasons, Louis could not admit the duke of Lorraine to the peace negotiations.[97] The king's original instructions that had accompanied his plenipotentiaries to Cologne ruled out negotiating over Lorraine: "His Majesty's intention is that nothing shall be dealt with except those affairs that have arisen since and as a consequence of the war begun with the States General."[98] Pomponne reminded the plenipotentiaries about Louis's position on Lorraine so that there could be no mistaking it: "His Majesty has noticed, Sirs, that the Dutch ambassadors are proclaiming that they can no longer . . . separate their interests . . . from those of the emperor, Spain, and the duke of Lorraine. He has thought it necessary to remind you of the orders that he gave you in your instructions, that you should tell the mediators that you have no authority to listen to anything concerning the duke of Lorraine."[99]

Courtin not only thought that a peace settlement would be in France's best interests; his honor, pride, and vanity were at stake in the negotiations at Cologne. He argued, in perhaps the most remarkable of his letters to Louvois, that the representatives of the dispossessed duke of Lorraine should be admitted to the peace conference. Courtin began by declaring that Louis could not deny representatives of the duke of Lorraine admittance to the peace conference without "incurring universal blame that he wishes to retain Lorraine by an unjustified (as you well know) usurpation." Then he sallied forth with remarks that would have endangered his position as a royal diplomat, if the king had seen them: "Permit me to add, Sir, that the king's conduct has recently appeared so arrogant and domineering toward other states that it is absolutely necessary, if the king wishes to retain friends, that he fully explain his intentions."[100] Courtin was surely fortunate that Louvois was too loyal a friend to show these comments to Louis.

Courtin concluded this extraordinary and prophetic letter with a protestation that he had taken this liberty with the best of intentions, and that he was only saying what many persons thought but had not the courage to express. Courtin, obviously, added this plea to ensure that Louvois would keep his confidence, but he was correct when he claimed that most French diplomats concurred in his views. Robert de Gravel, for example, the tough and shrewd French representative at the Imperial Diet, wrote to the duke of Vitry, French special envoy in Munich: "Finally, Sir, everyone, even our friends and allies, fear His Majesty's too great power and wishes not to support it and thereby render, so it is thought, the balance of power too unequal."[101]

It is noteworthy that Gravel, who had one of the keenest minds in the French diplomatic service, should have written explicitly about a balance-of-power structure in Europe at this time. Although many European statesmen no doubt had some inchoate concept of a power balance by the mid-seventeenth century, Louis XIV did not begin to think in these terms until his realm had been battered by several more decades of war. In 1673, the king was not concerned with such fine points of international relations.

Although Courtin, Wilhelm von Fürstenberg, and Count Tott persuaded Louis to accept a third party of neutral German princes to help work for a peace settlement, the most the king would concede on Lorraine was that the entire question of the duchy's control could be arbitrated after a general peace had been signed; the dispossessed duke, who had eagerly allied himself with the Dutch, would not be recognized as a sovereign prince, nor would he be permitted to send delegates to the peace conference. This was Louis XIV's definitive, official position, conveyed to his plenipotentiaries by royal dispatch on 18 November.[102]

The king's personal attitude about Lorraine and the third party, however, was best summarized in an unofficial letter that

Louvois wrote to Courtin about the same time. The letter began by describing Louis XIV's most basic feelings about Lorraine: "Understand that the king would rather wage war for the rest of his life than retract the orders m. de Pomponne has sent you."[103] Louvois then continued, making it explicit to Courtin that Louis was preparing to wage a long war, the "good long war"[104] that Louvois had foreseen with a certain relish six weeks earlier: "The king has no hope that what he has done either regarding Lorraine or the third party will bring us peace. But he does expect to have destroyed any pretext that the Swedes and his other allies had for not fulfilling their treaty obligations, and that he will either reap this fruit . . . or get rid of the burden of the subsidies that he is providing them."[105]

Lisola, the imperial diplomat, would later remark that the negotiations in Cologne collapsed over the problem of whether the duke of Lorraine's representatives could attend the conference.[106] Louis was closer to the truth, however, when he saw that the peace conference was already defunct when the question of Lorraine arose. The debate whether to seat the duke's delegates was merely a symptom of a deeper malaise; this same problem was brushed aside five years later at Nijmegen when everyone needed and wanted peace. The willingness of the French and the Dutch to subvert the negotiations over Lorraine shows that neither side was prepared to negotiate seriously late in 1673. Neither side had had enough fighting and the war was fated to be a war of attrition. Lisola's other explanation for the failure of the Cologne Conference, that the bellicose French nation "would have consumed itself in inactivity or discharged its bile internally"[107] were it not engaged in foreign war, may have applied to some of the French nobility but not to the French king, for Louis was motivated not so much by aggressiveness as by a thirst for military glory.

The peace conference dragged on until February 1674, when the spectacular kidnaping of Wilhelm von Fürstenberg on the streets of Cologne by imperial soldiers gave Louis XIV a convenient pretext to recall his negotiators. In effect, however, the Cologne Conference had failed by October 1673.[108]

Somewhat paradoxically, as the peace conference disintegrated the correspondence between the French court and the French ambassadors at Cologne became more intense and revealing. This was true not only because there was a certain desperation on the part of the ambassadors to prevent the utter collapse of the conference but also because the duke de Chaulnes, titular head of the French delegation, was recalled to France early in November to attend a meeting of the estates of Brittany, where he was governor.[109] Honoré Courtin, who had begun as the chief French negotiator, was left as the formal head of the French mission in Cologne. This hypertense diplomat thus had more freedom to maneuver in trying to save his negotiations, and his correspondence with the king and the royal ministers reveals much about the personalities and politics of the French governing circle as the first crisis of Louis's reign engulfed them.

In mid-November, Don Emanuel de Lira, the Spanish envoy at Cologne, advised the Swedish mediators that if Sweden and Louis XIV's German allies entered the war on the French side, the imperial army would have to withdraw from the lower Rhine in order to protect Emperor Leopold's hereditary lands. If this happened, Lira said, the Spaniards would be vulnerable in the Low Countries and would thus be interested in a bilateral settlement with the French—provided that Louis XIV was willing to barter away some of the forward fortresses he had acquired in the Spanish Netherlands by the Treaty of Aix-la-Chapelle (1668). The mediators, in turn, approached the French ambassadors with this tentative proposition, and Courtin duly informed Louis XIV that, although he had not flatly rejected the concept, he had told the Swedes that there were numerous obstacles to any settlement between France and Spain.[110] When Louis XIV received Courtin's dispatch, he was enraged.

> First, I will tell you . . . that your dispatch of the 14th of this month has angered me greatly. . . . I am not surprised that a Spanish minister should risk making such a proposal, but I find it strange that my ambassadors have even considered it, . . . when you should have flatly rejected it the moment it was made. Did you think that your powers to negotiate with the Dutch extended to include the Treaty of Aix-la-Chapelle? Is it possible that you thought the powers you were given to negotiate over my conquests of last year could be broadened, without my express consent, so that you could accept a proposal for an exchange of those lands that I conquered from Spain in 1667? . . . Make amends . . . for your ill-advised conduct and in the future never again begin any such discussions.[111]

This explosive reaction to Courtin's seemingly innocent talks in Cologne was out of character for the usually imperturbable Sun King, but a combination of events had ruffled his customarily placid facade. In general, Louis was undoubtedly becoming edgy as his Dutch War began to go sour in autumn 1673. He was experiencing the first setbacks of his reign, and his civil servants had to bear part of his frustration. More specifically, the king was jealous of his conquests in the Spanish Netherlands—the first of his career—and he did not want them to be bargained away in Cologne. Finally, Louis did not want his diplomats to start making executive decisions on their own initiative and thus usurp the power that belonged to him alone.

Louis's furious letter was accompanied by one from Pomponne, in which the latter gave Courtin and Barrillon an ominous warning that if Louis were provoked by "other such cases, it could be extremely prejudicial to you."[112] Pomponne did not make such threats to his ambassadors unless he had compelling reasons to do so.

On 5 December, Courtin was in his study in Cologne, writing to Louvois concerning a letter he had received from a mutual friend of his and Pomponne's. The letter, Courtin wrote, related that Pomponne had commented recently "that he had known for a long time about my private correspondence with you [Louvois], and that blood and friendship had induced me to go beyond the limits of my official station."[113] In the midst of writing to Louvois, Courtin received the dispatches from Louis and Pomponne that castigated him sharply for his conversations with the Swedish mediators concerning a settlement with Spain. Courtin, who was becoming nervous and suspicious as the negotiations with which he identified so closely were inexorably failing, seemed to snap; his emotional stability was shaken. Courtin began to fulminate against Pomponne: "One's master [i.e. Louis] is always right, and I have nothing to say about that. But m. de Pomponne insulted us even more by remarking that other such cases . . . could be extremely prejudicial to us. Those were his very words, which make me see what I must expect from a man who was looking for an opportunity to show me his power and punish me for my correspondence with you."[114]

As Courtin should have known, this was a wildly inaccurate portrayal of Pomponne and his motives. But after brooding over his situation for several days, Courtin sent another fiery letter to Louvois. He inveighed against Pomponne for several paragraphs, claiming that he, Courtin, had done all the successful negotiating in the past while Pomponne had reaped all the honors. Courtin concluded with the most farfetched of all his charges: that Pomponne must have been responsible for the king's furious and threatening letter.[115] Courtin's nerves had clearly gotten the better of his judgment, and he was indulging in juvenile accusations and wallowing in self-pity.

Although in 1679 Courtin came close, he could never fulfill his ambition of becoming foreign minister to Louis XIV. He allowed his feelings to rise too close to the surface. If his conversation was anything like his writing (usually witty and candid, sometimes personal and petulant), Courtin had made enough enemies to block his climb to the top of the royal bureaucracy.

Courtin bitterly denounced Pomponne in his letters to Louvois, but he did not forget that Pomponne was still his immediate superior and might well, despite what had happened, influence Courtin's future career. The same courier who carried Courtin's letters to Louvois also delivered personal letters to Pomponne: "I humbly beg you, Sir, to believe that there is nothing that could make me unfaithful to our friendship of twenty-five years. I have written nothing from here that has not been witnessed by someone whom you can trust. We hope, Sir, that the friendship with which you have honored us will lead you to support our position and make it appear sound."[116] In view of his philippics to Louvois, Courtin's letters to Pomponne were hypocritical and cowardly. Courtin was, of course, sorely threatened by the phrase "extremely prejudicial" and was fighting desperately to maintain his position as a royal diplomat, for he saw politics as his life's work.

When the routine duplicates of Louis's and Pomponne's dispatches of 26 November (in which Courtin and Barrillon had been taken so severely to task) were sent out from the court, the diplomatic pouch also carried a personal letter from Pomponne to the plenipotentiaries. Pomponne wrote of the pain it had caused him to carry out the king's orders by chastising and threatening Courtin and Barrillon, then closed his letter with a poignant sentence: "I am not giving you my opinions, particularly those concerning you; you know them well enough and know that no one is more true to you than I."[117] This was not merely a seventeenth-century rhetorical flourish, for Pomponne went to the trouble to send a special letter, outside the regular diplomatic correspondence. Suspicion and resentment had so closed Courtin's mind, however, that he rejected Pomponne's proffered hand; it was after he received the foreign minister's sincerely sympathetic letter that he attacked Pomponne most unreasonably and bitterly in his letter to Louvois of 8 December.

Courtin had lost his perspective, and two blunt letters, one from Louvois and one from Pomponne himself, were required to jolt him out of his paranoiac fantasies. These letters told Courtin, in the clearest terms, of Pomponne's true position, both politically and with regard to Courtin personally. With admirable frankness, Louvois informed Courtin that both the king's letter and Pomponne's accompanying letter had been dictated by Louis and "there was not a single word about which m. de Pomponne had any choice. And, although I cannot respond to you from his heart, I can nonetheless assure you that in that affair and in everything else that I have witnessed . . . he has spoken for you before the king more skillfully than I could have."[118] Pomponne responded the same day with equal candor—and more emotion:

You have done me a wrong, Sir, for which I have the right to ask for justice. . . . You should judge me more favorably and not accuse me of something that pained me in knowing that it pained you. All that I have done is to follow orders in the way prescribed for me. I did not desire, as did His Majesty and all those who have the honor of sitting on his council, that you should have rejected categorically the overture that was made to you. . . . Please believe that I always try to make your zeal and usefulness known and be assured that I did not forget what you might expect from our long friendship in this instance nor will I forget in the future. . . . For the rest, I hope that you believe that peace is not less dear to me than to you.[119]

These two letters are critical for understanding French politics during 1673, for they reveal some of the positions advocated in the council of ministers, whose proceedings were secret. Although one cannot state with absolute certainty that Pomponne stood alone in Louis XIV's high council as the sole advocate of a moderate policy during 1673, that is the gist of these letters to Courtin from Louvois and Pomponne. The latter wrote explicitly that he agreed with Courtin when he urged flexibility in the French negotiating posture, which might have rejuvenated the peace conference. Both ministers wrote that Pomponne consistently supported Courtin in the high council, and we have seen Courtin argue repeatedly and vigorously for moderation of the French terms at Cologne. Pomponne seems to have been an isolated figure within Louis's high council during 1673.

Louvois, when he responded to Courtin's complaint that Pomponne was angry about the unofficial correspondence between the ambassador and the war minister, dwelt upon the growing difficulty of Pomponne's position. Louvois told Courtin that Pomponne had been tormented by the effort to do his job and to keep others from interfering with it. The war minister suggested that this might be because of Pomponne's nervous temperament, and assured Courtin that "he can do you no harm so long as you do not furnish him with the materials. All of your dispatches are read in His Majesty's presence, and he judges them and decides what to respond."[120] Louvois relished ridiculing someone when he found the least opportunity to do so, and the basis of his mockery of Pomponne in this instance may be largely fabricated. Nevertheless, Louvois was accurate in maintaining that Pomponne was functioning under considerable strain during the turmoil of 1673. His nervous tension was probably brought on by having to fight the king and Louvois on one decision after the other during the year's campaigns and negotiations. The foreign minister, who had lost all the debates in the council—on Trier, the Alsatian cities, the German princes, and the negotiations in Cologne—was understandably a bit shaken.

In 1673, under great pressure and adversity, Pomponne maintained his civility, whereas Louis XIV, Louvois, and Courtin succumbed to the pressure and lashed out in rage and petulance. Civility is not, of course, the only test of a politician, and Pomponne failed to persuade the king's council to adopt his policies and misjudged Sweden's intention to make war. Yet, Louis XIV would ultimately vindicate Pomponne's stature as a statesman, when—after dismissing him in 1679 for "weakness and stubbornness"—he recalled him to his high council in 1691.[121] By then, in contrast to the situation during the Dutch War, Louis was forced to rely more upon his diplomats and less upon his army.

∽∽∽

V

War with Spain:
An Old Conflict Renewed

During the reign of Louis XIV, the Spanish Netherlands was a logical objective for French expansionary ambitions. For centuries French kings had sought to push their northern and eastern frontiers outward, for these were the frontiers of the realm that were closest to the capital and most dangerous. Acquisition of territory to the north and the east—in Flanders and the Franche-Comté of Burgundy—would provide more protection for the heartland of France, the Ile de France and Paris itself.

In addition to this basic geopolitical factor, Louis XIV had established a dynastic claim, through his wife, to parts of the Spanish Netherlands. According to the customary law of devolution in Brabant, Malines, and Namur, three provinces in the Spanish Netherlands, a child of the first marriage bed, even a female child, took precedence over children of later marriages in matters of inheritance. But Louis's wife, Marie Thérèse, eldest daughter of Philip IV of Spain, had renounced all claims to the Spanish inheritance in her marriage contract, which was incorporated into the Peace of the Pyrenees.[1] After Philip IV's death in 1665, however, Louis XIV's legal experts announced that Marie's renunciation was null and void because her dowry (500,000 écus) had never been paid and because renunciation was contrary to the nature of hereditary monarchy.[2] Louis's claim to parts of the Spanish Netherlands was thus a deadly serious matter with the

French. If Louis XIV were to wage war, and in the seventeenth century it was usually taken for granted that war was a king's *métier*, the Spanish Netherlands was an obvious arena of action for him.

The Dutch, however, objected strongly to French attempts to expand into the Spanish Netherlands. The Bourbons had aided the Dutch in their eighty-year struggle for independence from the Spanish Hapsburgs, but the Dutch did not want the French for neighbors; *Gallus amicus non vicinus*, the Frenchman for a friend but not for a neighbor, was an old proverb that the Dutch used to explain their position. They feared any strong neighbor on the southern flank of their republic. During the 1660s, Johan de Witt, the great but ill-fated Dutch statesman, tried to solve the problem of the Spanish Netherlands through diplomacy, but he failed. The lengthy negotiations between France and the Dutch Republic had foundered upon Louis XIV's willfulness.[3] The king wanted to resolve the problem in his own way, and until the latter part of his reign he always preferred to settle international problems with soldiers rather than diplomats.

In spring 1667 Louis launched an attack upon the Spanish Netherlands. This War of Devolution over Louis's claim to his wife's inheritance ended abruptly with the Peace of Aix-la-Chapelle in May 1668. Two diplomatic agreements, concluded earlier that year, apparently persuaded Louis XIV to make peace with the Spaniards rather than pursue the war. First, on 19 January Louis's special envoy at the imperial court, Jacques de Grémonville, signed a secret treaty of partition with Emperor Leopold's government whereby Louis and Leopold would divide the Spanish inheritance upon the death of sickly Carlos II. No one expected Carlos to produce an heir to the throne or to live much longer, and both Louis and Leopold had dynastic claims to the Spanish inheritance. According to this secret treaty, Louis's share would consist of the Spanish Netherlands, Franche-Comté, Navarre, Naples, Sicily, and the Philippines.[4] Second, on 23 January England and the Dutch Republic signed an alliance at The Hague (called the First Triple Alliance after Sweden joined in April) whose purpose was to preserve the territorial integrity of the Spanish Netherlands.[5] Although Louis would later wage war against a coalition of states with a certain relish, in 1668 neither the king nor his foreign minister, Hugues de Lionne, wished to confront the principal powers of northern Europe as well as Spain; Mazarin had taught them to fear diplomatic and military isolation, and France had had enough trouble dealing with Spain by herself just ten years earlier. Thus Louis accepted the Treaty of Aix-la-Chapelle in 1668 with the thought that he could eventually acquire the Spanish Netherlands peaceably and with the knowledge that further military conquests would bring a major European conflict upon him.

Where, then, did the Spanish Netherlands fit into the French king's plans during the 1670s, the decade of the so-called Dutch War? When Louis planned the Dutch War, the ultimate conquest of this territory was likely one of his objectives. The Dutch had been presumptuous enough to oppose the king's entry into the Spanish Netherlands when they joined the Triple Alliance of 1668, and Louis was becoming impatient waiting for his share of the Spanish inheritance when Carlos II should die. When Louis launched his attack upon the Dutch Republic in spring 1672, he expected to neutralize Dutch resistance so that he could continue the conquest of the Spanish Netherlands that had been interrupted in 1668.[6] As Louvois wrote in November 1671, when he was acting as interim foreign minister following Lionne's death, "the true means of conquering the Spanish Netherlands is to slap down the Dutch and if possible to crush them."[7]

In summer 1672 the French armies seemed well on their way to crushing the Dutch Republic. At the Doesburg meeting in June 1672 the Dutch were probably willing to cede territories to Louis that would have given him the strategic position from which he could overrun the Spanish Netherlands at his leisure. Louis, goaded by Louvois,[8] rejected this settlement for two probable reasons: First, he had become swept away on the euphoria of his first easy victories in the United Provinces and for the moment had forgotten his principal target, the Spanish Netherlands; the means to the end, crushing the Dutch, had momentarily become the end in itself. Second, Louis was worried about England. The English were France's most important allies in 1672 and they strongly opposed a war with Spain, their principal trading partner.[9]

Louis XIV's thoughts, however, were driven back to the Spanish Netherlands late in 1672, when the prince of Orange laid siege to Charleroi. This strategic fortress had been a French enclave within the Spanish Netherlands since the Treaty of Aix-la-Chapelle. A siege so close to his frontier was enough to force Louis

XIV to act, but the siege at Charleroi had a peculiarly galvanic effect on the king because the Dutch were aided by the impetuous governor of the Spanish Netherlands, the count of Monterey. The situation in December 1672 was ripe with possibilities, and Louis wanted desperately to take advantage of them. When rumors arrived at the French court that Charleroi had been invested, the king sent Louvois to Flanders to appraise the situation. Louis wrote regularly to his war minister, often completing dispatches in his own hand, through which the king's thoughts can be followed closely. As soon as Spanish involvement at the siege had been confirmed, Louis drew up a memorandum that swarmed with excited proposals: a winter campaign would have great *"éclat"*; Brussels might be taken; affairs at court could be handled by Le Tellier and Colbert, and Louis himself would march to the northern frontier personally to direct the war against the Spaniards.[10]

Louis left Saint-Germain and moved north up the valley of the Oise. He wrote to Louvois with the hyperbole of a person who lusted for action: "I consider this juncture as one of the most important that I will ever witness."[11] The king moved carefully up the Oise because, although he was rambunctious enough to think of a winter campaign, his concern with how he would be judged made him cautious: "If there is any chance to take revenge upon the Spaniards, stay where you are and make the preparations, . . . so that I can act without being reproached for it."[12] On 23 December the king advanced to Compiègne and demanded news from Louvois because he was "furiously impatient."[13] It appeared that an open break between France and Spain was inevitable. Louis was already planning a two-front effort against the Spaniards, and he ordered the prince of Condé to gather intelligence on the defensive positions of Franche-Comté.[14]

Then, almost as quickly as it had risen, the king's bellicosity subsided. When Orange and Monterey discovered that Charleroi was too strong to take, they gathered up their siege train and slipped off into the winter mists of the Low Countries. As soon as the threat to Louis disappeared, his rhetoric became hesitant and tentative. He wrote to Louvois on 24 December: "I wonder if we should hotly pursue the plans concerning Burgundy [Franche-Comté]? Give me your advice."[15] Louvois advised a moderate course. The war minister often pandered to Louis's taste for war, but his grasp of military affairs was strong enough in this instance

for him to see that an attack upon the Spaniards during winter
1672/73 would have been foolish; no troops had been assembled
and no logistical bases had been established. Moreover, the cere-
bral stroke that Le Tellier had sustained while accompanying the
king to the northern frontier left him partially paralyzed. Le Tellier
knew more about military affairs than any other man in France,
and Louis and Louvois, who were relatively inexperienced at
large-scale warfare, were no doubt reluctant to begin a major new
conflict while Le Tellier was ill and unable to function at full
capacity. By the morning of 26 December the king was planning
to leave Compiègne and return to Saint-Germain. He wrote to
Louvois: "I am beginning to agree with you, and your father
wrote me a letter yesterday . . . that will show you that he feels
the same way you do."[16] Louis was highly agitated and the next
day he changed his mind, deciding to stay at Compiègne until he
received the official Spanish reaction to Monterey's provocative
actions. Then he changed his mind again, and by the end of December was on his way back to Saint-Germain. He wrote simply
to his war minister: "When you return we will have lots to talk
about."[17]

Spain was certainly one of the issues that the king and Louvois
talked about during that winter of 1673, for soon after Louvois
returned to Saint-Germain from Flanders he wrote to Condé:
"The Spaniards have been as quiet as a mouse since the Charleroi
incident. . . . After examining everything, His Majesty has decided
not to undertake anything between now and spring time. . . .
Nonetheless, it will be a good thing for the men [i.e. spies] that you
have in Franche-Comté to finish their trip so that we will be better
informed for the future."[18] Thus the Charleroi affair had not
been forgotten at Saint-Germain but had merely been shelved,
to be used against Spain at a more convenient time.

On 1 April 1673, Louvois wrote a tantalizing letter to Turenne,
who was still stationed with his army in Germany: "The Spaniards
are very perplexed. They have no idea what to do because the
Dutch are in no mood or condition to continue the war, and the
only order they have received from Madrid is to prevent peace
from being made. . . . If I could have the honor of talking to you
for but fifteen minutes, I would tell you some things that would
certainly not displease you."[19] What were these mysterious matters
about which Louvois could not write to Turenne but which the

war minister was confident would please the marshal? A clue is provided in a letter Louvois wrote some three weeks later to a French cavalry commander who was stationed in a defensive position on the frontier of the Spanish Netherlands. The war minister told him that the king did not wish to let the Spaniards act with impunity. "If the count of Monterey . . . touches the least little bit of the king's territory, His Majesty wants you to tell him that you have orders not to allow it."[20] Thus we see that in spring 1673 the French were quietly but persistently seeking to increase tensions between France and Spain and were looking for a pretext to provoke an incident.

However, Louis XIV's intentions vis-à-vis Spain are best seen in the instructions for his ambassadors who were preparing to depart for the peace negotiations in Cologne. Louis was permitting Spain to send representative diplomats to the peace conference, but the French ambassadors' powers to treat with the Spaniards were rigidly prescribed by their instructions; they were free to discuss only one of the French king's grievances: the aid that Monterey had given William of Orange at the siege of Charleroi in December 1672.[21] This was the grievance about which Louis had been most vocal and which, it had seemed, might lead to open war between France and Spain. The French diplomats were instructed that any dispute that had arisen between France and Spain *before* the outbreak of the Dutch War, especially the sinking of a French merchant ship in Cadiz harbor, was emphatically *not* negotiable in Cologne. Moreover, the French plenipotentiaries were to "employ their skill to choke off all memory of that affair, in such a manner that . . . the Spaniards believe that His Majesty . . . is no longer even thinking of asking compensation for what occurred off the Spanish coast."[22] Louis XIV was thus engaged in what he felt was a clever stratagem. He would lull the Spaniards into thinking he was prepared to live amicably with them by settling his most obvious complaint, the Charleroi affair. At the same time, he would keep a trump card, the Cadiz incident, which he could play to justify any move he might wish to make against the Spaniards, either in Flanders or in the Franche-Comté of Burgundy.

Louvois was confident that the matters would "not displease" Turenne. When Turenne's advance into the Spanish Netherlands during the War of Devolution had been halted by the untimely (in

Turenne's opinion) Peace of Aix-la-Chapelle, he had reacted "as though struck by a club."[23] By April 1673, however, Louis XIV was seriously thinking of turning his attention once more to the northern possessions of the atrophying Spanish monarchy.

Louis's thoughts about renewing a war with the Spaniards seem to have been part cause and part consequence of his changing disposition toward the Dutch. The king's sudden willingness in spring 1673 to dictate a settlement to the Dutch was probably prompted by his awareness that the Spanish Netherlands, not the Dutch Republic, was the logical target for his expansionary efforts. After all, Spain had always been the primary opponent of the Bourbons. Out of pique and passion for military glory, Louis had considered trying to destroy the United Provinces of the Dutch Republic, but by April 1673 he was preparing to develop a different war policy, based on the dynastic and state-interest policy of extending French frontiers at the expense of the Spanish Hapsburgs. On the other hand, once the war with the Dutch had become burdensome—politically, because Sweden and Brandenburg opposed it and militarily because of the flooded countryside and the extended lines of supply—Louis had to find a new opponent, who would be more accessible and less likely to attract sympathetic allies. The king's thirst for martial glory was unslaked, and if the Dutch accepted his terms and made peace, the Spaniards would become his adversaries. Louis was not finished with the Dutch in spring 1673; but if he could have things his way, he would impose a crippling settlement on them and move again against the Spaniards in Franche-Comté and Flanders.

What precisely did Louis have in mind for the Spanish Netherlands, the object of so much fruitless negotiating in the 1660s? John B. Wolf has suggested that as early as the 1670s Louis and his advisors wished to create a rationalized line of frontier fortifications across the north of France.[24] His suggestion is perhaps based upon the famous letter Vauban wrote to Louvois from Flanders in January 1673: "Seriously, Sir, the king must think some about creating a *pré carré* [literally a squared field]. I do not like this pell-mell confusion of fortresses, ours and the enemy's. You are obliged to maintain three for one; your men are plagued by it; your expenses are increased and your forces are much diminished. . . . Therefore, Sir, either by war or treaty, always advocate the *cadra-*

ture [square], not the circle but the *pré*."²⁵ Extrapolating from these admonitions, the suggestion that the French began to strive for linear frontiers as early as 1673 is attractive, but it will not hold up under scrutiny. First, when Vauban wrote of a *pré carré* he was thinking of the frontier as an area, not as a line. Vauban wanted to "rationalize" the frontier, but there is no indication in his writings that he was thinking of linear boundaries for the Flemish frontier when in 1673 he wrote about rectifying its "pell-mell confusion of fortresses."

Indeed, given Vauban's conception of the use of frontier fortifications, a linear frontier would have been a logical impossibility, for the great engineer conceived of border fortresses as fulfilling two functions, one external and one domestic. In December 1673 Vauban wrote to Louvois, advocating that the fortifications at La Fère, in the valley of the Oise near the northern frontier, be strengthened: "It [La Fère] is the only secure fortress on the frontier that covers the Île de France and the better part of Picardy. It is (I say) a secure fortress against all disorders of state wherever they may come from, *whether from within or without*."²⁶ Thus the royal government could not plan a rigidly linear frontier of fortresses until it was confident that the realm had been fully reduced to obedience within. The government did not have this confidence at the time of the Dutch War.

Second, Vauban envisioned a rationalized frontier purely as a defensive matter, which was not what Louis XIV intended in 1673. Louvois replied clearly to Vauban's letter of 19 January: "Everything in your letter looks good to me, but things cannot be done as quickly as one would wish. You must be patient and hope that, after some time, your advice will be useful."²⁷ Thus, Louvois was telling Vauban that the engineer and the king were interested in different issues. In all of the many letters that Vauban and Louvois exchanged during winter and spring 1673, while the fortifications expert moved from town to town inspecting the fortresses along the northern frontier, the *pré carré* was never mentioned again. After the Charleroi incident, Louis began to consider eliminating some unnecessary frontier fortresses, and Condé as well as Vauban urged this action.²⁸ A number of superfluous fortresses were thus abandoned and razed, but Vauban's suggestion for a clean, defensive cordon was brushed aside.²⁹ In 1673 the king was not concerned with establishing a defensive barrier between his realm and the Spanish Netherlands. Louis had other plans for the Spanish Netherlands.

Sometime during the campaign of 1673, after the siege at Maastricht, Louis and Louvois drew up tentative plans for the campaign of 1674. In this *Projet pour 1674* five fortresses are listed in the order the king wished to attack them.[30] Namur, in the Spanish Netherlands on the Meuse River, headed the list. Then came Mons, Condé, Cambrai, and Bouchain, all Spanish fortresses in the valley of the Scheldt. Finally, the *Projet* says "one could also think of clearing the Meuse by taking all of the Spanish fortresses and outposts from Liège down to Grave."[31]

Thus Louis XIV's strategy as projected into 1674 from summer 1673 had two objectives: (1) to open a broad avenue along the Meuse, from his logistical bases in France to the occupied territories in the Dutch Netherlands; (2) to penetrate the Spanish Netherlands via the Scheldt River Valley. The plans for 1674 never materialized as Louis envisaged them—but in any event the king was not planning, in summer 1673, to tidy up his frontier with the Spanish Netherlands. The notion of sweeping down the Meuse was discarded after Louis decided in October 1673 to withdraw his troops from the conquered Dutch territory, for there was no longer any reason to clear a corridor into the Dutch Netherlands; but in fall 1673 the king was thinking more and more about the Spaniards. As we have seen, when his negotiators in Cologne showed interest in proposals presented by the Swedish mediators that would have somewhat rationalized the border between France and the Spanish Netherlands, the enraged Louis ordered Pomponne to inform the diplomats that even listening to such proposals in the future would jeopardize their careers. Louis himself wrote to Courtin that he should "discourage in every possible way any negotiation about this subject [that is, the Flemish frontier], and do not give the Spaniards the least suspicion that I wish to withdraw from their heartlands, for I believe that the war they have just declared will give me the opportunity to penetrate much deeper."[32]

Thus it is apparent that at no time during the early 1670s did Louis XIV consider creation of a rationalized frontier between his realm and the Spanish Netherlands. Rather, he was preparing to march into Brussels' Grand' Place and lay claim to those territories that were justly his, both by dynastic right and strategic necessity. Vauban's concept of a rationalized frontier, consisting of blocks of fortresses to provide a defensive barrier, began to materialize only at the end of the Dutch War, in 1677–78.[33] A linear frontier, as such, did not develop until the latter third of the eighteenth century.[34] In 1673, Louis was thinking of neither.

What, then, prevented war between France and Spain in spring 1673? Before renewing his war with Spain, Louis wanted to establish his place in history as the conqueror of Maastricht. An immediate break with Spain would deny Louis the opportunity to concentrate his forces against Maastricht and might give the French military initiative in the Low Countries back to Condé and Luxembourg—a disagreeable alternative when 1673 was to be Louis's year of glory on the battlefield. Second, although Louis had persuaded Charles II of England to declare that Spain had broken the Peace of Aix-la-Chapelle in the Charleroi affair,[35] the French king knew that neither Charles nor Parliament wanted war with Spain. The prosperity of English merchants depended heavily upon commerce with Spain, and the English king's revenues were derived largely from the customs duties upon this trade.[36] Louis had no desire to lessen his principal ally's appetite for war, or perhaps even give him cause to make a separate peace. This need to maintain the English alliance explains Louis's statement in his military memoirs: "The Spaniards were surely my enemies, but not overtly. I therefore dissimulated with them, wishing that they should be the first to begin the war."[37]

Duke Philippe de Navailles was from an old and distinguished military family but had disgraced himself in the abortive French attempt to assist the Venetians against the Turks on Crete in 1669. The duke was looking for an opportunity to recoup his honor, and he wrote to Louvois early in June that "the king will never have such a fine opportunity. It seems to me that when he has such superb armies His Majesty does not have to dicker but can fall directly upon Brussels. . . . Brussels would be a very good place to winter."[38] Although Louis doubtless tended to agree with his *noblesse d'épée*, who saw war as their principal occupation, the king also had to work at statesmanship. Louvois responded to Navailles: "At this time I see no chance that His Majesty will decide to order you to march into the Franche-Comté, since he does not want to be the one to break the peace."[39] Open conflict with Spain would doubtless come soon enough, but spring 1673 was not a propitious time for the king to begin the war.

The Spaniards, for their part, appeared to be ready to accommodate Louis by abandoning their neutrality and breaking openly with France. Louvois was perhaps correct when he suggested that Turenne's victories in Germany lessened the Spaniards' appetite for war, but the count of Monterey was eager, and it was questionable how long the divided and confused councils in Madrid could hold him in check. The council of regency for the young and half-witted Carlos II was nominally headed by the queen mother, Maria Ana, and she was wholly under the influence of her Jesuit advisors. Under pressure from both the imperial and the Dutch ambassadors, several of the Spanish ministers of state were in favor of open war with France after the fall of Maastricht. The duke of Villars, Louis's ambassador in Madrid, reported that the Spaniards were harassing all Frenchmen, including his own servants, and that "everything appears as if they [the Spaniards] are trying to goad Your Majesty into declaring war."[40] Thus in midsummer 1673 the French and Spaniards tried to lure each other into making the first lunge. The Spaniards may well have gone ahead, if it had not been for the persistent and realistic opposition of Count Peñaranda, who repeated acidly in the Spanish councils of state that "he was quite willing to accept war with France, provided that he could be shown the money, the men, and the officers necessary to undertake such an enterprise with any hope of success."[41]

Shortly after Louis XIV had assumed power in the French monarchy in 1661, his mettle had been tested by one of the innumerable confrontations over precedence that plagued diplomats during the seventeenth century. The French and Spanish ambassadors, with their entourages, arrived simultaneously at a bottleneck in a street of London; swords were drawn to decide the issue; several French lackeys wound up dead on the cobblestones; and the Spaniards passed in triumph. The Spanish triumph was short lived, however, as Louis XIV compelled the sickly King Philip IV of Spain to send a special ambassador to Paris to apologize to Louis before the assembled French court and foreign diplomatic corps at the Louvre. The Spaniards promised that henceforth the French would take precedence over them on all occasions.[42] Louis thereby avenged himself. He formally established the premier position of his crown in the rules of European protocol, and for a time there was no need to insult the Spaniards and make them lose face.

In summer 1673, however, Louis's ambassador in London, Colbert de Croissy, was the sort of man who liked to aggravate matters. Approaching Whitehall Palace one night in July in an ordinary coach with two footmen, Croissy discovered that the Spanish ambassador, the Marquis Pedro Fernández del Fresno, was about to enter the gates in his state coach with complete and liveried retinue. Because it was nighttime and Croissy was traveling informally, Fresno did not at first recognize him as the French ambassador and did not withdraw for Croissy as speedily as the Frenchman desired. The result was that Croissy made a formal complaint to the Spanish court about the conduct of its ambassador, and Fresno was so angered by Croissy's action that he vowed never again to enter the French ambassador's house or to attend the Italian comedy, which performed in the courtyard of the embassy.[43] It was a minor incident but it shows the tension that existed between the French and Spanish crowns during summer 1673.

By August 1673, Louis XIV looked for war with Spain more eagerly than at any time since Monterey's provocative act to aid the Dutch at Charleroi. Louis's thrust against the Dutch at Maastricht had proved a brilliant success, and he thought that the Dutch were ready to accept his terms at Cologne. Moreover, by late August Louis commanded his own army just north of Franche-Comté, the Spanish possession that was his objective in 1673.

The great Condé, who had been relegated to a holding action for Louis's siege of Maastricht, was to perform the same menial duty during Louis's invasion of Franche-Comté. Late in August, when the French heard that the regency council in Madrid was preparing to order Monterey to begin open warfare with France, Louvois reinforced Condé's forces in Flanders with ten squadrons of cavalry from Luxembourg's army, which was still stationed in Utrecht.[44] However, Louvois refused to send Condé the additional infantry that he had requested, for the principal action against Spain was not to be pursued in the Low Countries: "Because Your Highness knows the king's intentions if the Spaniards declare war [i.e. Louis's intention to invade Franche-Comté] . . . Your Highness can easily see that it will be impossible to send you four battalions, and if the Spaniards do not break openly with us they would be useless to you."[45]

Louis, or more probably Louvois, realized that the prince of Condé might weary of serving as Louis's lackey in a profession (that is, war) that was the prince's specialty, and Louvois wrote to mollify him: "His Majesty will consider Your Highness's services on this occasion as if they were great victories over his enemies and realizes full well the sacrifice Your Highness is making to him in agreeing to do that which serves him best at the present."[46] This was small consolation for the man who had beaten the Spaniards at Rocroi and Lens. But what recourse did the prince have? After all, he was also the man who had joined the Spaniards and fought against the French king's armies during the chaotic years of the Fronde. Condé had to consider himself fortunate to receive the mediocre command; he was still expiating his past misconduct.

During the first days of September, on his return to Lorraine from the triumphal march through Alsace, Louis was so excited about the prospect of invading Franche-Comté that he considered forgoing the diplomatic and propaganda advantages of allowing Spain to begin the war. Louvois wrote to Condé that "in case His Majesty sees that the Dutch do not want peace and that the Spaniards are determined to break with us, it is possible that His Majesty will order you to provoke them to do it promptly, so that he can seize Burgundy [the Franche-Comté] before it can be reinforced with more troops."[47]

During the second week of September, while Louis maintained faint hope that the Dutch ambassadors at Cologne would abandon their intransigence and accede to the French and English terms, Louvois and Pomponne busily prepared for the invasion of Franche-Comté. On 12 September Louvois wrote to Saint-Romain, the French ambassador in Switzerland, that the king would be in Franche-Comté within two weeks with an army of 18,000 men and that nothing must be spared to prevent the Swiss cantons from giving passage and providing aid to any Spanish troops that might wish to pass through Switzerland to reinforce the Spanish garrisons in the Burgundian province. During September, Saint-Romain attended a meeting of the diet of the Swiss cantons at Baden (near Zürich) and Louvois pleaded with him to bribe the delegates so that the diet would adjourn before the end of the month. "If you can prevent the Swiss from allowing aid to Franche-Comté, the king will be absolutely master of it by October 20. You can see how important it is that the diet adjourns before news arrives of His Majesty's entry into Franche-Comté."[48] While Louvois urged Saint-Romain, Pomponne wrote to Colbert and informed the finance minister how many livres had to be delivered to pay off the Swiss.[49] Swiss mercenary pikemen no longer controlled the battlefields of Europe, but the Swiss—as venal as ever—were still turning a profit from war because of their strategic location at the crossroads of the Continent.

For the final two weeks of September 1673, Louis and his court remained in Nancy, received dispatches from Turenne (who had begun his intricate maneuvers with Montecuccoli on the Main River), prepared for the invasion of Franche-Comté, and awaited news that Monterey had initiated war with France. Finally, on 24 September, Louis XIV became impatient, and he ordered a declaration of war against Spain drafted.[50] The declaration was based upon two arguments: Spain had broken the Peace of Aix-la-Chapelle (most flagrantly when she assisted the Dutch at the siege of Charleroi in December 1672), and the treaty Spain signed with the Dutch at The Hague on 30 August 1673 (which stated the allies' intention of reestablishing the Flemish frontier on the basis of the Peace of the Pyrenees, thus undoing the Peace of Aix-la-Chapelle) demonstrated that the Spaniards had no desire to maintain peace in Europe. Like most declarations of war, the French claims had a certain plausibility, but the words were largely contrived to legitimate actions that Louis XIV perceived to be in his own interest.

The day after the declaration of war against Spain was drafted, Louis XIV abruptly cancelled his plans for invading Franche-Comté. In long dispatches to Condé and Turenne, Louvois explained that the army Louis had gathered in Lorraine would be split up—part to be sent to protect ducal Burgundy, part to proceed via the bridge over the Rhine at Philippsburg to reinforce Turenne's army, part to remain in Lorraine, and the largest part to march under Louis's personal command northwestward to Flanders.[51] The war minister enumerated the reasons that had persuaded the king not to invade Franche-Comté in fall 1673: the emperor's army in Germany was stronger than had been anticipated (which obliquely admitted that Turenne would need reinforcements from Louis's army); the Swedes and the English would be alienated if France initiated war with Spain; and Louis was concerned lest Monterey and Orange join forces and "undertake something against His Majesty's lands."[52]

These were eminently sound reasons for calling off the invasion of Franche-Comté, but from the first Louis had known that the Swedes and the English had fierce objections to his starting a war with Spain. Thus the strategic problems that Turenne faced in Germany and Condé faced in the Low Countries must have dictated the king's abrupt change of plans on 25 September.

At precisely the same time that Louis and Louvois planned the invasion of Franche-Comté, Turenne and Montecuccoli were engaged in their fateful maneuvers in Franconia. It was on 21 September that Turenne wrote to Louvois, explaining that the bishop of Würzburg had thrown his support to the Imperials and that Turenne had no choice but to fall back and look for flour to feed his army.[53] The French strategic position in Germany had suddenly worsened and neither Louvois nor Louis could fail to recognize this. Turenne's dispatch must have arrived in Nancy just after Louis had the declaration of war against Spain drafted. Then, within hours of the arrival of Turenne's dispatch, Louvois received a dispatch from Condé, who was stationed in Tournai on the border of the Spanish Netherlands:

> I have told you about the condition of my army. The infantry could not be in worse shape, and assuredly it would be no pleasure to lead it into combat. If the prince of Orange sends some troops to the Spaniards and they withdraw theirs from Holland, you can surely see that I would be forced to cross the Scheldt River and station myself upon French soil.[54]

Just two years before Louis XIV's birth in 1638, Spanish *tercios* had penetrated France as far as Corbie on the Somme and threatened Paris. Customarily, Louis's ministers of state read dispatches to him, and the king must have remembered Corbie when Louvois read Condé's dispatch.[55] Louis had a more compelling need than most men to maintain his hold on what belonged to him, and despite the acute disappointment of postponing the conquest of Franche-Comté he had to abandon that objective for another year and use his army to support Condé and Turenne, who were protecting French soil.

Thus Louis XIV's plans for martial glory were confronted by harsh reality during the last week of September 1673. He had been campaigning flamboyantly for four months, with his mistress, Mme. de Montespan, as a spectator, but now he had to narrow his far-flung operations to protect the more tangible and immediate interests of his realm. The king abandoned his plans for invading Franche-Comté and sent reinforcements to Condé in the Netherlands, to Turenne in Germany, and to Elector Max Heinrich of Cologne, his principal ally in the Rhineland.[56]

While Louvois was redeploying the royal armies, Pomponne wrote enthusiastically to the French ambassadors in Cologne: "You can easily judge, Sirs, that something momentous will happen when His Majesty's army joins the army commanded by the prince of Condé."[57] Pomponne was relieved. He had counseled against the rash and improvised campaign that Louis and Louvois had begun after Maastricht fell to the French at the end of June. Now Pomponne did not have to worry about justifying another adventure to the princes of Europe. Moreover, on the same day that Louis decided not to invade Franche-Comté he agreed to send major concessions to Cologne; his aim was to convince the Swedes that the war was justifiable and that Sweden should march into Germany in support of the French.[58] Pomponne was thinking that Louis was beginning to see the validity of his arguments: bring Sweden into the war at any cost; cease antagonizing the Germans with a provocative policy in the Rhineland; then prepare to turn the French armies back to Spanish Flanders, where the true interests of the French monarchy could best be served. However, Pomponne's optimism in September 1673 was largely unfounded. The king was thinking of rekindling hostilities with the Spaniards in Flanders, but he could not confine the growing war to Flanders and Franche-Comté. Five more years of European warfare lay ahead.

On 26 September Pomponne forecast "momentous" happenings once the king's army joined Condé's in Flanders. On the same day, Louvois wrote to the prince: "His Majesty is well aware that the season and our lack of infantry will not permit him to begin a siege. But he believes that it should be possible to seize some position that will greatly inconvenience the Spaniards."[59] Within two days, however, Louvois notified Condé that the king had changed his mind; only Louis's cavalry would be sent to reinforce Condé's army, and Louis was retiring with his ministers to Saint-Germain to prepare for the coming year's campaign.[60]

The king's decision not to join Condé for an autumn campaign in the Spanish Netherlands was dictated largely by the news from Madrid. Villars, the French ambassador to Spain, had written that the Spaniards were in no hurry to enter open war with France, and, in any case, would not do so until Montecuccoli had made a good showing against Turenne in Germany.[61] Thus even had Louis marched to Flanders he could not have attacked the Spaniards without bringing reproaches upon himself for having initiated a new war. Undoubtedly, Louis's desire for a final thrust to conclude the campaign of 1673 was also dulled because he did not wish to share the honors of any victory with the prince of Condé; this was a policy to which the king had adhered throughout the year.

In foul weather, during the first week in October, Louis rode with his cavalry as far north as Saint-Quentin in Picardy. Then, sending his soldiers to join Condé in Flanders, he quickly retired southward, arriving at Saint-Germain on 13 October and Versailles two days later. When a defensive posture rather than a triumphal march was called for, Louis, quite naturally, preferred the château to the battlefield.

At Versailles, Louis impatiently awaited news from the northern frontier and from Germany, and did not have long to wait for news from the north. From his advanced position in French Flanders, Condé had been sending foraging parties into the Spanish Netherlands, and the Spaniards finally reacted to this provocation. As Condé reported to the governor of Maastricht, they "came this morning with a quantity of troops and pillaged some villages in the area around Ath. . . . My orders from the king are to inform all the governors if this should happen. I am informing you so that you can begin hostilities with them [the Spaniards] and start taking contributions in their territories."[62] Thus Flemish peasants, who did not care who their sovereign lord was, were the first to suffer from renewed war between the French and Spanish monarchs.

According to Louvois, Louis XIV judged that the Spaniards had begun hostilities: "I received the letter from Your Highness [Condé] . . . in which it appears that the Spaniards with no warning have begun the war. The king approves the orders that Your Highness has sent out directing his troops to begin hostilities and demand contributions."[63] The same day, Louvois sent a circular letter to the other royal commanders, expressing his relief that the long-awaited clash had come. "I have dispatched this courier to inform you that the Spaniards have at last begun the war."[64]

On 20 October 1673, by order of La Reynie, the lieutenant general of police in Paris, "the warre with Spain [was] very solemnly proclaimed all over this city."[65] While Condé opened hostilities against the Spaniards in Flanders, the imperial army, under the command of Montecuccoli, swept across Germany and invaded the electorates of Cologne and Münster, Louis XIV's Rhenish allies. Lord Arlington's correspondent in Paris wrote that he had gone "to salute his Maty yesterday at Versailles, where Monsr. de Louvoy lookt very merry upon the farther engagement in a warre."[66] Indeed, a new and larger phase of the so-called Dutch War had begun.

Marquis de Louvois (1641–1691),
engraving by Pierre Simon
(courtesy of Roger-Viollet)

The End of the Dutch War: Louis XIV's First Setback

The opening campaign of Louis XIV's Dutch War is well known. Every history of the Sun King's reign describes the blitz of the royal armies up the corridor of the bishopric of Liège into western Germany and then down the valley of the lower Rhine into the Dutch Netherlands. The crossing of the Rhine in June 1672, one of the great feats of French military history, is immortalized by a Gobelin tapestry and by Coysevox's bas-relief that dominates the Salon de Guerre at Versailles. However, the hurried withdrawal of French forces from Dutch territory just eighteen months later is little studied and virtually forgotten.[1] Historians have tended to neglect the French retreat ever since Louis XIV glossed over it in his military memoirs.[2] Although from the French viewpoint, the account of their withdrawal from the Dutch Netherlands makes a less rousing story than the invasion, it is in some respects of more interest to the historian, for the pressure of defeat laid bare certain aspects of Louis XIV's war policies that the flush of easy victories had left unexposed. An examination of the events of autumn 1673 tells us much about the king, his advisors, and the nature of the Dutch War.

Louis had pursued the campaign of 1673 at a frenetic pace. He had marched on and conquered Maastricht, crushed the independence of the Alsatian cities, overseen the invasion of Trier, and laid plans for a new war with Spain. In late September 1673, the king was retrenching. The plans for invading Franche-Comté were shelved and Louis assigned the troops that had been under his personal command to the armies led by Condé in Flanders and Turenne in Germany. The trimming of the king's military ambitions was in part the result of prudent French strategy devised by Louis XIV and Louvois. But their prudence was largely imposed upon them by the situation they had created by autumn 1673; in absolute terms, they no longer had sufficient numbers of troops to sustain all of their far-flung operations.

On 1 September, Luxembourg, who had been given command of the French army in occupied Utrecht after Condé was withdrawn to guard the Flemish frontier, wrote to Louvois about his predicament: "As animals do certain things during each season of the year, so the Dutch are in movement this season. And it so happens that this is the season during which I am in the weakest position."[3] Luxembourg's army could not be reinforced, and within two weeks he informed Louvois that the prince of Orange had invested Naarden, the most advanced French-held fortress in the Dutch Netherlands. This news did not disquiet the French war minister because he thought that Luxembourg might relieve the siege and that, "in any case, if Naarden should be taken it would not be the first time that a place has been lost."[4] By 17 September Louvois, in a less cavalier mood, had reconciled himself to the eventual loss of Naarden and was only hoping that Orange would "pay dearly enough for his conquest that he will have no cause to rejoice."[5] On 20 September news of Orange's disconcertingly fast conquest of Naarden reached Nancy, and Louis XIV wrote a personal letter to Luxembourg, ordering the court-martial of Du Pas, the governor who had surrendered Naarden after little resistance.[6]

Although Du Pas had surrendered too quickly, his hurried capitulation was not the fundamental cause for the fall of Naarden. Luxembourg explained this in a remarkable letter to Louvois, and he began by telling the war minister that he had already written "a fine letter, Sir, as one does to a minister. Now I am writing as a friend." Luxembourg then explained that because he had been obliged to send most of his cavalry to the king's army for the attack on Trier, he had been impotent in the face of the Dutch counterattack. "This prompts me to ask you," Luxembourg concluded, "'My God, why hast thou forsaken me? . . .' Did you not know the strength of the Dutch and did you not think that they would try something?"[7] Louis XIV and Louvois were so deeply absorbed in their own projects in autumn 1673 that they did not appreciate the positions and capabilities of the other royal armies. Luxembourg was always an obedient commander but he was hurt and confused by the king's muddled strategy.

Although it was increasingly apparent that the French armies were overextended, Louis XIV was not prepared to withdraw his occupying force from the Low Countries and thus sacrifice his prized Dutch conquests of the preceding year. He had as yet suffered no serious military setback, and he was planning to hold his position in preparation for new conquests in the coming year's campaign. The intensity of the king's feelings about his Dutch conquests was expressed by Louvois on 21 September: "In the king's present mood he would rather give up Paris or Versailles than Maastricht."[8]

The Dutch conquests were indeed a delicate subject at the French court during autumn 1673. In mid-October Louvois sent a curious letter to Luxembourg, who was still commanding the royal armies in the Dutch Netherlands: "This is a response to the letter that you took the trouble to write the 6th of this month for me personally. I wish you would have given me your opinion about what I told you in the letter that you returned to me, and you will be doing me a big favor if you will do so as soon as possible."[9] It was customary for ministers of state to carry on unofficial correspondence with ambassadors and generals, and Louvois frequently did so. Yet the cryptic tone and style of this letter are strange if not unique in Louvois's correspondence.

Luxembourg replied to Louvois's request for advice by advocating that most of the French-held fortresses in the Dutch Netherlands be razed and abandoned in preparation for war with Spain.[10] In the nonextant letter that Luxembourg returned to Louvois, Louvois had apparently discussed the possibility that the Dutch conquests might have to be sacrificed to the exigencies of an expanding war. Louvois needed expert advice and he had taken Luxembourg into his confidence on a topic (the Dutch conquests) that was taboo at Louis XIV's court. Luxembourg knew that his future in the royal army depended upon Louvois and thus he proved his loyalty to the war minister by returning the compromising letter so that Louvois could destroy it with his own hands.

Louvois secretly corresponded with Luxembourg because he was afraid to confront Louis openly with the painful fact that his conquests from the campaign of 1672, which were so important to the king's self-image, should be given up. All of the Louvois–Luxembourg *sub rosa* correspondence is not extant, but what remains makes it clear that Louvois was shirking his responsibility as war minister when he failed to rouse his courage and speak bluntly to Louis XIV about the need to withdraw and regroup the French armies. As war minister, Louvois had a large role in bringing on the increasingly unmanageable war of 1673 and producing the predicament that faced the French in the fall of that year. Thus he found it difficult to confront Louis XIV with the unpleasant facts. Louvois, ambitious and proud, had to risk incurring the king's wrath and to admit failure to himself.

Turenne, on the other hand, had strategic sense and a soldierly quality of plain speaking, and first dared to mention the evacuation of Holland. "His Majesty will permit me to say that if war with Spain is foreseen with certainty I believe that the sooner Holland is evacuated the better." Turenne concluded this letter by saying, "I note this only in passing, for the king was doubtless considered it at length."[11] Thus the marshal was obliquely questioning the judgment of Louis and his war minister, for his last sentence implied that they had *not* been making the necessary contingency plans.

Louvois, who had returned to Versailles with Louis, responded to Turenne on 20 October: "The king recognizes perfectly well the necessity of withdrawing some troops from Holland, and I think that I will be able to inform you within eight or ten days of his decision on that question."[12] Louvois responded to Turenne's query with great sureness, but his confidence rings hollow; he was attempting to conceal the indecision and vacillation at Versailles. Perhaps Louis XIV had seen the overriding necessity of relinquishing most of his Dutch conquests when Louvois wrote to Turenne, but probably he had not. If Louis had been "perfectly well" aware of this necessity, why did he delay his decision for eight or ten days? It was probably only after receiving Turenne's letter that Louvois decided he had to face Louis with the problem of evacuating Holland. Turenne's perceptive strategic advice helped to sweep away the confusion that had surrounded Louis's decision making during September 1673. The clear-sighted ordering of priorities that the Dutch War demanded in autumn 1673 came from a general in the field rather than from the king or his war minister at Versailles.[13]

Louis XIV had vastly overextended himself by autumn 1673, and no one could find solutions to all the strategic problems created by six months of expansive and careless campaigning. Louvois was unable to combine the variables of geography, logistics, and troop strengths in an effective formula for deploying the royal armies while the French and their allies were pushed into a defensive posture. Louvois had handled the offensive war of 1672 admirably, but the setbacks of 1673 demanded new skills that he had not acquired. His correspondence with the French generals during October 1673 shows that he did not have the knowledge or experience to direct a war that was rapidly changing in character. On 15 October Louvois wrote to Condé, who was still in Flanders, that the Spaniards could not delay going to war without losing face, but if they did not openly break with France in order to aid the Dutch more effectively, "the king's intention is that you should advance into their country [the Spanish Netherlands] . . . to prevent them from giving any troops to the prince of Orange."[14]

Condé snapped back: "It would be difficult for me to advance without leaving the country entirely open to their [Spanish] incursions, particularly the frontiers of France. . . . Their ability to mass troops much more easily than I can creates many problems."[15] The same day that Condé wrote, Louvois was compelled to turn his attention to the lower Rhine, where the lands of the elector of Cologne, Louis XIV's German ally, were threatened by the imperial army: "Because the loss of Bonn or Anderach would be of cardinal importance, His Majesty correctly believes that he has no more urgent business to attend to; he cannot recommend too strongly to Your Highness to do everything in your power to prevent our enemies from attacking them."[16] Condé refused Louvois a second time, replying that Luxembourg, if anyone, could go to the aid of Bonn, the elector of Cologne's threatened capital.[17]

For the time being, Louvois was not giving orders; he was desperately trying to save Louis's conquest, the French allies, and his own position in the government. Louvois needed to wring a decision from the king in order to save himself.

On 20 October, Louvois wrote to Rochefort, who commanded the French army in occupied Trier, that "the king will deliberate today on abandoning Utrecht, and . . . I believe that I can say, just between the two of us, that it will be decided upon and carried out in a very brief time."[18] The pressure of events was forcing Louvois and Louis XIV to make a long-overdue decision. On 21 October, Louvois dispatched to Luxembourg a preliminary sketch of plans to abandon all of the French-held Dutch territories except a few scattered fortresses along the Meuse and Rhine rivers near the German frontier. Louvois and Luxembourg often spiced their letters with repartee and badinage, but now the war minister tried to conceal his uneasiness, from himself and from Luxembourg, by belittling William of Orange: "While the prince of Orange entertains himself muddying his boots in Flanders, you can evacuate Crévecoeur and Woerden."[19] The French minister might scorn the young Dutch leader, but it was the French army, not the Dutch, that was retreating.

After the war, Louis XIV would complacently analyze his decision to evacuate Holland:

My troops were deployed in Germany, in Holland, in Flanders, and on my frontiers, with but a few inside the realm. My enemies were posted in order to prevent me from carrying out the withdrawals and regroupings that I desired. . . . I had to do something in order to turn the tables on them. This was not easy, but my diligence prevented any mishap from occurring. . . . I resolved to forfeit almost all of my advanced conquests so that I could turn my attention to areas where I could attack [my enemies] and defend myself.[20]

When the king wrote these words five years after the events, he was apparently trying to obliterate bad memories, for this account from his memoirs bears little resemblance to the agitated dispatches of 1673. Louis minimized the impact, on himself and on his war, of Luxembourg's withdrawal from the United Provinces. What happened in late autumn 1673 was that Louis was goaded and pushed into abandoning all the hopes and plans that had preoccupied him for the five preceding years. Indeed, he was abandoning the Dutch War.

During 22 and 23 October, the *commis* in Louvois's war office rubbed numb hands as they drafted voluminous orders for a grand plan of retreat and relief: Luxembourg was to assemble the French army that occupied Utrecht and lead it toward the Rhine. As Luxembourg's army approached the river, a large detachment of cavalry from the army that Condé was using to guard the

Flemish frontier was to join him; this task force would then be prepared to cut off the prince of Orange and prevent him from joining
forces with Montecuccoli, sweeping into the electorate of Cologne
and gaining control over the lower Rhine.[21] The overriding significance of these orders was impressed upon Luxembourg when the
king took the unusual step of personally confirming Louvois's
directives: "Cousin, having ordered the marquis of Louvois to
explain my intentions about assembling an army . . . and abandoning some of the fortresses . . . that I conquered last year from
the Dutch, I am sending you this note to tell you to execute what
he orders you to do."[22] A passage from Louvois's dispatch to
Luxembourg reveals the war minister's frantic state of mind at the
moment that Louis XIV belatedly decided to withdraw from the
Dutch Republic in order to support the elector of Cologne and
hold the line of the Rhine: "You can easily imagine what the king
hopes to achieve with the army that he is ordering you to assemble,
which is to prevent Montecuccoli from crossing the Rhine. . . .
Everything depends upon the arrival of an army near . . . Bonn as
soon as it is humanly possible."[23]

If the job were to be done, Louvois had the appropriate man
in the right place. Bold but not foolhardy, seasoned but not yet
gouty, Luxembourg was probably the best tactical commander in
the French army. Although he occasionally succumbed to a sadistic
impulse,[24] he did not allow this darker side of his personality to
impair his professional effectiveness. However, it was not "humanly possible" even for a Luxembourg to evacuate and raze
fortifications, extort contributions from the Dutch, and prepare
an army to march in a short time.[25] The very length of the orders
that were rushed to Luxembourg (some 35 folio pages) shows
the hopelessness of the mission assigned to him by a distraught
Louvois. Moreover, Luxembourg's operations were delayed by
another, unforeseen factor, which he explained to Louvois as soon
as he received the orders of 23 October: "I am not answering your
dispatch today, Sir, . . . for the code in which it was written was
left in Utrecht because it was no longer being used."[26] The French
military cipher had been routinely changed in mid-October, but
Louvois in his vexed condition or one of his overworked secretaries had coded the critical dispatches to Luxembourg in the out-
dated cipher. Luxembourg's intendant soon had the dispatches
decoded, but this small drama indicates that Louvois had not only

lost track of the locations and capabilities of the various French armies, his war office was in chaos.

The mix-up of the ciphers did not, however, ultimately affect the denouement of the drama on the Rhine, where armies from all of Europe were converging upon the electorate of Cologne. Luxembourg, although he tried valiantly, could not assemble his scattered army and march quickly enough to save Bonn, Elector Max Heinrich's capital. In fact, Luxembourg did not evacuate Utrecht until after Bonn had fallen to the Dutch and imperial armies. Louvois had not only misjudged the effective strength of the French army in the Netherlands, according to the intendant Robert, but the decision to evacuate the Dutch Republic had come too late to stop the allies on the Rhine.[27]

As for Turenne, he had been trapped in Franconia south of the Main River, without access to a bridgehead. Having been forced to swing his march southward to cross the Rhine at Philippsburg, he was now slogging northward through the rugged and rain-soaked countryside of the Rhineland and Saar. Louvois wrote to him on 1 November, suggesting that he try to join forces with Luxembourg to intercept the armies of Orange and Montecuccoli.[28] Turenne answered calmly from Bad Kreuznach in the Rhenish Palatinate with the assurance of one who knew that he was not responsible for the debacle on the lower Rhine and that no effort of his could salvage the situation for Louis XIV and his threatened ally, Elector Max Heinrich: "Because you have seen the countryside surrounding Trier you can surely understand that, given the relative locations of the armies, Luxembourg and I cannot hope to join forces."[29] Once again Turenne was questioning Louvois's competence, for if the war minister were in command of the situation, he would not propose that his soldiers accomplish the impossible. The full scope of Turenne's disenchantment with the young war minister would be seen when Turenne returned to Paris from the field.

The last week in October, Montecuccoli, the wily commander of the imperial army, had begun to build a bridge with barges on the Rhine River just below Mainz. This project, however, had been an elaborate bluff, and Montecuccoli soon broke up his half-completed bridge, embarked part of his infantry and artillery on the river boats, and swept down the Rhine with an improvised flotilla. The imperial infantry followed the right bank of the Rhine north to Koblenz and crossed to the left bank, using the elector of Trier's bridge. With brilliant timing—considering the logistical problems of the period—the imperial forces joined with the Dutch, led by the prince of Orange, and on 4 November the allies invested Bonn, the capital city of the elector of Cologne.

Bonn was unable to withstand a siege. In desperation, Louis sent some troops from Trier into the city to reinforce the garrison, but they found a deplorable situation. The peasants who had been recruited to work on the fortifications in the final effort to prepare the fortress fled when they heard that the prince of Orange was approaching. It must have encouraged the prince to know that someone was fleeing his army rather than that of the French. When the siege began, the German soldiers' wives tried to drag their men from their posts, and the commander of the French troops was physically attacked on the streets.[30] The citizens of Bonn had nothing to gain from a protracted siege. On 12 November, after only a week of open trenches, Bonn fell to Orange and Montecuccoli. Although the siege was almost perfunctory, it was the culmination of a brilliant campaign by the imperial general. Montecuccoli is most famous for his victory over the Turks at Saint-Gotthard in 1664, but the autumn campaign of 1673 has rightly been called his masterpiece.[31]

Although a French army arrived at the Rhine in time to prevent the electorate of Cologne from being entirely overrun, the fall of Bonn was a powerful strategic and psychological victory for Louis XIV's enemies. It dispelled the mystique of French invincibility; it broke the French domination of the course of the Rhine; it encouraged the vacillating German princes to join the growing anti-French coalition; and ultimately it was an important factor in convincing the German Diet to declare a *Reichskrieg* against France the following May. After the fall of Bonn, the many diplomats and agents who canvassed Germany for Louis XIV, pleading the French case and spreading French gold, could not prevent the great majority of the imperial princes from throwing in their lot with the Hapsburgs. Since the Peace of Westphalia, the German princes had ever less need to look to France for help in checking the ambition of the Hapsburgs to consolidate their power in the empire. With the final destruction of Hapsburg attempts to create a unified absolute state in Germany, the individual princes could align themselves, more or less freely, with whoever offered the most security, and after the campaign of 1673 there was a flight toward Vienna.

Pierre de Chassan, the French envoy at the duke of Saxony's court, wrote to Pomponne from the vantage point of Dresden: "It is certainly true that the Imperials have made the most out of Bonn's capitulation. They are boasting all over Germany as if they had conquered Philippsburg or Breisach. In the meantime, the Dutch are claiming as conquests all the places that the duke of Luxembourg has evacuated."[32] Louvois, who as war minister was largely responsible for the misjudgments that led to the debacle at Bonn, understated the case when he grudgingly conceded "that it would have been better if this had not happened."[33] Louis sneered at the capture of that "wretched fortress,"[34] but it is apparent that this defeat for royal arms was a trying experience for the king. The secretary to the English embassy in Paris reported to Lord Arlington that Louis had gone into seclusion at Saint-Germain to "xercise at the heads, with Lance, saber, dart, arrow & pistoll," with "no body . . . admited to see him xcepting some few intimates."[35] Louis's first major setback had shaken him.

A contemporary French military expert, Antoine de Pas de Feuquières, later wrote about the fall of Bonn:

This single Event . . . change the Constitution of the War in Germany; obliged the King of France to abandon the Places he had taken in Holland; gave the Emperor's Army an Opportunity to secure Winter Quarters between the Rhine and the Maes; enabled them in the next Campaign of 1674, to join the Troops of Spain and Holland, who by this considerable Reinforcement, had almost changed the Nature of the War, so as to render it Offensive on their Part, against France.[36]

Feuquières, who was a soldier, may have exaggerated the significance of this defeat for French arms. But it is true that the capture of Bonn by Louis's enemies had repercussions beyond the purely military.

In the free imperial city of Cologne, where French, English, Dutch, and Swedish diplomats had been trying vainly for five months to hammer out a peace settlement, the advance of Montecuccoli and Orange toward Bonn halted the negotiations and caused a near panic. When the news arrived in Cologne that Montecuccoli had maneuvered around Turenne, Honoré Courtin wrote to Louvois with his usual combination of self-mockery and pointed advice. He began his letter by offering several pages of gratuitous strategic suggestions, and continued: "As for me, Sir, I have decided to set an example for them [the French generals] and fling myself into Bonn or Neuss. To get serious with you, we have an ally here [the elector of Cologne] who is very frightened and whose affairs are in a miserable shape."[37]

Poor Elector Max Heinrich! He had placed so many hopes upon his alliance with France, and now he had been humiliated. The French and English diplomats at Cologne feared that the elector might succumb to the offers of the importunate Lisola and agree to a unilateral settlement with the emperor; they wanted Max Heinrich to flee Bonn for Kaiserwerth, where there was a French garrison and where French influence on his policies could be maintained. Instead, the elector sought refuge in a Benedictine monastery in Cologne, where he brooded over Louis XIV's desertion of him in his hour of need.[38]

After Brandenburg entered the war in summer 1672, the elector of Cologne concentrated his military efforts upon Frederick William's Rhenish territories. Contiguous to lands belonging to the electorate of Cologne, they made Brandenburg a more logical opponent than the Dutch for Max Heinrich. The archbishop had been so loath to make peace with Brandenburg that he continued hostilities after Louis XIV and Frederick William struck an armistice. As Turenne remarked to Louvois, "when things were going badly for the elector of Brandenburg, they [Cologne and Münster] were ready to take advantage of him."[39]

In spring 1673 the French feared that their impending peace with Brandenburg would discourage the elector of Cologne and induce him to quit the war. Thus Louis XIV, who needed allies, decided that he must renew his offensive alliance with Cologne. Late in March, Verjus de Crécy, the French envoy in Bonn and one of several versatile diplomats who specialized in German affairs for Louis XIV, received instructions and full diplomatic powers to push through a new alliance with the elector of Cologne.[40] During the first week of April 1673, Verjus "negotiated" a renewal of the offensive alliance between France and Cologne with Wilhelm von Fürstenberg. After his initial talks with Verjus, Wilhelm dispatched a letter to Pomponne that lays bare not only Cologne's dissatisfaction over the French settlement with Brandenburg but the remarkable patron-client relationship that bound Cologne to France: "With regard to M. Verjus's report to the elector of Cologne that he has orders to pay no subsidies if I balk at signing the treaty, . . . the elector has told me that it is evident that no further remonstrances, however just and reasonable, could have any effect. Therefore, I am blindly to sign everything that M. Verjus, or rather the orders that have been sent to him, prescribe for me."[41]

Fürstenberg's words summarized the plight of Elector Max Heinrich of Cologne, and indeed the plight of all of Louis XIV's German client princes. Impecunious and dependent upon French gold, they simultaneously resented the disdainful way in which the French treated them. Quite aware that they were being bought by Louis, they did not like to fawn for their subsidies. Desirous of being aligned with the mighty Bourbon monarchy, they did not want to serve simply as Louis's lackeys. Fürstenberg in effect told Pomponne that it was possible to buy the Germans but that the French did not have a right to abuse them because they were venal. The Germans were probably asking the impossible.

As word spread that a settlement between France and Brandenburg was imminent, Elector Max Heinrich of Cologne made an obsequious and pitiful plea to Louis XIV, imploring that he delay peace until Cologne's strategic position vis-à-vis Brandenburg had improved. Otherwise, according to Max Heinrich, "peace would appear as honorable for the elector of Brandenburg as it would be disgraceful for Your Majesty's allies, . . . especially for me, who has had my states entirely ruined for Your Majesty's sake."[42]

In the same diplomatic pouch as the elector's letter came a more carefully conceived brief, addressed to Pomponne from Franz Egon von Fürstenberg, who was already bishop of Strasbourg and who wanted to be appointed coadjutor of Cologne. He told Pomponne that since France began negotiations with the elector of Brandenburg the elector of Cologne's attitude had changed dramatically. Franz Egon was "afraid that the recommendation for the coadjutorship that the king gave me will do me no good either with the elector or with the cathedral chapter. There it is believed, even amongst those who were my best friends, that Prince Wilhelm and I convinced the elector to ally with France only for our personal ends."[43] Fürstenberg could not suppress a remark on the mercenary quality of the work that he and his brother performed for France, but the bishop's main point was that if France ignored Cologne's interests in a treaty with Brandenburg, the powerful influence that Louis XIV's paid agents, the brothers Fürstenberg, exerted in the electorate's politics could be destroyed and French influence and power on the lower Rhine might in turn be seriously impaired.

Franz Egon argued the case better than the elector of Cologne. Rather than simply throw himself on Louis XIV's mercy, he argued that it was in the best interest of France to deal generously with Cologne, that it was sound politics for Louis to placate Elector Max Heinrich. This was not a negligible argument, and doubtless Louis and his ministers considered it. However, they were not persuaded to postpone peace with Brandenburg. Max Heinrich's only satisfaction was a conciliatory reply, signed by Louis XIV and in his foreign minister's smoothest prose.[44] The elector was informed in the most diplomatic way of something he could hardly accept: an immediate peace with Brandenburg was in the best interests of France and her allies, Cologne included.

When Louis XIV's policies antagonized and alienated his allies, Pomponne did what he could to soften a harsh policy with courteous words. In response to Wilhelm von Fürstenberg's complaint that the French were taking advantage of Cologne, Pomponne replied in his usual accommodating style. After excusing his tardiness, he explained that Louis XIV "considered it a great advantage for the common cause to disarm a prince [the elector of Brandenburg] who has provided the principal support for the Dutch," and that Louis "believed that he was showing his strong desire for peace in the empire . . . when he decided to give up his conquests there."[45] Though Pomponne's letter convinced neither Fürstenberg nor the elector of Cologne that a settlement with Brandenburg was in Cologne's best interests, Pomponne's civil prose contrasts sharply with Louvois's blunt, disdainful, and brutal manner of dealing with Wilhelm von Fürstenberg.

Because of his position on the high council, his wide-ranging administrative correspondence as war minister, his interim tenure as foreign minister in 1671, and the sheer thrust of his personality, Louvois had a large influence on the conduct of French diplomacy.[46] While Pomponne tried to placate Wilhelm von Fürstenberg during the French negotiations with Brandenberg, Louvois seemed to relish compounding harshness of policy with brutality in expression:

You must not, if you please, consider quartering any troops in the county of Mark [Brandenburg's possession] because you have orders forbidding it. The day that any troops enter there you can count on a frightful reduction in your subsidies. . . .

If you were here, I would read you a long chapter about your accusations that we have been harsh to the king's allies. But, as one cannot explain oneself so well in writing as in person, I will be content with telling you that they have received everything that was coming to them. . . . Although at present you are a loyal German, you would not disagree with me if I could talk to you for half an hour.[47]

Louvois, who could not forgo sneering at Fürstenberg's uncertain loyalties as a mercenary diplomat, did not convince Wilhelm with this letter that his complaints about the harshness of French policy were ill founded. As pressure mounted with the near collapse of the French military position during 1673, Louvois became even more overbearing with Wilhelm von Fürstenberg, and his gratuitous abuse would ultimately have repercussions far beyond the electorate of Cologne.

In fall 1673, when Wilhelm von Fürstenberg informed Louvois of the elector of Cologne's plight, Courtin wrote to Louvois, warning him that the Fürstenberg brothers were becoming anxious. Courtin recommended that it would be wise "to placate the bishop of Strasbourg [Franz Egon] and Prince Wilhelm a bit. . . . Because the elector of Cologne will often be tempted to make a settlement . . . it is important to spare those who govern him."[48] Courtin, finely attuned to nuances in the interplay of personality and politics, gave Louvois shrewd advice. However, before Courtin's counsel reached Louvois, the war minister had written to Wilhelm von Fürstenberg, venting his frustration over French military and diplomatic setbacks and, in his usual manner, relying on threats rather than persuasiveness: "Since, so contrary to the spirit of the treaties between the elector and the king, the elector is listening to the enemies' proposals and negotiating with them behind the king's back, you better understand that the king would be justified in treating the elector's territories like those of his enemies. It must be you who is trying to force the king to do your bidding because I do not think that your brother or the elector could do such a dastardly or stupid thing."[49] Is it any wonder that Wilhelm Egon detested Louvois?

Several weeks later, Courtin wisely advised Louvois to apologize for his biting rebuke of Wilhelm by exempting the estates of Wilhelm's mistress, the countess of Mark, from contributions by the royal army: "Put yourself in his [Wilhelm's] place, and consider how you would feel if a person whom you loved fiercely were being ruined by contributions; this is like thrusting a dagger into the breast of this poor prince who is risking all in order to serve His Majesty." According to Courtin, to exempt the countess's estates from contributions would be "a great boon to our affairs, for I think that without her he [Wilhelm] would not remain in the service of the elector of Cologne."[50] Fürstenberg, the mercenary diplomat, was not "risking all" to serve Louis XIV *per se*, but was risking his position in Cologne so as to continue being paid by the French king to further French interests in Germany. Courtin's point was valid in any case.

Although Courtin on this occasion convinced Louvois that part of a statesman's task is to consider the sentiments and sensibilities of other persons, much harm had been done to the French cause when Louvois baldly stated that Louis XIV's allies existed solely to serve the king. The elector of Cologne no doubt remembered this point when he abandoned France and made his separate peace with the Dutch and the emperor in May 1674. It might well be asked: what difference should it make to France if a relatively weak prince, such as the elector of Cologne, chose to make peace with Louis's enemies or even decided to join forces with them? This would have been an obvious question for Louvois, who, though precocious in the mechanics of warfare, had no profound or far-ranging grasp of international relations. Courtin, who knew how Louvois reasoned, anticipated the war minister's question and answered it for him: "You will perhaps say, what difference does it make if we lose them [Cologne and Münster], since they will only be a burden in the future? I would respond that this matter is so important for our position that if they should abandon us we would no longer be able to count on the third party, or on Sweden, or Bavaria, or Hanover."[51] Courtin's prophecy proved remarkably accurate; only Sweden entered the war on the French side, and France fought the last five years of the Dutch War in virtual isolation.

Louvois was overwrought during autumn 1673 because his military plans for Germany and the Netherlands were coming unstuck, and with his blast at Wilhelm von Fürstenberg we see him at his most destructive. Although a mercenary diplomat of Wilhelm's stripe invited contempt, Louvois's harsh treatment of him served French interests poorly. Wilhelm, who saw his influence and credibility crumbling with both the elector of Cologne and Louis XIV, seized an opportunity to strike back at his tormentor by trying to foment a rift between the English and the French, whose alliance had been riddled with suspicion and recriminations since the naval battle off Texel on 21 August.[52] Fürstenberg scurried to the English plenipotentiaries in Cologne and spread Louvois's intimidating and demeaning letter before them. The English diplomats were properly shocked by Louvois's abusive language and immediately reported to Lord Arlington, Charles II's secretary of state for foreign affairs:

> We have heard Prince William, more than once, charging the French ministry with having neglected this Elector [Cologne] all along this War. . . . Prince William hath gone further with us, and in Confidence showed us a Letter, which M. de Louvoy had written to him . . . which we could not but be sorry to see. . . . It was written in such a Stile and Language, as that we did not understand how the one could well give it, and the other take it; but that he professed, he hath been long used to receive Mortifications of this Kind, and at the Hands of that Minister. This he left us a great Secret, and we beseech your Lordship to use it accordingly; because it appears that he had placed his Hopes and Fortunes wholly upon France, and that it may be a Prejudice to him, if this should come round.[53]

The English diplomats in Cologne made it as clear as they dared that the French were not congenial allies. Charles II, who at home faced a vehemently anti-French, anti-Catholic Parliament, had determined to abandon his French alliance before November 1673, and his ambassadors' reports from Cologne surely confirmed Charles in his decision. With Louis XIV clearly willing to disregard the interests of his allies, Charles II did not require Parliament's compulsion to dissolve his alliance with France in February 1674.[54]

Allies whom Louis XIV had bought were discovering that working for the king of France was unrewarding employment; thus the French, who had isolated the Dutch in preparation for the war, were now isolating themselves. Using allies for one's own purposes is doubtless a customary and perfectly legitimate aspect of foreign relations, and Louis XIV's principal task was not to look after the welfare of England or Cologne. However, when he pursued a policy of self-interest to the point of alienating his allies and isolating himself, Louis perverted sound reason-of-state policy into self-defeating nonpolicy. Any ruler who consistently practices a policy of state interest will necessarily recognize that all sovereign states have interests to protect and promote; rational politics demands that a statesman consider both the interests of his allies and those of his enemies. Louis XIV had great difficulty doing either during the early stages of the Dutch War.

The king's inept statesmanship in 1673 was aggravated by his overreliance upon Louvois. Louvois had that peculiar personality that thrives on servility on one hand and cruelty on the other. According to Wilhelm von Fürstenberg, he repeatedly used language that served only to relieve his own rage and sense of frustration. Louvois came down brutally on the Fürstenbergs, yet he was too much the sycophant to risk confronting the king with the hard choices the strategic situation demanded of the French in autumn 1673. Because of the war minister's miscalculations, masses of royal soldiers were immobilized, holding Louis's conquests in the Netherlands, while the Dutch and imperial armies joined forces and seized the line of the Rhine.[55] Louvois, the youngest member of the king's high council, was making a bid to become Louis's omnicompetent minister, but despite his technical virtuosity he failed signally on the larger matters of war and diplomacy. Courtin, who was Louvois's friend, despite the two men's radically different conceptions of foreign policy, drew the war minister's attention to his narrowness of political vision: "I believe, Sir, that you have good reasons for doing what you do as secretary of war, but consider, if you please, that you are a minister of state."[56] Courtin was making a subtle but important distinction between the responsibilities of a secretary of state and a minister of state. He was implying that Louvois should be more than an efficient bureaucrat who uncritically executes policy without regard for its broader consequences.

The spectacular march of the royal armies into the Dutch Republic during the campaign of 1672 promoted the fortunes of Louvois, who, with the help of his father, Le Tellier, had planned the logistics of the march. The two Le Telliers had done their work well, and the campaign was conducted as the king desired: fast moving, eye catching, and with few casualties. Although the flooded countryside was soon to swamp Louis XIV's adventure into the Dutch Republic, this was not immediately apparent, and

Louvois's reward for his role in the campaign was that he became the king's closest collaborator. By midsummer 1672, there is little doubt that Louis was depending more upon Louvois than any other man for military and political counsel. The king was preoccupied with war in summer 1672, and it was natural that he should depend upon his war minister for advice. But Louvois's influence went beyond purely military affairs. At the critical Doesburg negotiations in June 1672 the king preferred Louvois's opinion on dealing with the Dutch to that of his foreign minister, Pomponne.[57] Louis and Louvois, warrior king and war minister, were already collaborating, and they would be the duo that directed the French monarchy through the Dutch War.

When the prince of Orange attacked Charleroi and provoked a small crisis in December 1672, Louis acknowledged his dependence upon Louvois and gave him remarkable leeway to act according to his own best judgment. By 22 December, Louvois had advanced almost to Charleroi and the king had left Saint-Germain and was heading for Compiègne. Le Tellier had just suffered the stroke that would leave him immobilized for many months, and Louis wrote to Louvois: "In light of what has happened to your father, I do not know quite how to use you; I find you very necessary where you are, . . . and yet I would be much comforted if you were with me. I will give you no orders, . . . and will be content if you only do what you think is best for my service."[58] The pressure was mounting in late December 1672, and obviously the king was depending upon Louvois to assist him.

The following January, Louvois had enough confidence in the security of his position that when Condé requested that Vauban be sent to help him evaluate the fortifications in Alsace, the young war minister could dismiss the prince's request by replying that Vauban still had a month's worth of work to accomplish in Flanders.[59] It is not remarkable that Vauban's work in Flanders had higher priority than the fortifications in Alsace, but it is significant that a request from a man who was both a prince of the blood and the most prestigious soldier in France could be so sharply rejected by a thirty-two-year-old upstart.

The triumphal siege of Maastricht in June 1673 enhanced Louvois's position. He, of course, planned the logistics and his protégé, Vauban, who was rapidly becoming the king's man, conducted the siege. In summer 1673, although the Dutch War was about to take a sudden turn for the worse, Louvois's influence was greater than ever before. The king and Louvois were ruling France that summer, and indeed it sometimes appeared that the war minister, because of his greater intelligence and energy, was the more important partner.

When the king marched his army southeastward after the siege at Maastricht, Louvois left the king's entourage and preceded him to Nancy, the capital of Lorraine. Although removed from the king in person, Louvois did not fail to dispatch detailed instructions to Louis XIV. On 18 July he wrote to the king and advised him to establish a special courier route to Cologne to expedite the peace negotiations that were proceeding haltingly in the German city. In the same dispatch, Louvois also told the king how to quash an effort by the Spaniards to break up the Anglo-French alliance.[60] These two matters were diplomatic affairs, and clearly within Pomponne's jurisdiction, but Louvois did not hesitate to instruct the king on how to cope with them. Louis XIV, who was approaching Nancy from the north, received Louvois's dispatch the following day and answered obediently: "I just received the letter that you wrote from Nancy, where I see that you have found everything in order, which pleases me. I have also seen the news that you sent and what you propose for England and Cologne, which I will have executed immediately."[61]

As much as Louis disliked the earlier tutor-pupil relationship between Richelieu and his father, this later exchange of letters resembles Louis XIII's correspondence with the great cardinal-minister. Louis XIV was the source of all political power in the French state, but Louvois, ambitious and energetic, was assuming a commanding position in the king's counsels by midsummer 1673. As the Savoyard ambassador, who accompanied the king's army throughout the campaign of 1673, remarked, "when it comes to war no one functions like him, and in the absence of his father and Colbert he is all-powerful."[62]

In September, the siege of the city of Trier did not proceed as swiftly as the king expected, and he became angry at Louvois, who had planned the operation. On 7 September Louis wrote to his war minister that "the siege of Trier is not progressing as one might wish, and this upsets me a great deal."[63] Two days later, Saint-Maurice reported that Louis reprimanded Louvois in open court at Nancy about not having sent enough cannons to Trier.

Louvois made excuses, and the king repeated his reprimand. "He [Louvois] looked chagrined to be chastised in public, . . . and the entire court rejoiced inwardly."[64] It seems as though Louis may have resented his dependence upon Louvois and felt a need to take him down a peg, although it was uncharacteristic of Louis to rebuke his servants in public. If the king's dependence on Louvois's expertise earned the war minister a rebuke, it also meant that Louvois had become virtually indispensable to the king. Saint-Maurice concluded his report by noting that he did not think Louvois's position had been "prejudiced."[65]

Despite his qualities, or perhaps because of them, Louvois helped to bring about the stunning military setbacks that the French experienced in autumn and winter 1673. He erred in strategic judgments because he was relatively inexperienced and, more importantly, was willing to promote the king's personal campaign, and thus his own ambitions, at the expense of the overall French military posture. Louvois's personal style—abrasive, supercilious, disdainful—meant that he could not make such mistakes and walk away from the campaign of 1673 unscathed. He had made powerful enemies who would have delighted to see his ambitions founder with the wreckage of the Dutch War. When the soldiers came in from the field in December 1673, Louvois's position in the royal government was threatened.

Three generals—Turenne, Condé, and Luxembourg—commanded French armies independently of the king during the campaign of 1673. All three of them had good reason to be irritated by the manner in which Louvois managed the campaign. Turenne's maneuvers in Germany had come to disaster at least in part because of the war minister's miscalculations. Condé, shuttled from garrison duty in Utrecht to garrison duty in Flanders, had not been provided enough troops to carry out anything but minor foraging operations.[66] Luxembourg's occupying force in the Netherlands had been kept so small that he had no opportunity to show the audacity that had characterized his movements in 1672.[67] None of these generals, the best France had, participated in any of the king's conquests of the 1673 campaign—not Maastricht, not Alsace, not Trier. Perhaps it was Louis, rather than Louvois, who had planned the campaign exclusively for his greater glory and to the chagrin of the generals, but the king could hardly be attacked, and thus Louvois caught the brunt of the generals' wrath.

Luxembourg did not have the status to move against a minister of state—and, moreover, was young enough to expect future opportunities for advancement and honor. But Turenne and Condé were different: they had earned enormous stature and prestige independently of the king, and they were distressed to see their brilliant careers come to an end as they played lackey not only to the king but also to a bureaucrat from a family of the robe nobility.

There is no doubt that Turenne worked at Louvois's disgrace and removal from the high council in December 1673.[68] The precise extent of Condé's collaboration with Turenne will never be known, but it seems likely that the prince was at first sympathetic to crushing Louvois, and that Le Tellier, a virtuoso at court intrigue, intervened to help save his son's career.[69] In the extended maze of servants, clients, and advisors that surrounded the great families in seventeenth-century France, there was inevitably some lapping over of personnel. Thus Marshal Villar's remark that Condé's chaplain, who was a sometime creature of Le Tellier, functioned as an intermediary in bringing the prince and Louvois together is plausible.[70] Perhaps Jean Héraut de Gourville, the memoirist, who was on good terms with both Condé and Louvois, served as a reconciler. (Gourville's correspondence in January 1674 shows that he was acting as some sort of go-between for Louvois and Condé.)[71] Perhaps Condé was placated with promises of a military command for his son, the duc d'Enghien, in the coming year's campaign.[72] In any event, Condé did not follow through in supporting Turenne's effort to unseat the young minister.

Camille Rousset commented that Louvois came perilously close to falling from power in the crisis of late 1673: "Never, in his long career, was Louvois's fortune so seriously threatened."[73] Villars, who knew all three men, thought that if Condé had strongly supported Turenne, Louvois would have been lost.[74] Rousset and Villars may have been correct in their assessments, but the latter also pointed out that Louis XIV was satisfied that none of Louvois's mistakes was grievous. Indeed, the king would have had difficulty judging Louvois guilty of cardinal errors when the two of them had collaborated so closely on the 1673 campaign. How could Louvois have fallen from grace when his partner in failure had been the grace-giving source itself—the Sun King? Although rumors of Louvois's impending fall spread far and wide in Europe, Louvois himself wrote: "The rumors . . . that are circulating about me are substantial enough to upset some courtiers who, after having placed me first for a year, have now done me the favor of disgracing me, while I have not budged from my place."[75] Yet this remark is somewhat disingenuous, for it is apparent that the courtiers who had announced Louvois's rapid rise during 1673 had been correct.

The anti-Louvois party nevertheless forced Louis XIV to establish a war council, consisting of all of the great generals and presided over by the prince of Condé, to plan and manage military affairs.[76] The *chansonniers* of Paris were quick to side with Turenne, the aristocrat, against Louvois, the bureaucrat:

> *Turenne confronted Louvois*
> *With what everyone else was thinking.*
> *He dared to tell the king*
> *That this grandson of a lawyer*
> *Was causing all the troubles for France.*
> *He said to the insolent constable* [Louvois]
> *Who was acting like God on earth,*
> *That he was not a true soldier*
> *But was really a quartermaster.*[77]

Despite what the wits in Paris were saying, the check to the absolutist tradition of reserving executive power to the individual ministers of state—which the war council represented—was short-lived. Louvois apparently reached a tentative accord with Turenne in January 1674 by admitting to some errors in judgment, and within a matter of months he was back in control as Louis XIV's full-fledged war minister.[78] Turenne, of course, had only limited leverage because he too had erred grievously in judgment during the 1673 campaign.

In any event, as a step in consolidating his power, the king had established firm ministerial control over his generals. Never again during the Old Regime would a general enjoy the autonomy that Turenne and Condé once had.

VII

Charles II and Louis XIV:
The Manipulator Manipulated

Since the days of Cardinal Wolsey, England's role in western Europe was pivotal, and she made alliances with France and Spain as need and circumstance dictated. During the 1620s, Richelieu had sent an ambassador to London to seek an alliance with England in the hope of breaking the vise of Hapsburg power that encircled France. But the duke of Buckingham's anti-French policy, sustained by Francophobia among the English, helped to prevent the consummation of Richelieu's plans, and soon England was engulfed by domestic political storms that precluded involvement in Continental affairs.

The military alliance that was concluded between France and England in 1657 to wage war against Spain must be seen as one of Mazarin's great achievements. This alliance looked highly improbable in 1649, when the English executed King Charles I and created a Protestant republic. Not only had Charles been the husband of young Louis XIV's aunt, Henriette of France, but Spain, swallowing its distaste for the Puritans, had quickly recognized the Commonwealth, thus apparently dimming the prospects for any future Anglo-French accord. As the Fronde petered out, however, Mazarin began to think of an alliance with Cromwell, and soon he explained to the queen mother, Anne of Austria, his justification for treating with the English regicides: "The laws of honor and justice should never lead us to do anything contrary to the dictates of prudence."[1] Reason-of-state politics therefore brought the cardinal and the great Puritan together, first in a treaty of amity in 1655 and then in the military alliance of 1657.

After the Peace of the Pyrenees, when it became clear that the Spanish Hapsburgs were no longer a political threat, the English and French monarchs, Charles II and Louis XIV, were drawn together by mutual dislike of the Dutch. Although the Franco-Dutch treaty of 1662 bound the French to protect the Dutch from all foreign aggressors, Louis XIV was reluctant to aid the Dutch when they became embroiled in their second naval war with England in 1665. After all, it was in the French king's best interests to stand by and allow his cousin Charles II to try to destroy Dutch domination of the high seas. When Charles participated in the Triple Alliance of 1668, ostensibly to stop French expansion into the Low Countries, his real intentions were largely otherwise; he wished to show Louis XIV that his English friendship was valuable, and he also wished to arouse the French king's anger against the Dutch, whose leaders Charles managed to make look like the instigators of the anti-French alliance. In this way Charles was preparing Louis to enter into an anti-Dutch compact, which the English king wanted to secure an easy victory in foreign policy that would, in turn, strengthen his position at home.[2]

The secret Treaty of Dover (22 May 1670 o.s.) was the last Anglo-French alliance to be signed for half a century, although there were several brief periods of entente between the two powers. In this treaty the French and English agreed jointly to attack the United Provinces of the Dutch Republic, to expropriate parcels of Dutch territory, and to leave Prince William of Orange, Charles's nephew, as sovereign of a rump state.[3] When the French and English launched their joint attack upon the Dutch in spring 1672, everything seemed to conspire for their success and their continued close relations. As late as February 1673, the earl of Shaftesbury made his famous *delenda est Carthago* speech in Parliament in which he advocated destruction of the Dutch Republic, as Cato had urged the destruction of Carthage, and was well received by the Commons.[4] Yet within a matter of months opinion in Parliament and in the English nation at large would turn sharply and demand an end to the French alliance and peace with the Dutch.

Parliament, upon which King Charles depended for funds to run his government and wage war, reflected public opinion, however imperfectly. Scholars agree that the rising clamor of the

English public against Catholic France played a decisive role in compelling Charles to abandon his alliance with Louis XIV early in 1674. K. H. D. Haley concluded that a propaganda pamphlet, *England's Appeal from the Private Cabal at Whitehall to the Grand Council of the Nation, The Lords and Commons in Parliament Assembled*, "did more than anything else to identify the French alliance in foreign policy with the danger of Popery at home, and consequently to lead public opinion . . . to turn against the war."[5] His emphasis on the importance of religious factors in the motivations of seventeenth-century Englishmen is certainly correct. On Easter Sunday 1673, John Evelyn made this entry in his diary:

I staied to see whither (according to custome) the Duke of York did Receive the Communion, with the King, but he did not, to the amazement of every body; This being the second yeare he had forborn & put it off, & this being within a day of the Parliaments sitting, who had Lately made so severe an Act [the Test Act] against the increase of Poperie, gave exceeding griefe & scandal to the whole Nation; That the heyre of it, & the sonn of a Martyr for the Protestant Religion, should apostatize: What the Consequence of this will be God onely knows, & Wise men dread.[6]

Spring 1673, when the Test Act was passed (which forbade Catholics from holding governmental office), was a turbulent season in England. The Venetian envoy in London decided that it was "the nature of this people to cherish nothing but change & confusion, which now reign here more than ever."[7] *England's Appeal*, written by Pierre du Moulin, an embittered Huguenot, and distributed in England by his propaganda machine was, then, part of the maelstrom's mix; but Haley's claim that "the *Appeal* immediately attracted much attention"[8] must be rejected. One searches almost in vain in contemporary writings for references to this pamphlet; neither Evelyn nor the Venetian envoy, for example, mentions it. It seems not to have had the impact in England that Haley, who discovered and analyzed the manuscript, claims for it. Indeed, Colbert de Croissy, the French ambassador in England, wrote to his brother Jean Baptiste about Du Moulin's pamphlet, which Croissy thought had been co-authored by Lisola: "The book I am sending to m. de Pomponne that was written by Lisola and his friend, little Du Moulin, contains no worse calumnies than are being voiced in the House of Commons."[9]

Complex factors turned the English public against the French alliance in 1673; but nothing was more critical than the failure of the Anglo-French fleet to defeat the Dutch at sea. This failure was far more important than any propaganda pamphlet. Indeed, the conduct of the French during the crucial naval battle was the subject of several propaganda attacks against the French alliance, and they attracted more attention than *England's Appeal*.

Englishmen, particularly the influential and vocal London merchants, were well aware that any benefit they might derive from England's third Dutch War depended on destroying the Dutch supremacy at sea; and when, in their view, the French fleet failed them, English opinion turned irreversibly against the alliance with Louis XIV. With the northern seas dominated by De Ruyter's stout figure on the quarterdeck of his flagship, *Seven Provinces*, a nation whose economy was increasingly dependent on overseas trade demanded peace with the Dutch. Bishop Gilbert Burnet wrote of the English reaction to the naval battle that was fought off Texel in August 1673: "This opened the eyes and mouths of the whole nation. All men cried out, and said, we were engaged in a war by the French, that they might have the pleasure to see the Dutch and us destroy one another, while they knew our seas and ports, and learned all our methods, but took care to preserve themselves."[10]

In 1673 Louis XIV was keenly aware of his need to preserve his alliance with Charles II of England. Sweden was disappointingly slow in coming to the aid of France in accord with her treaty obligations, nor were Louis's Rhenish allies, Münster and Cologne, proving of much help to the French cause. Moreover, the French navy was not equal to the Dutch, and Louis needed English naval power if he were to have any hope of controlling the northern seas.

When Louis concluded the Treaty of Dover with King Charles, he planned not only to acquire a military ally but also to serve the cause of Catholicism in England through the Stuart brothers: Charles, a crypto-Catholic, and Duke James of York, who practiced his Catholic faith openly. Partly because of Louis's urging, Charles had issued a Declaration of Indulgence in March 1672 that provided for limited freedom of worship for both Dissenters and Catholics. But in spring 1673 the English Parliament was intent on forcing Charles to revoke the declaration, before it would vote more funds to support the Dutch War and thus the French alliance.

In March, Croissy reported from London that Parliament had met to discuss the religious issue and all "those on the king's side were forced to remain silent. . . . To tell the truth, Sir, the great zeal of the duke of York causes all this trouble for the king his brother."[11] Pomponne responded by saying that Croissy's reports made him "painfully aware of the agitation in the English Parliament, but I hope that it will soon disappear, and that Parliament will soon pass the money bill that it promised to the king of England when he gave the assurances concerning religion."[12] Charles had assured Parliament that he had no intention of attempting to re-Catholicize England, but though the king was telling the truth, Parliament was not satisfied and continued to agitate for revocation of the Declaration of Indulgence. Charles and James (particularly the latter) seemed prepared to fight Parliament over the declaration, but Louis XIV had no desire to watch his English ally become embroiled in domestic troubles that might undermine his capacity to wage war. By special courier on 13 March, Louis sent Croissy orders to advise Charles to yield to Parliament on the religious issue and revoke the Declaration of Indulgence.[13] Croissy met with the English king and within a matter of days the declaration was revoked. Croissy then wrote to Louis XIV: "Never has advice been better received, more punctually followed, or had such speedy results as that which Your Majesty has had me give to the King of England."[14]

The duke of York and his Catholic following in England were enraged that their religious cause had been sacrificed to the demands of war. They "made it clear that we [the French] have sacrificed the interests of religion and the honor of the English king to politics when we advised him to abandon his declaration, and that this is an irreparable prejudice to Catholicism."[15] Thus, although His Most Christian Majesty of France was alienating his co-religionists and natural allies in England, he was delighted to see his cousin Charles compromise religious principles to obtain Parliament's support for England's continued participation in the war. Louis XIV needed his English ally to finish the Dutch War quickly and successfully.

From Saint-Germain, Pomponne wrote jubilantly to one of his ambassadors in Germany about "the news that just arrived for the king by special courier from England that everything has worked out there. The king of Great Britain conceded some points to Parliament concerning the declaration on religion, and Parliament passed an Act providing the king with seventeen millions for the war against Holland. This should convince the States General, when they see their hopes collapsing on every side, to accept the peace that His Majesty wants very much to give them."[16] Always expecting peace, Pomponne continued to delude himself. He underestimated the tenacity of the Dutch and the arrogance of his sovereign.

When the French plenipotentiaries left Paris for Cologne at the end of April 1673, their instructions from Louis XIV included a section on how to deal with the English representatives at the peace conference. The Frenchmen were to take pains to maintain cordial relations with Charles II's ambassadors and were unreservedly to support the English demands on the Dutch, whatever they might be.[17] Louis XIV persisted in this position even after Count Tott's ominous visit to Maastricht early in July, when Tott had bluntly expressed Sweden's abhorrence of the English demand for cautionary towns on the Dutch coast. Louis ordered Croissy to tell of the French king's "determination not to separate my interests from his [Charles's] and to support them with continued vigor. . . . I do not wish you to emphasize to the English king or his ministers that their demand for coastal towns might be an insuperable obstacle to a peace settlement. Simply inform them what Count Tott has said."[18] Louis sent the same orders to his plenipotentiaries in Cologne: Do not press the English to lower their demands; leave that task to the Swedish mediators.[19] Thus it is apparent that Louis XIV valued the English alliance and was willing to take some pains to preserve it.

After the Dutch fortress of Maastricht fell to Louis XIV's army on 1 July, the English expected Louis to assist them in their effort to seize a beachhead on the coast of Zeeland. The French king had taken his share of Dutch territory, and now, the English felt, it was their turn. The Venetian envoy in London reported that "all England was flattering herself that when Maastricht was taken and the Most Christian King was at liberty he would lend a helping hand to the English troops destined for the landing [in Zeeland]."[20] As early as the first week in June, Charles assembled an army on Blackheath Common (east of London) in preparation for a waterborne assault on the seacoast of the United Provinces.[21]

To further the English plans, Lord Arlington, Charles II's secretary of state for foreign affairs, ordered William Lockhart, the English ambassador accompanying the French court, to ask Louis XIV to provide a diversion by land to support the English attack from the sea. As Louis and his entourage proceeded up the Moselle River toward Nancy late in July, Lockhart replied to Arlington, explaining the French king's position. Louis told Lockhart that the prince of Condé had been ordered, and would again be commanded to march his army into Dutch Brabant as far as Breda. The Dutch, alarmed by the prince's advance, would draw their forces away from the coastal region and open the way for an English landing in Zeeland. However, Louis explained to Lockhart, the swollen floodwaters in the Netherlands and the need to maintain a supporting force for Turenne's army in Germany prevented the French from offering the English additional assistance.[22]

Louis XIV was trying to placate Arlington with lies and half-truths, for Condé had been ordered to march south into French Flanders and not north into Dutch Brabant.[23] Clearly, as Louvois bluntly revealed to Turenne, Louis XIV did not want to push the Dutch so far and so hard that they would have to surrender coastal towns to the English.[24] The French wanted English assistance for coping with Dutch naval power, but it was not in France's best interests to allow England to acquire a series of enclaves on the Continent.

The difficulty was that Charles II viewed a foothold on the Dutch coast as one of his principal objectives of the war. Charles hoped that by gaining control of seaports in Zeeland he could stimulate English overseas trade. This in turn would strengthen his position at home, both because the royal customs revenues would increase and because the powerful London merchants would profit and, therefore, become more supportive of the crown.

An important provision of the secret Treaty of Dover guaranteed certain Dutch towns to the English if the war aims of Charles and Louis succeeded.[25] Accordingly, Louis XIV was caught between his promises and his interests—what he had been willing to grant in the secret treaty he was not willing to pursue in the war. Louis wished to keep his cousin Charles as an ally, but he did not wish to help him win one of his chief goals of the alliance. The

French king's only way out of this dilemma was to attempt to persuade Charles that his project for an English landing on the Dutch coast had full French support.

Louis was trying to manipulate Charles, and he was assisted by his ambassadors at the Cologne peace conference. On 1 August, the French plenipotentiaries in Cologne wrote to Condé, who was still stationed in the Netherlands, to inform him that the Anglo-French fleet had put to sea and that soldiers for the projected landing in Zeeland were already embarked in England. The plenipotentiaries then told Condé that it was of utmost importance to keep the English negotiators deluded with the hope that Charles could expect help from Louis in his effort to conquer territory on the Dutch coast, and that, to promote this delusion, Condé should write a spurious letter to the French diplomats that they could show to their English colleagues as "proof" of Condé's intention to use his soldiers to assist the English expeditionary force when it landed in Zeeland. The letter to Condé then went to a personal matter: "We are aware, Sir, of the problems created by flooding and your lack of troops; but this is the very reason why it is necessary to show a little ingenuity and that Your Highness can be an ambassador when it is not within your power to be a general of the army."[26]

Only Honoré Courtin could have written to the prince of Condé with so much verve and wit. His reference to Condé's lackluster assignments during the 1673 campaign was a deft stroke by which Courtin buffered his mockery of the great Condé with empathy, for, in Courtin's mind, Louis XIV was neglecting Courtin's talents as a diplomat and Condé's talents as a soldier. In Cologne, Courtin's thwarted ambitions made him sensitive to Condé's frustrations and to the king's compulsion to pursue the war to acquire personal glory. Indeed, this letter of Courtin to Condé reveals that Louis's vainglory was virtually a standing joke, though a bitter one, among certain royal generals and diplomats.

Condé followed Courtin's instructions to the letter, and on 8 August the English plenipotentiaries in Cologne wrote to Lord Arlington: "The French Ambassadors, upon our first Advices of his Majesty's Fleet being put to Sea, offer'd themselves . . . with great Zeal and Heartiness, to give the Prince of Condé notice of it; . . . Yesterday the Ambassadors received an Account their Letter had come safe to Hand, and that the Prince would not fail to give all the Help he could in that Occasion."[27]

Courtin's elaborate ruse worked on this occasion, but the English were nevertheless becoming suspicious of French intentions, for bland reassurances, spoken and written, could do only so much. Sooner or later the English would demand something for their war efforts—or they would quit the French alliance and the war.

The Fürstenberg brothers had been sorely abused by Louvois for their attempts to moderate French policy in Germany and thereby ease the pressure that was building on themselves and on the elector of Cologne. In August the Fürstenbergs began to take their revenge; they whispered in the ears of the English plenipotentiaries, Williamson and Jenkins, and the English in turn reported to Lord Arlington in London: "We . . . crave leave to add one Word of an Afternoon Conversation, which we have had this Day with the Bishop of Strasburgh [Franz Egon] . . . of Measures already taken, to satisfie France, and to leave the rest of the Allies to shift for themselves as well as they can."[28] Arlington had never liked the French alliance, and one can imagine that he was happy to read the letter from Cologne to King Charles II.

The English diplomats in Cologne sent a similar letter to their colleague William Lockhart, who was still with the French court in Nancy, and he replied soberly that "if the Bishop of Strasbourgh had foreseen, what he now doth, fifteen moneths agoe, it might have been much to his own advantage, *and perhaps to others too*."[29] Fifteen months took Lockhart's thinking back to the start of the Dutch War in the spring of 1672. Thus Lockhart was the first of Charles's ambassadors to hint openly that it would have been better for England if she had not aligned herself with France to attack the Dutch. However, Lockhart's sentiment was soon echoed throughout England and the English government; the French alliance was condemned and an end to the war was demanded.

Although Courtin had duped the English with Condé's trumped-up letter early in August, Courtin was too astute to think that the English would continue to be so credulous. Shortly after giving the English plenipotentiaries Condé's reassuring letter, Courtin wrote to Pomponne somewhat cryptically: "Take care, if you please, with regard to the king of England because things could wind up as they began. We are not saying this, Sir, without grounds, for we have some reason to doubt . . . if our accord with the English is holding up so well in the negotiations as it has thus far in the war."[30] Courtin thus alluded to the Triple Alliance of 1668, referred to the English suspicions of French objectives at the Cologne peace conference, and, in his last phrase, hinted that the Anglo-French military alliance could collapse. His premonition proved accurate, for open strife between the English and French admirals at sea soon eclipsed the minor quarrels between the delegations at the peace conference.

When the English and French fleets first joined forces in 1672, the duke of York had been given command of the joint fleet for two reasons. The French navy that Colbert was desperately trying to develop, despite Louis XIV's lack of interest in naval affairs, had no one with the talents requisite for an allied command. If the duke of York was not a brilliant admiral, he had at least received thorough grounding in naval operations during the Anglo-Dutch War of 1665–67. Also, Louis XIV wished to assure himself of Charles II's alliance by deferring to the English on naval matters. Thus when the English Parliament passed the Test Act in spring 1673, which forced the Catholic duke to resign his position in the admiralty, Charles's cousin, Prince Rupert, replaced the king's brother as commander of the Anglo-French fleet. Colbert chose the count d'Estrées to lead the French squadron of the combined fleet. Estrées was not the most capable French seaman available, but to Louis XIV the navy was simply an adjunct to the royal army and Estrées had the distinguished lineage considered necessary for a position of command.

Two indecisive battles were fought off the Dutch coast during June 1673.[31] The Dutch fleet, commanded by Michiel de Ruyter and Cornelis Tromp (men of differing political bent, whom the prince of Orange had reconciled after the De Witt brothers were murdered in 1672), held its own against the larger, joint Anglo-French fleet. The allies were nonetheless satisfied with their performance. Prince Rupert wrote to Lord Arlington from his flagship that the "French . . . behaved themselves very bravely."[32] J. B. Colbert was highly pleased with the bravery shown by his French seamen,[33] and his brother, Croissy, wrote to him from London that "our seamen have spoken very favorably of the English . . . and very modestly of their own actions, which makes them very popular here. There is room to hope that this solid union between the two nations will produce some glorious results if the enemy can be joined on the high seas."[34] Croissy was hoping that if the

Dutch fleet could be lured away from the treacherous shoals and sandbars of the Dutch coast the larger Anglo-French fleet would have an easy victory. He was soon to be disabused of these fanciful hopes.

On 26 July (N.S.), Charles II, York, and Arlington attended a council of war aboard Rupert's flagship, *Royal Charles*, as it lay at anchor off Gravesend in the Thames. The following morning the Anglo-French fleet stood out of the Thames estuary on the ebb tide, while Charles watched from the royal yacht at Middleground. Newcastle colliers sailed with the warships, carrying 8,000 infantry for the anticipated landing on the Dutch coast. On 12 August the prince of Orange boarded De Ruyter's flagship, *Seven Provinces*, anchored off Scheveningen, and gave the admiral written orders from their High Mightinesses, the States General, to accomplish two tasks: prevent an English landing on the Dutch coast and protect a convoy of Dutch East Indiamen, which was expected soon in the North Sea. The prince remained aboard until De Ruyter had fired his crew's enthusiasm with a short speech. Then the Dutch fleet set sail immediately. This was the background for what a recent historian has called "perhaps the turning point of the war."[35]

During ten days in mid-August, the Anglo-French and the Dutch fleets tested each other on the narrow seas between England and the Continent. Dutch peasants, expecting an English invasion, fled inland; but the feared invasion never came. On 21 August, just after dawn, De Ruyter perceived that the wind was favorable, and he made his move away from the protective shoals of the Dutch seacoast.

Although the combined Anglo-French fleet outnumbered the Dutch, both fleets consisted of three squadrons. De Ruyter, running with the wind, bore down on Rupert's squadron, and Tromp attacked the other English squadron, which Vice Admiral Edward Spragge commanded. Estrées kept his French squadron close-hauled to the wind, with the supposed intention of beating past the Dutch fleet in order to catch it in a crossfire. Because of sheer incompetence, or because of the mist and fog that hung over the North Sea, or because he lacked the stomach for a pitched battle, Estrées remained aloof from the fight. For most of the day the battle took the form of a strange triptych: Estrées meandered aimlessly through the mist and fog; Spragge and Tromp engaged in a ferocious running battle, during which both admirals had to change their flags several times when they were obliged to leave sinking or immobilized ships (Spragge was drowned when a cannonball shattered his dinghy); and Rupert's squadron, caught between De Ruyter and the Zeeland squadron, gave and took broadsides simultaneously from starboard and port. This was the longest, largest, and bloodiest naval battle of the war, and by the afternoon of 21 August the sea was littered with wreckage and bodies.

Late in the afternoon, Rupert and De Ruyter, sailing on the same tack, rejoined the melee that continued between Tromp's squadron and the remnants of Spragge's. As De Ruyter prepared to capture some disabled English ships, Rupert rallied his vessels to mount a renewed attack. At this moment Estrées's squadron, all but unscathed, sailed into view, and Rupert saw an opportunity to strike a crushing blow at the Dutch before nightfall. He ran a blue signal up his mizzenmast: all ships were to rally to the commander of the fleet immediately. The marquis of Martel, second in command of the French squadron, ordered his ships to heave to "while waiting for M. Estrées to arrive so that the entire squadron could swoop downwind on the enemy and send fire ships into him."[36] Estrées, however, sailed blithely by, and Martel was compelled by his orders to follow suit. "It was," Rupert wrote later, "the greatest and plainest opportunity ever lost at sea."[37] Night fell on the flotsam-strewn North Sea, and the naval action for 1673 was over.

De Ruyter, punning triumphantly on the name of his flagship, remarked that "the enemy still stands in awe of *Seven Provinces*.[38] Colbert's remark that De Ruyter was "the greatest admiral ever to sail the seas"[39] may be hyperbolic but it did not come from a friend, and the Dutch admiral's contribution to the preservation of the Dutch Republic in 1672–73 can hardly be exaggerated. Outnumbered, De Ruyter had not won smashing victories, but his brilliant defensive action precluded a landing on the Dutch coast and made the northern seas relatively safe for Dutch merchantmen, whose cargoes of goods and gold from Spain, the Baltic, and the East Indies were the lifeblood of the small republic. The Dutch navy had achieved its highest moment of glory.

Although the naval action for the year was over by nightfall of 21 August, the political repercussions of that day's great battle were only about to begin, repercussions that would culminate in

February 1674 when England withdrew from the French alliance and the war. Prince Rupert immediately dispatched a scathing denunciation of Estrées's conduct to the English court,[40] and by 28 August Croissy reported from London that rumors were abroad in the city that the French had conspired with the Dutch to prevent an English victory at sea.[41]

Eugene Sué, the French novelist and would-be historian, tried to make a case that Estrées had received secret orders from Louis XIV to keep the French squadron out of the main action and thus prevent a Dutch defeat, which would have allowed the English to land troops on the Dutch coast.[42] Although several shreds of evidence seem to support this contention,[43] they are not substantial proof. Louis XIV did not want the English ensconced on the Continent, but he did want glory brought to his arms, by sea as well as by land; moreover, by August, Louis was convinced that Charles II wanted peace badly enough to drop his demands for Dutch coastal towns.[44] Charles had sold Dunkirk to France in 1662, and Louis doubtless found it hard to believe that Charles, bedeviled by a refractory Parliament, had the power, the perseverance, or the money to establish a permanent foothold on the Dutch coast. Not Louis XIV's orders but Estrées's incompetence cost the French and English a victory at sea.

At first, Rupert's sharp criticism of Estrées had worried Croissy in London, but by 31 August he was writing with noticeable relief to Colbert: "I will not continue to din you with a subject which, by its unsettling effect in the city, has caused me much grief. I can only assure you that His Britannic Majesty is very satisfied with the account Major Hérouard of the French squadron has given him and very discontent with the way Prince Rupert has acted and written, so that we need not worry that he will command next year."[45] Croissy's reports, however, blew hot and cold, according to the climate of opinion in London, for on 7 September he wrote: "Because the [English] people are very susceptible to any calumnies that can be concocted against France, you can imagine what a bad effect the present ones have had. . . . I see that this affair is not finished and that . . . if he [Prince Rupert] should make a comeback, it will be very difficult to maintain the French alliance during Parliament's next session."[46] Thus Colbert de Croissy, writing with more candor to his brother than to his sovereign, Louis XIV, or his superior, Pomponne, first mentioned the possibility that the political repercussions of the sea battle off Texel might cost France the English alliance. However, when Croissy wrote this on 7 September, the worst had not yet happened.

Within three days the agitated Prince Rupert came up to London from the fleet to renew his imprecations against Estrées. What was worse, however, was that he carried a condemnation of Estrées written by none other than Estrées's subordinate, Martel, and Rupert circulated this document around London and Whitehall. Croissy wrote to his young nephew Seignelay, who was still with Louis XIV on campaign, that "this defamatory libel is doing more harm to the king's interests here than anything the Dutch and Spanish are doing to destroy the French alliance. It is being said openly that the count d'Estrées would never have acted in so cowardly a fashion if he had not received secret orders from His Majesty, that France is in collusion with the Dutch, and that England can expect to gain nothing from our alliance."[47] Before Colbert learned about the circulation of Martel's condemnation of Estrées in England, he had written to Croissy: "I would like to believe that all of the accusations and counteraccusations . . . about the last battle are finally finished."[48] Colbert was soon to learn that Martel's account of the battle (the English translation of which may have been edited by anti-French propagandists)[49] had rekindled the controversy and invective with explosive intensity.

The marquis of Martel had several possible motives for savagely condemning Estrées and for giving Prince Rupert a written copy of his denunciation (which he seems to have done). Martel, a fiery and aggressive captain, was incensed by Estrées's listless performance during the battle ("more prudent than valorous," the other French captains called it).[50] When Martel had come from the French Mediterranean fleet to join Estrées's command in July 1673, Estrées—as he was wont to do with all of his subordinate officers—had treated Martel contemptuously and rudely; Martel, who had more than thirty years' experience at sea, did not take kindly to snubs from a count who barely had his sea legs. It is also possible (as Estrées claimed) that Martel hoped to discredit Estrées and replace him as commander of the Atlantic fleet—although Colbert's response to that suggestion was that "of all the lunatics in the Petites-Maisons [a Parisian insane asylum], none of them is far enough gone to have dreamt up something like that."[51] Whatever Martel's motives, there can be no doubt that his and Rupert's savage denunciations of Estrées caused a great stir in England.

When Prince Rupert came up to London from the fleet in the second week in September, public opinion in the city was reported to Williamson in Cologne by a London friend. The Londoners were saying that the French and English fleets would never again fight together because the English sailors were persuaded that the Frenchmen had not done their duty.⁵² Moreover, "a translation of what was printed in Amsterdam of the late fight is read in our coffeehouses, which sayes that the French . . . fought bravely, but lost not one man, and that will be the beliefs of all the English till Doomes Day."⁵³ At the time that these reports were sent to Williamson, Croissy wrote to Colbert: "The accounts that are circulating throughout England over M. Martel's name, and which have been translated into English, are arousing the entire nation against us. . . . I do not think that M. Martel can ever repair . . . the damage that he has done the king's affairs in this country."⁵⁴ From London, Croissy and Williamson's correspondent vouched for Charles II's continued goodwill toward France and Louis XIV, but both the Frenchman and the Englishman clearly saw the tide of anti-French sentiment welling up among the English people in the aftermath of Texel. The Venetian envoy in London remarked, shortly after the battle, that "unless the king's prudence finds some vent for the peccant humors generated by the present crisis . . . he will scarcely be able to apply a remedy when they have taken root."⁵⁵ Even from his distant vantage point on the Continent, Abraham de Wicquefort, that shrewd observer of affairs, thought that the failure of the English and the French at sea would create a rift in their political alliance.⁵⁶

Because he was misled by inaccurate reports or because he could not understand representative government, Louis XIV often misjudged English public opinion and its importance in the functioning of the English polity. However, Louis's ambassador in England, Colbert de Croissy, misjudged neither in 1673. As early as the spring of that year, he had written to his brother: "Everything that is taking place in Parliament, Whitehall, and London makes me see all too clearly that the Anglo-French alliance is like sailing against both wind and the tides."⁵⁷ Croissy soon recognized that there were only two ways in which Louis could maintain the English alliance: either settle the war on reasonable terms at Cologne or give the English some hope of profit from continued war. Both possibilities were finally dashed in August 1673. Croissy, with the French plenipotentiaries at Cologne, had urged Louis XIV to make a reasonable settlement, but they had not succeeded;[58] and De Ruyter's successful defense of the Dutch coast and shipping dashed all hopes that England might gain territory or commercial advantage from the war.

Croissy was an ambitious man, with the right family connections, and his principal task as ambassador in England was to keep the Anglo-French alliance intact—but failure in one's assigned mission was not in the interests of such an ambitious man. Croissy's sudden "ill health" early in September is one of the best proofs of Texel's importance in alienating England from France in 1673.[59] Frequently, ambassadors use the excuse of ill health to remove themselves from discomforting situations, and Croissy doubtless found sitting helplessly in London, awaiting the inevitable parting of ways between England and France, acutely uncomfortable. He anticipated the break and wanted to dissociate himself from a job that he correctly foresaw was doomed to failure. Croissy managed to leave his post in England just one month before Charles II left the French alliance in February 1674.

In mid-October the Venetian envoy reported from London that "all measures are paralysed by the approaching session of Parliament,"[60] and its absolute intractability, when it met in late October, forced Charles II to expedite a separate peace with the Dutch. As soon as Parliament convened, it was obvious that it would not vote more funds for the war, and even the wealthy King Louis of France could not provide his cousin Charles with the staggering sum of money (1,400,000 pounds sterling) he demanded to remain Louis's partner in the war.[61] Louis could not subsidize Charles singlehandedly when the former was provoking a general war on the Continent. Indeed, by autumn 1673 the wealth of the French monarchy was sorely taxed by the demands of the war.

Writing a routine report to the doge and Senate of Venice in November 1673, the Venetian envoy in England remarked that "no one is able to explain why the people of England detest the French alliance so violently or why they wish for peace with Holland at any cost."[62] Indeed, there seemed to an irrational and pervasive Francophobia in England, that no one could (or can) explain. However, some factors that contributed to the growing opposition to the French alliance in England during autumn 1673 can be explained. The first was religious, and one can excuse the

Venetian envoy for not comprehending the mind of the English Puritan. English fear and loathing of Roman Catholicism had waxed and waned for over a century, according to the seriousness of the Catholic Church's threat to launch a comeback in England. In 1673 Englishmen perceived such a threat, and their dislike of Catholicism emerged in aggravated form. Charles II's brother James, duke of York, and one of the royal ministers, Lord Clifford, were forced to resign their government offices after Parliament passed the Test Act in May.[63] In addition, there was the Stuarts' relationship with Louis, who was the greatest threat to Protestant Europe in 1673. By autumn Englishmen knew that he had selected and paid the dowry for the duke of York's new Catholic wife, Mary of Modena, whose eventual offspring might return a Catholic dynasty to the English throne.[64] In November 1673, Croissy wrote to Louis XIV that "there are not four persons in that assembly [the House of Commons] who do not think that the only way to maintain the Protestant religion is to make a separate peace with Holland."[65] To the English, Louis XIV's Catholicism was intertwined with his absolutism, which his Stuart cousins so much admired. Religion and politics were almost inseparable in the seventeenth century, and the extension of French power was anathema to most Englishmen on both counts.

Also, the English may at first have been able to justify their third war against the Dutch within twenty years on economic grounds, as an extension of their heated commercial rivalry. But this justification remained valid only so long as Spain, England's largest trading partner, was not involved. When it appeared likely that Louis XIV would declare war upon Spain during the Charleroi incident in December 1672, Croissy notified Louis that all members of Charles II's privy council thought that war with Spain would be ruinous for England.[66] By October 1673, France was openly at war with Spain, and the English wanted no part of Louis XIV's new war. As the Venetian envoy justly noted: "What the people fear is war with Spain because of the stagnation of trade."[67]

Finally, there was a general sentiment among the English that Louis XIV was using them. The brightest wit among the "merry gang" of wits at Charles II's court, John Wilmot, earl of Rochester, summarized his countrymen's feelings:

Has not the French King made us Fools,
By taking Maestricht with our Tools?
But Charles what could thy Policy be,
To run so many sad Disasters:
To join thy Fleet with false D'Estrees,
To make the French of Holland Masters?
Was't Carewell, brother James, or Teague,
That made thee break the Triple League?[68]

Since the naval battle off Texel, when it seemed that the French had deserted the English fleet in its moment of potential triumph, Englishmen increasingly felt that the alliance with the French was not reciprocal. When a member of the autumn Parliament recalled the naval battle by saying it was as "if the English and Dutch had been gladiators for the French spectators,"[69] he was summing up the frustrations of a nation that had watched its ally receive all the spoils of their joint war efforts. On 15 November, the anniversary of the Gun Powder Plot, an effigy of the pope was burned in London, and an effigy of a Frenchman was "shot at because the French are accused of having shirked their duty in the sea fights."[70] These anti-French and anti-Catholic views were exploited in the propaganda that Pierre du Moulin's underground press published and distributed.[71]

The English public was vehemently opposed to the French alliance as early as August 1673, and Parliament echoed public opinion when it met in October. A rapid settlement with the Dutch was therefore a necessity for Charles. Nevertheless, it is interesting to speculate at what point Charles became convinced that he should break off his engagement with France. In mid-September Croissy wrote to Pomponne about Charles's growing anxieties: the attack on Trier, the equivocations of the elector of Bavaria, and the fact that France was creating so many new enemies.[72] Charles perceived Louis XIV's unslaked thirst for war, and had no interest in the major conflict that Louis was provoking in Germany.

Croissy, who had been trying for weeks to sound out Charles's position on the war, wrote to Pomponne on 25 September:

Sir, he [Charles II] has spoken to me (if I may say so) in a rather embarrassed and confused manner, making me to understand that Lord Arlington, who does not want the Prince of Orange humiliated, has all too much softened the king toward the prince, and that this minister will support his [the prince of Orange's] interests even at the expense of those which the king, his master, has in common with France.[73]

Of the many great actors on the Restoration stage, none was more accomplished than Charles II. He concocted for Croissy the story that he had lost control of English politics to Lord Arlington, and Croissy apparently believed it! Charles had to be cautious. "The separate peace must be made with the French king's consent, to avoid any chance of Louis's disclosing the treaty of Dover, and this meant that Charles must avoid all appearance of wanting peace: *he must be the victim of overwhelming pressure.*"[74]

Clearly, from Croissy's letters to Louis and Pomponne during late September, Charles II, though no one but Charles knew it, had reconciled himself to a separate peace with the Dutch as early as September 1673. Croissy's task of keeping England within the French orbit was even more impossible in fall 1673 than he realized. Although neither one knew it, the obtuse duke of York was Croissy's only important ally in England. King Charles, though he put up a good front, was preparing himself for peace several months before Parliament forced his hand. As well as any member of the Parliament, Charles knew where the interests of his realm lay.

Louis XIV did not take Croissy's increasingly pessimistic reports seriously, and he hoped that his cousin Charles's goodwill and desire for French gold would keep England bound to France in alliance. But in mid-October Louis received a report from Nicolas de Sève d'Aubeville, the French ambassador in Portugal, that he could not ignore. This report told of a conspiracy involving England, Spain, and Alfonso, the dispossessed king of Portugal. The object of the conspirators was to overthrow Pedro, Alfonso's brother and regent, after which Alfonso would regain the Portuguese throne. England was to receive as her share of the spoils all of Portugal's colonies immediately upon Alfonso's resumption of the throne, and upon Alfonso's death the Portuguese throne would escheat to Spain.[75]

Louis, who received this news from Lisbon just after he had declared war on Spain on 20 October, was understandably taken aback. He quickly dispatched complicated instructions to London, advising Croissy how to draw Charles out. Croissy was to relate the entire story of the conspiracy to Charles—save the alleged English complicity. As Croissy was speaking, he was to observe

Charles very closely, for "if the story is true and he [Charles] has worked closely with the Spaniards in an affair of this nature, it will be difficult for him . . . not to give himself away by showing some embarrassment or surprise."[76] Croissy followed Louis's orders to the letter and wrote back to Versailles on 30 October that he had confronted Charles face to face:

I told him all of the circumstances of the enterprise, . . . and during this time I observed his eyes, his face, and his whole demeanor. But, in truth, he appeared no more troubled or upset than at any other time that I have spoken to him about affairs which his ministers had not briefed him on. I noticed no change in his color or emotion; he simply remained pensive with a trace of a smile on his lips while I was speaking to him. . . . Without responding to me about Portugal, he expounded at great length everything that he foresaw about the coming session of Parliament.[77]

No wonder Croissy wanted to leave London. Although the conspiracy in Lisbon was immediately quashed, Aubeville confirmed Charles's complicity in a second letter to Louis XIV.[78] The conspiracy amounted to nothing. Yet this melodrama shows that Louis XIV could not always fool his allies. Charles II was often a step ahead of Louis and his ambassador, Croissy. The English king was actively aware of his own interests and refused to remain his powerful cousin's stooge interminably.

Historians have long paid tribute to the abilities of Venetian diplomats, to their sharp perceptions, good judgment, and accurate reporting. Girolamo Alberti, the Venetian envoy in London during the early 1670s, was no exception to the usual high quality of the diplomatic corps in which he served; but on one subject his astuteness failed him. During autumn 1673 he repeatedly commented that Charles II was determined "to persevere in the French alliance at any cost."[79] Alberti said that Charles gave every semblance of such determination, and the Venetian accepted this appearance because "the king does not understand art."[80]

In fact, Charles was a crafty politician, and his artifices succeeded in gulling Alberti (among others). Charles not only was preparing to leave the French alliance long before he formally did so (in February 1674) but he had made his decision even before Parliament convened in late October 1673. The king was merely keeping his own counsel and dissembling, for if he wanted to remain Louis XIV's pensioner in the future, he had to ease himself out of the war and the alliance with his wealthier and more powerful cousin.

On 9 February Pomponne wrote dolefully to Robert de Gravel at the German Diet that "doubtless they [the Imperials] will make much of what has just happened in England. . . . The peace party has won out over the word of honor that obliged both king and nation not to make peace without France."[81] Pomponne's rhetoric is peculiar for a man who knew as well as anyone that interest rather than honor usually governs the making and breaking of treaties. Thus, the peace between England and the Dutch was signed in Lord Arlington's office on February 19 (O.S.).[82]

Texel was the occasion for England's vehement rejection of the French alliance, but it was not the fundamental cause. The English people and the Parliament objected to Louis XIV's Catholicism and absolutism and to the war's destruction of English commerce. King Charles II, although he admired his French cousin's religion and style of government, saw that continued war in alliance with France was contrary to his interests. He could no longer cope with his domestic situation when his people were so heatedly anti-French, but, more important, he understood that he was being used by Louis XIV. Charles would have quit the war even if Parliament had not pressured him and even if Arlington, whose foreign policy was based on friendship with Spain,[83] had not badgered him; for Charles could no longer hope to profit by the conflict. Neither the war in Germany nor the war with Spain would strengthen his position at home or increase the revenues from his customs grant. The war on the Continent was increasingly Louis XIV's private war and no other prince had any interest in joining him.

Charles's separate peace with the United Provinces in February 1674 was one of Louis XIV's two major diplomatic defeats of the Dutch War. Together with the Alliance of The Hague (30 August 1673), which bound the emperor, the Dutch, and the Spaniards in union against France, England's withdrawal from the war left Louis standing alone against a coalition of European states. A pattern of failure in Louis's conduct of foreign policy thus emerges: he tried to use England, while ignoring Charles II's vital interests, just as he tried to use Cologne while ignoring Elector Max Heinrich's interests. This shallow, manipulative foreign policy could only succeed in the short run; and by the end of 1673 Louis was virtually isolated in a war that was already a burden to his people and his government.

VIII

Louis XIV and France

Johan de Witt remarked in 1664 that France "has a twenty-six-year-old king, vigorous in mind and body, . . . who possesses a kingdom inhabited by an extremely bellicose people and which contains considerable wealth." Such a king would have to "possess an extraordinary, almost miraculous, moderation, if he thrust aside the ambition which is so natural to all princes . . . and did not extend his frontiers where they are most constricting and where France has always been troubled most by her enemies."[1] In short, Johan de Witt said it was inevitable that Louis XIV would wage war to extend the frontiers of France to the north and the east.

Louis XIV did not disappoint De Witt: he waged long and costly wars and extended his frontiers where they were "most constricting" and where France had "always been troubled most by her enemies." This happened in the so-called Dutch War of the 1670s. In the peace settlements of 1678/79, France's frontiers were extended to the north and the east at the expense of the Spaniards. All French statesmen, and probably most European statesmen, would have agreed that these extensions were in the interests of Louis XIV and his kingdom. Thus in the Dutch War it might appear that Louis simply executed a policy that Richelieu and Mazarin had visualized, that contemporary statesmen agreed with, and that De Witt had predicted a decade earlier.

After the war, Louis wanted to think of the conflict of the 1670s in these terms; he wanted to think of the Dutch War as an effort that he had conceived principally to acquire strategic territories from the Spaniards. In his military memoirs, which he wrote shortly after the war, the king remarked that as early as the summer of 1672 he had been contemplating evacuating the Dutch Netherlands in order to prepare for war with Spain:

> I wish . . . to say that an inner premonition that the burden of the war would finally fall on the Spanish Netherlands and that the territories that would be ceded to me by the peace would better serve to enlarge and secure my realm than those in Holland, which I could hold only with great trouble and expense and which I would perhaps be obliged ultimately to abandon, convinced me to refuse peace on the terms that were offered to me [in June 1672].[2]

This analysis of the Dutch War conveniently corresponds with the fact that, in the peace settlements of 1678/79 at Nijmegen, the French were rewarded exclusively at the expense of the Spaniards, not the Dutch. Louis XIV, like many other public figures of great vanity, wrote "history" in order to furnish posterity the most flattering image of himself and his actions. When, after the Dutch War, the king wrote the above passage, he was attempting to conceal the basic error in his policy during the first phase of the war. Louis's account of his reason for rejecting the Dutch offers in June 1672 is nonsense. He did not reject a favorable settlement because he had an "inner premonition" about the Spanish Netherlands, or because his Dutch conquests were then too difficult to hold. On the contrary, if Louis had been planning an attack on the Spanish Netherlands during summer 1672, he would have seized the opportunity to make peace with the Dutch, for they were prepared to cede territory that would have given the French the strategic position from which to overwhelm the Spanish Netherlands at their convenience.[3]

Louis rebuffed the Dutch peace offers in 1672 because he felt that he had the Dutch at his mercy and that he could continue his triumphal march toward Amsterdam and The Hague; even as late as spring 1673, Louvois was urging Condé to push across the flooded polders of Holland.[4] There is no evidence that Louis considered withdrawing his occupational forces from the Dutch Netherlands before late October 1673.

The Dutch War had begun, like Charles VIII's invasion of Italy in 1494, as a war to enhance the glory of the prince, with little regard for the interests of the French state. The fundamental military problem of the French monarchy in the century preceding Louis XIV's reign had been the defense of the northeastern frontier of the realm. When Louis attacked the Dutch in 1672, he more or less turned his back on that basic problem in order to win military glory and to revenge himself on the Dutch for their presumption in standing up to him. The year 1673 was a time of transition in the so-called Dutch War. During this year a personal war was transformed into a war that was more in keeping with the policies of Richelieu and Mazarin, with the fundamental interests of the French kingdom. To extend the frontiers to the north and the east by attacking the Spaniards was in the interest of the state, and had a legal basis in the king's Spanish marriage. This was a combination with which Richelieu would have cherished working: raw interest of state buttressed with plausible juridical arguments.

Implicit in the remarks of Johan de Witt is the idea that wars should be waged in the interest of the state and that the ambition of the prince and the needs of the state should perfectly coincide. De Witt apparently did not think in terms of distinguishing the interests of the prince from those of the state, and assuredly Louis XIV did not. We in the twentieth century have difficulty understanding the motives that drove Louis: the desire to promote his family's fortunes; the need to achieve personal *gloire* on the battlefield; his belief that he was serving the interests of the entire French nation when he demonstrated the prowess of his arms. We should not condemn Louis's impelling motives *simply* because it requires a leap of the imagination to comprehend them. As Victor-L. Tapie has written: "It is very difficult to discover moments when Louis XIV saw a distinction between his private person and his kingly office. . . . His *gloire* concerned his entire realm. . . . To explain his taste for *gloire* as individual egotistical ambition seems inadequate."[5]

Tapie was correct. It is not satisfactory simply to explain Louis's desire to achieve glory as an outgrowth of a capricious egomania. Nevertheless, it is a fact that the king's subjective policies did thrust the problem of distinguishing between the interests of the prince and those of his realm into the thoughts of his contemporaries—indeed, into the thoughts of statesmen who were serving in the royal government. This problem was analyzed by the most brilliant of contemporary French diplomats, Honoré Courtin:

The king is doubtless the world's greatest . . . prince. He can remain so with a peace settlement that all Europe would consider very honorable for him and very advantageous for his state. Thus I have trouble under-standing why his Majesty wants to jeopardize this happiness and risk ex-posing himself to future troubles, which might indeed serve to show off his courage and valor but will doubtless be the ruin of his subjects. . . .

If . . . one wishes to reflect in all seriousness and good faith on the internal affairs of the state, is it not recognized that funds are depleted, that most of the money has left the kingdom and will not return while the war continues to ruin commerce? Can it not be understood that the taxes on the people, who will become impoverished (in fact already are), cannot be raised without violence that is very dangerous when we have so many enemies abroad? . . . The authority that the king has exercised so absolutely (*souverainement*) up to this time, being attacked from without will weaken within the kingdom.[6]

Courtin, who was a keen observer of economic and social currents, foresaw in 1673 the problems that would plague France during the latter half of Louis XIV's reign. Although these prob-lems cannot be attributed solely to the king's adventuresome for-eign policy, Courtin, who had served as a provincial intendant, knew well the havoc that war could wreak upon the French people, and his association of enlightened despotism and reason-of-state politics is noteworthy. He had no objection to absolute monarchy on philosophical or on practical grounds; he simply could not comprehend the king's inner drives—his compulsion constantly to prove himself on the battlefield at the expense of his state. To Courtin, Louis XIV's search for military *gloire* was incredibly shortsighted because, in trying to achieve it, the king was precisely destroying his instrumentality for future *gloire*, that is, the richness and well-being of his realm.

The French diplomatic corps was not the only locus of dis-enchantment with Louis XIV's policies during 1673. Jean-Baptiste Colbert wrote to his younger brother, Colbert de Croissy, just before the latter returned to France from his embassy in London in January 1674, and in this cryptic letter the finance minister obliquely expressed his discontents: "I cannot help telling you that you sometimes misinterpret affairs over here [in France]. . . . I cannot say more, but rather often I have had a strong desire to talk to you for a few minutes about all that is happening, for assuredly that would be necessary before you could recognize the situation here, with which you are wholly unfamiliar."[7] Colbert was informing his brother, as openly as he dared in a letter, that radical change had occurred in France during Croissy's absence and that Colbert did not like it.

Croissy had been ambassador in England for five years and therefore had not witnessed firsthand the changes in Louis's government and in royal policies. During those five years, Lionne had died and Louvois had entered and quickly risen to preeminence in the high council. The team that had been recruited and trained by Mazarin no longer ran the French state. Lionne was dead, Pomponne and Colbert were being conspicuously ignored, and two relative neophytes, Louis XIV and Louvois, were in full command—much to Colbert's discomfort.

Colbert was just as displeased with the Dutch War by late 1673 as the French diplomats were. During the 1660s he had imposed some measure of order and discipline on the royal finances. The tax burden on the peasantry had actually been lightened, the year-by-year governmental expenses had been met without using the next year's revenues, and increasingly less recourse had been had to *affaires extraordinaires*—that is, the sale of offices, loans from private persons, alienation of the royal domain, and creation of new excise taxes.[8] Colbert probably, although with some reluctance, had endorsed the Dutch War at its outset, for he had seen it as a possible means of expanding the French economy at the expense of the Dutch.[9] As early as 1672, however, Colbert had been forced to curtail his plans for colonial development and inform the royal intendant in Canada that he could not expect to receive any funds from Paris that year.[10] By autumn 1673 it was apparent that the Dutch War was not proceeding in accord with Colbert's plans, that Louis XIV's expanding European war was destroying the finance minister's hopes for economic growth and reform. Colbert was a tough-minded mercantilist but not a warrior, and by the end of 1673 he had ample cause to be displeased with the condition of the French economy.

Indeed, Colbert's economic program had been destroyed. While Louis was still on campaign in August, the finance minister wrote to tell him it would be necessary to raise "twenty millions [livres] by extraordinary means."[11] "Extraordinary means" were the measures that Colbert particularly dreaded, not only because they put additional pressure on an already war-burdened economy but because they would throw his budget calculations for the future into chaos.

Two months later, when Louis had returned from the field, William Perwich, the secretary to the English embassy in Paris, made several revealing remarks about the state of royal finances. He wrote to Arlington that Colbert had been "feeling the pulse" of the tax farmers for an advance of fourteen million livres but they had replied that such an amount was unthinkable "because of the deadnesse of trade."[12] Two weeks later Perwich observed that since the king's return from the campaign, the judges of the royal law courts in Paris had traveled to Versailles to compliment him. "The President of the Court of Aydes made a very fine harangue, but at ye later end, represented ye poore condition of the his people, . . . with many wishes that his Majy would make a Peace & then take off ye tax upon paper."[13] It is humorous and typical that the president of the Cour des Aides (a royal court for handling extraordinary taxation) should complain to the king about the plight of the people and then ask for the repeal of a stamp tax that primarily affected the legal community, of which the president was a principal representative. But the president's fundamental point, that the war was ruining the French economy, was valid.

Charles Cole, in his comprehensive study of Colbert and French mercantilism, indicted the Dutch War: "It was this war that ruined the Company of the North, the Insurance Company, the Levant Company, all but ruined the East India Company, and checked the progress of the West Indies. It was this war that reduced the value of the inspectors of manufactures, by making their remuneration partially dependent on local fees."[14] (Indeed, Courtin's prophecy to Louvois in 1673, that the war would bring upheavals in the French state, was fulfilled two years later when new war taxes helped to precipitate widespread and bitter revolts in Brittany.)[15]

Colbert no doubt foresaw the long-term consequences of a prolonged war, and he informed the king of his views. Perhaps because he had risen to prominence and power under the auspices of a first minister, Mazarin, rather than under the Sun King himself, Colbert, unlike Louvois, did not shrink from presenting the king with the facts. Louis, who preferred flattery to criticism, did not appreciate this quality in the finance minister as much as he might have. By mid-December 1673, Perwich could write to Lord Arlington from Paris that "Monsr. Colbert . . . has been a long while in a small disgrace."[16] Colbert remained a minister of state because Louis recognized that he was almost indispensable for handling the financial apparatus of the royal government, but the king and the finance minister were in fundamental disagreement on policy.

When Louis personally assumed the reins of power in the French state in 1661, Colbert offered to turn his personal dream for France into a reality for the king. Colbert proposed to create an integrated realm, which would be rich in commerce and manufacturing and would dominate its European neighbors, not so much with arms as with economic power. This dream could not have been fully realized even under ideal circumstances of peace, domestic stability, and favorable weather; but as Ernest Lavisse remarked: "how the country and the king received Colbert's offer was the capital question of Louis XIV's reign."[17] For a decade, Colbert made headway. Then, with the Dutch War, Louis rejected his finance minister's offer once and for all. The king's *gloire* was not to be achieved by calculations of revenues and expenses in the countinghouses of Marseilles, Bordeaux, Nantes, or Rheims. Louis XIV dreamed of being a warrior prince, not a merchant prince.

Under the pressure of events during the Dutch War, a profound conflict developed at the highest levels in the French government. This conflict, which Honoré Courtin came closest to articulating, centered on the eternal problem of the relationship of the ruler to the state. Although Louis XIV never said *L'état, c'est moi*, he did see the state as a projection of himself. A recent authority on reason-of-state has remarked that Louis's "strong tendency to equate his personal interests and glory with those of the state . . . was not unknown in earlier periods of French history, since it was a natural concomitant of monarchical rule; but it reached its furthest development under Louis XIV, and may be regarded as the logical end product of personal absolutism."[18]

It has been suggested that later in his life Louis regretted the war of 1672–1678/79, that he matured and perceived the errors of his youth.[19] This may be true; but at the time of the Dutch War the king was prepared to use the powers of the French monarchy to satisfy a rather puerile desire for self-aggrandizement. However, highly placed men in the royal government had radically different views about the state and its ruler. These men (who included many diplomats and two ministers, Pomponne and Colbert) saw the French state, in greater or lesser degree, as an entity that transcended the king and even his dynasty. The patently subjective nature of Louis's policies during the Dutch War compelled these men to begin thinking of the state in different, more modern terms, in the sense that they saw themselves as civil servants who labored for the strength and well-being of the entire French nation.

During the Enlightenment it was popular to think that monarchy was an inherently bellicose form of government. Montesquieu wrote in his *De l'esprit des Lois* that "the spirit of monarchy is war and the enlargement of dominion,"[20] and Thomas Paine's indictment of monarchy was stronger: "In the early ages of the world, . . . there were no kings, the consequence of which was there were no wars; it is the pride of kings which throws mankind into confusion."[21] Despite the silliness of Paine's remarks, there continues to be a sense of the close ties between monarchy and warfare. Recently, Pierre Goubert has written: "The impression remains, very clearly, of the profound taste of kings for war, a passion traditional and mystical at the same time. It was in the exaltation of war, the epic charge, the clash of steel, the smell of powder, . . . that the oldest, the most intense, perhaps the essential royal function was realized."[22] At the outset of the Dutch War, Louis XIV was acting within this latter tradition, playing out a "mythology, versified, engraved, sculpted, painted and sung, of the king on a steed at the head of his troops, of the king always victorious and gilded . . . with triumph."[23] But insofar as Louis XIV was acting out this tradition and mythology, he was backward-looking and increasingly out of date.

The modern, bureaucratic aspect of Louis's rule has been described in some detail,[24] but the king was Janus-faced, looking forward to the modern world as a *roi-bureaucrate* and back toward the medieval world as a military chieftain. The time had passed, however, when European monarchs fought great wars in order to embody an ancient ideal of the king as warlord. None of Louis XIV's contemporary princes did. The prince of Orange, for example, was as combative as any man of the seventeenth century, but his pugnacity sprang from political ambitions that had little to do with the laurels of chivalric combat. Frederick the Great, a century later, would have smiled sardonically to see Louis XIV marching about in pursuit of military glory, with his queen and two mistresses in tow. Frederick may have loved warfare but he never romanticized it; he always fought for real objectives.

Louis XIV stood at the head and as leader of a social and legal class, the French *noblesse d'epée*. The *raison d'être* of this class had been to wage war. As the first nobleman of the realm, it was no mere whim that drove Louis to achieve his identity on the battlefield. John B. Wolf has remarked: "The king of France was a soldier, and a king of France born during the Thirty Years' War, when all the talk in the court concerned battle and heroes, would inevitably want to play out the role of soldier-king."[25] In a similar though more abstract vein, Joseph Schumpeter explained that Louis's bellicose policies stemmed from "the necessities of [the] social structure, from the inherited dispositions of [the] ruling class."[26] Thus we have Schumpeter's analysis of warfare as social atavism, as a product (in the case of Louis XIV) of the primordial drives and longings of the old nobility in France. These men, including of course the king himself, did not fight for material acquisitions or specific goals but rather because it was only in battle that they could fulfill themselves and achieve their identities, as dictated by the traditions of their social class.

In reviewing the ideas of Goubert, Wolf, and Schumpeter on the enormous traditional pressures that pushed Louis to seek military glory, one might conclude that the king's particular personality was negligible; that any man who might have been king in France during the second half of the seventeenth century would have conducted himself precisely as Louis XIV did. But this would be a too rigidly deterministic analysis; the man *did* count, for there were not only social imperatives behind Louis's belligerence at the time of the Dutch War but psychological necessities as well. The king's own words demonstrate this. When, toward the end of December 1672, a renewal of war between France and Spain appeared to be a necessary concomitant of the Dutch War, Louis's imagination played with heroic designs. He wrote to Louvois and described his dream of glory:

I swear that I would find it beautiful if—while the emperor, Spain, Holland, and Brandenburg are trying to frustrate my projects—m. de Luxembourg should cross the ice in Holland, m. le Prince [de Condé] should seize part of Burgundy, and I should drive all of their [Spanish] troops out of Flanders. . . .

I station myself in Flanders because, as you know, I now must command an army for myself.[27]

Louis's grandiose plans were tempered by his councillors and the strength of his enemies, and he never realized this project. But the king's fantasies tell us as much about the nature of the Dutch War as an elaborate analysis of Colbert's tariff policy would, for Louis's need to fulfill himself on the battlefield was an important cause of the war. The king's need was so intense that he not only insisted upon personally leading an army but found it necessary to denigrate his other generals, seemingly to cast a more favorable light on his own leadership. Thus, at the same time he explained to Louvois his compulsion to command an army on his own, Louis wrote contemptuously of Turenne, who was about to begin a brilliant winter campaign in Germany: "The best reason that my cousin, le vicomte de Turenne, gives for not crossing the Rhine is the impossibility of doing it that he mentions in every letter."[28] Louis was not a man who customarily indulged in sarcasm, and this invidious remark about Turenne shows how much the king wished to see himself as the foremost soldier in France.

There is a paradoxical twist in Louis's and Louvois's successful effort to domesticate the French generals, to force the semiautonomous military leaders of the feudal nobility to submit to the civilian, centralized control of the war ministry, for the "modern" army, thus created, did not serve a "modern" state, as one might suppose. At least during the early stages of the Dutch War, this army was used principally as a tournament weapon by the first nobleman of the realm, King Louis XIV. To speak of a policy of jousting would be a contradiction in terms, for policy implies a larger and more rationalized vision of the world, and it was precisely the absence of an explicitly articulated policy that plagued the French war effort during the initial stages of the Dutch War. Louis seemed determined to ignore his advisors and ministers who possessed the training and the temperament, the wisdom and the experience, to formulate a coherent policy for the French state. Ruling his kingdom with no firm guideline of state interest, Louis mismanaged both domestic and foreign affairs.

Louis destroyed Mazarin's greatest diplomatic achievement when he forced the two houses of Hapsburg to reunite in political alliance; he disregarded the interests of his fellow sovereigns in Europe, thus losing his allies and swelling the ranks of his enemies.

Perhaps Louis could not comprehend the interests of his allies, because he had difficulty conceptualizing a policy of state interest as a framework for his own actions. The king's thoughts and feelings about his war policy were more immediate, personal, and of narrower scope; his lust for action for its own sake, his love of the campaign and the siege, with all their concomitant details, took the place of a broader policy, rooted in state interest.[29] Louis could not decide with whom or for what specific political purposes he was waging war. The king played Mars during 1672 and 1673 as glitteringly as he had once played Apollo in the court ballets, but by December 1673 he was reduced to reacting to the threats of a vigorous and growing coalition of hostile powers that did have a sharply focused policy, based upon the specific objective of stopping French expansion. The very lack of focus in Louis's military operations deprived the French of the victories that should have been assured by the size and the quality of the royal armies.

Although the natural strength of the land and the resources of the French monarchy permitted Louis to withstand a pan-European coalition, and indeed to acquire territory from the Spaniards in the peace settlements of 1678/79, a long downward spiral of economic disruption and social instability began for France in the 1670s. Emmanuel Le Roy Ladurie has suggested that if it had not been for the economic slump (the "Phase B") of the late seventeenth century, the increased taxes induced by Louis XIV's wars would have been "painful, but endurable, and in certain cases stimulating because the intendants fed part of the tax revenues back into the economy."[30] But could not the formula be reversed: If it had not been for the crushing burden of taxes and the general dislocation brought on by war, Frenchmen could have better survived the economic slump, and perhaps in certain cases have acquired new ingenuity and strength in response to the challenge of a faltering economy? Who can say with certainty that it was not the wars, in adding to the problems of a sluggish economy, that pushed the life of the French peasant over the line from hardship into abject misery?

When Louis XIV could not distinguish between his personal desires and the interests of the state, he was guilty of a certain myopia, even within the context of seventeenth-century political values. That fault of vision meant that the king and his realm paid a heavy price for the territories acquired at the Peace of Nijmegen.

In the eighteenth century Voltaire commented, in his *Age of Louis XIV*, that Nijmegen found "the king . . . at the height of his greatness."[31] But Voltaire was probably wrong. The king's designs on the United Provinces were wholly shattered by 1678, and it seems easier to agree with Gaston Zeller, for whom "the Dutch War [was] a mistake, perhaps the greatest mistake of the reign,"[32] than with Voltaire.

~~~

Notes

Chapter 1

1. François A. Mignet, *Négociations relatives à la succession d'Espagne,* 1:1ii–1iii.

2. Herbert H. Rowen, *The Ambassador Prepares for War: The Dutch Embassy of Arnauld de Pomponne, 1669–1671.*

3. Albert Sorel, *L'Europe et la Révolution française,* pt. 1, pp. 253–61.

4. Gaston Zeller, "La monarchie d'ancien régime et les frontières naturelles," pp. 305–33.

5. Sorel, *L'Europe et la Révolution française,* pp. 280–83.

6. Adam Smith, *The Wealth of Nations,* p. 180.

7. See, for example, Elphège Frémy, "Causes économiques de la guerre de Hollande (1664–1672)," pp. 523–51; Simon Elzinga, *Het voorspel van dan oorlog van 1672: De economisch-politieke betrekkingen tusschen Frankrijk en Nederland in de jaren 1660–1672;* Henri Sée, "Que faut-il penser de l'oeuvre économique de Colbert," p. 186. Charles W. Cole, this century's leading authority on Colbert, remarked (*Colbert and a Century of French Mercantilism,* 2:551) that the Dutch War "sprang directly from the very core of his [Colbert's] type of mercantilism." Pieter Geyl's review of Elzinga's book (in *History,* n.s. 13 [1928]:162–63) contains one of the rare criticisms of the economic interpretation of the Dutch War.

8. Philippe Sagnac and Alexandre de Saint-Léger, *La préponderance française: Louis XIV, 1661–1715,* p. 147. Historians like Charles Wilson (*The Dutch Republic,* pp. 202–3), who approach French policy from the perspective of the Anglo-Dutch commercial wars, are understandably prone to err in attributing Louis XIV's Dutch War to Colbert's mercantile policies.

9. Rowen, *Ambassador,* chap. xiv.

10. Pierre Goubert, *Louis XIV et vingt millions de français,* pp. 85–95.

11. See, for example, Colbert's "Mémoire au roi sur les finances" (1670), in Pierre Clément, ed., *Lettres, instructions, et mémoires de Colbert,* 7:251. Professor Paul Sonnino, of the University of California (Santa Barbara) however, is preparing to make a case that Colbert did not advocate war upon the Dutch in 1672.

12. Ernest Lavisse, *Histoire de France depuis les origines jusqu'à la Révolution française,* 7:pt. I, 223, n. 1. It is remarkable that the editor of *Recueil des in-*

structions données aux ambassadeurs . . . *Venise*, Pierre Duparc, should find that "it is only with the coming of the eighteenth century that economic considerations appear regularly" in the royal directives provided for the French ambassadors accredited to the Republic of Venice (*Recueil . . . Venise*, p. x).

13. Gaston Zeller, "Politique extérieure et diplomatie sous Louis XIV," pp. 125–26.

14. Camille Picavet, *La diplomatie française au temps de Louis XIV (1661–1715); institutions, moeurs et coutumes*, p. 176.

15. Zeller, "Politique extérieure," p. 126.

16. Ibid., p. 131.

17. John B. Wolf, *Louis XIV*, p. 618.

18. Zeller, "Politique extérieure," p. 128.

19. Gaston Zeller, *Les temps modernes, de Louis XIV à 1789*, p. 7.

20. Zeller, "Politique extérieure," p. 128.

21. Gilbert Burnet, *History of My Own Times*, 1:394.

22. William Temple, *Works*, 2:25.

23. See John C. Rule, "Louis XIV, Roi-Bureaucrate," pp. 28–29, 53–54; Paul Sonnino, *Louis XIV's View of the Papacy (1661–1667)*, p. 5.

24. Paul Sonnino has examined Lionne's waning influence on Louis in the late 1660s in "Hugues de Lionne and the Origins of the Dutch War" (pp. 68–78).

25. Thomas François de Saint-Maurice, *Lettres sur la cour de Louis XIV*, 2:586.

26. Primi Visconti, *Mémoires sur la cour de Louis XIV*, p. 34.

27. Goubert, *Louis XIV*, p. 95.

28. Robert Mandrou, *La France aux XVIIe et XVIIIe siècles*, p. 238.

29. Two diplomatic agreements of January 1668 persuaded Louis XIV to accept peace with Spain in May of that year. The Triple Alliance was signed, and England, Sweden, and the Dutch Republic appeared ready to support the Spaniards in the Southern Netherlands; Louis's ambassador in Vienna signed the first of the partition treaties, whereby Emperor Leopold and Louis agreed to divide the Spanish inheritance upon the death of sickly Carlos II of Spain. See below, chap. 5.

30. Emmanuel Le Roy Ladurie, *Les paysans de Languedoc*, 1:531–32.

31. François de Salignac de la Mothe de Fénelon, *Ecrits et lettres politiques*, p. 147.

32. Louis de Rouvroy, duc de Saint-Simon, also saw the Dutch War as the beginning of Louis XIV's problems (*Mémoires*, 28:10–11).

Chapter 2

1. "Ingrates," from the French point of view, because Louis XIV considered Dutch support of his claims upon the Spanish Netherlands assured by the Franco-Dutch treaty of 1662, and because he attributed the Dutch victory over Spain overwhelmingly to French assistance. In his memoirs on the Dutch War Louis wrote, in reference to the Dutch involvement in the Triple Alliance of 1668: "In the midst of all good fortune . . . I found in my path only my good, faithful and old friends, the Dutch, who instead of welcoming my good luck . . . wished to impose rules upon me and compel me to make peace. . . . I avow that their insolence sharply irritated me and that I was ready . . . to turn my armies against that proud and ungrateful nation." Camille Rousset, *Histoire de Louvois et de son administration politique et militaire*, 1:519.

2. Charles II and Louis XIV had agreed to lop off pieces of the republic and leave the prince of Orange, Charles's nephew, as sovereign of a rump state. See article 7 of the Treaty of Dover (1670) in Mignet, *Négociations*, 3:261–62.

3. Pieter de Groot, son of the great Hugo Grotius (Huig de Groot), was the agent, if not one of the leaders, of the faction within the States General that favored appeasement (Pieter Geyl, *The Netherlands in the Seventeenth Century*, pt. 2, pp. 126–29). De Groot was one of the ambassadors sent by the States General to talk to the French at Doesburg, but later, in summer 1672, when the De Witt brothers had been murdered and the prince of Orange had assumed control in the republic, De Groot was forced to flee abroad. See Robert Fruin, *De oorlog van 1672*.

4. See below, chap. 5, n. 8.

5. "The decision to flood the entire country was a little extreme, but what doesn't one do to prevent foreign domination? I cannot help but admire and praise the zeal and strength of those who broke off the negotiations [at Doesburg], although their opinion . . . did much damage to my interests" (Rousset, *Louvois*, 1:532). It was, of course, easier for Louis to write like this in 1678, when the *Mémoire* on the campaign of 1672 was written. See Paul Sonnino, "Louis XIV's Mémoires pour l'histoire de la guerre de Hollande," pp. 29–50.

6. Turenne to Louvois, 9 Dec. 1672, Archives de Guerre (hereafter AG), A¹ 281, no. 142.

7. Vauban to Louvois, 19 or 20 Jan. 1673. The last time I saw this now famous letter, which is in Vauban's own hand, it was unbound in AG, A¹ 337, as no. 111.

8. Condé to Louvois, 12 Dec. 1672, AG, A¹ 281, nos. 205–9.

9. Louvois to Condé, 25 Jan. 1673, AG, A¹ 314, fos. 43–44.

10. Turenne was preparing to meet the armies of Brandenburg and Emperor Leopold. See below, chap. 3.

11. Saint-Maurice, *Lettres*, 2:503–4.

12. Louis XIV, *Oeuvres*, 3:303–6. For the dating of this portion of Louis's memoir on the campaign of 1673 see Sonnino, "Mémoires de la guerre," p. 42.

13. Wolf, *Louis XIV*, pp. 230–31.

14. Courtin to Condé, 21 May 1673, Archives de Chantilly, papiers de Condé, P 46, fo. 206. Condé responded from Utrecht (30 May 1673; ibid., fo. 399): "I will begin by assuring you that no one but my son and I will ever know what you have told me. You can trust me on that matter."

15. Mignet, *Négociations*, 3:705–7. Louvois went in person to Cologne to complete, with the bishops of Cologne and Münster, the negotiations for an offensive alliance against the Dutch. See H. Böhmer, "Forschungen zur französischen Bündnispolitik im 17 Jahrhundert: Wilhelm Egon von Fürstenberg und die französische Diplomatie in Deutschland, 1668–1672," pp. 225–59.

16. On the Fürstenberg brothers see Max Braubach, *Wilhelm von Fürstenberg (1629–1704) und die französische Politik im Zeitalter Ludwigs XIV*; John T. O'Connor, "Wilhelm Egon von Fürstenberg, A German Agent in the Service of Louis XIV," pp. 119–46.

17. Franz von Fürstenberg to Louvois, 28 Apr. 1673, AG A¹ 322, fos. 795, 800–801.

18. Louvois to Franz von Fürstenberg, 6 May 1673, AG A¹ 315, fo. 196.

19. Courtin to Louis XIV, 30 May 1673, Archives des Affaires Etrangère, correspondance politique (hereafter AAE), Allemagne 267, fos. 27–28.

20. A copy of the treaty is contained in AAE, Cologne 11, fos. 82–83.

21. Pomponne to Chaulnes and Courtin, 23 May 1673, AAE, All. 270 bis, fo. 25.

22. Grotius clearly acknowledges the right of passage (*The Law of Peace and War*, bk. 2, pp. 198–99). Emmerich de Vattel (*The Law of Nations or the Principles of Natural Law Applied to the Conduct and to the Affairs of Nations and Sovereigns*, pp. 274–75) is more inclined to recognize the rights of any sovereign to deny passage to protect his lands even against nonhostile forces.

23. "The king of England has given a written declaration . . . declaring that after what has transpired at Charleroi the king [Louis XIV] cannot be blamed for breaking the Treaty of Aix-la-Chapelle if he attacks the Spaniards." Louvois to Turenne, 8 May 1673, AG, A^1 315, fo. 203.

24. Louis replied to Monterey (20 May 1673, *Oeuvres*, 3:410): "Cousin, I was very pleased that you sent Don Franciso Antonio de Agusto as a representative of the queen regent expressly to welcome me to this country" (the Spanish Netherlands).

25. Paul Pellisson-Fontanier, *Lettres historiques, 1670–1688*, 1:276.

26. *Oeuvres*, 3:338.

27. J. B. Colbert's son, Seignelay, was on campaign with the French court and was ordered to write to his father about having a proper painter sent to record the great siege (Seignelay to Colbert, 12 June 1673, Bibliothèque Nationale [hereafter BN], nouvelles acquisitions françaises 9504, fo. 163). Van der Meulen's painting can be seen in the Louvre.

28. Monmouth to Arlington, 20 June 1673, Public Record Office, State Papers (hereafter PRO, SP), 78/137, fo. 113.

29. Vauban to Louvois, 28 June 1673, AG A^1 337, no. 223.

30. This is Louis XIV's description (*Oeuvres*, 3:390–91).

31. Louis XIV to Count d'Estrées, 30 June 1673, Archives Nationales (hereafter AN), série marine, B^2 21, fo. 24.

32. Colbert to Louis XIV, 4 July 1673, Louis XIV, *Oeuvres*, 3:412–13.

33. De Groot to Abraham de Wicquefort, 14 July 1673, in F. J. L. Krämer, ed., *Lettres de Pierre de Groot à Abraham de Wicquefort (1668–1674)*, p. 142.

34. Louvois to Turenne, 30 June 1673, AG, A^1 315, fo. 362.

35. Bertrand Auerbach (*La France et le Saint Empire romain germanique*, p. 80) wrote about Gravel as someone who "lived almost his entire life in foreign countries, depending upon himself alone, instructing his government more than he was instructed by it. He was one of the most remarkable examples of the type of diplomat that one meets in the seventeenth century. The places where he lived and the negotiations he conducted were not tempered by the boudoir and the salon the way diplomacy was in the eighteenth century."

36. Gravel to Pomponne, 3 July 1673, AAE, All. 266, fo. 12.

37. Courtin to Vitry (French special envoy in Munich), 5 July 1673, AAE, Cologne 11, fo. 130.

38. Louis's description (*Oeuvres*, 3:395–96).

39. Louvois to Condé, 12 May 1673, AG, A^1 315, fo. 219.

40. Condé to Louvois, 12, 20, 23 June 1673, AG, A^1 324, fos. 64, 139, 167.

41. The Swedes were heavily dependent on Dutch financial expertise and commercial power and were thus committed to preserving the republic. See below, chap. 4.

42. Louvois to Le Tellier, 24 June 1673, AG, A^1 315, fos. 341–42.

43. Louvois to Condé and Turenne, 1 July 1673, AG, A^1 316, fos. 1 ff.

44. Frederick the Great (*History of My Own Times*, 1:72) claimed that the French invented the portable copper pontoon in 1672. Most floating bridges, however, were still improvised from river barges.

45. Louvois to Turenne, 1 July 1673, AG, A¹ 316, fos. 4–5.

46. See below, chap. 4.

47. Louis XIV, *Oeuvres*, 3:397, n. 1.

48. Robert de Gravel to Louis XIV, 20 July 1673, AAE, All. 266, fos. 17–18.

49. Louis André, *Michel Le Tellier et Louvois*, p. 302; Georges Livet, *L'intendance d'Alsace sous Louis XIV, 1648–1715*, pp. 363–74.

50. Louvois to Fourilles, 23 July 1673, AG, A¹ 316, fos. 59–61.

51. *Recueil des instructions données aux ambassadeurs et ministres de France depuis les traités de Westphalia jusqu'à la révolution française, Mayence*, pp. 68–74.

52. Robert de Gravel's report (Gravel to Pomponne, 16 Feb. 1673, AAE, All. 265, fo. 42) of Johann Philipp's death gives us a remarkable portrait of a tough, seventeenth-century diplomat's mind. Gravel mixes piety with respect for a fellow statesman and with a shrewd awareness of his own master's best interests:

"I don't doubt that by the time this letter reaches you you will have learned of the rather sudden death of the elector of Mainz. . . . God rest his soul. He was a prince with great qualities . . . and he took affairs strongly to heart. . . . I revere his memory. But as a faithful and zealous servant and subject of the king, I cannot help myself from thinking, and indeed saying, that God has disposed of this prince at a time when he might have caused some damage to His Majesty's interests if he had remained in this world."

On Schönborn, see Georg Mentz, *Johann Philipp von Schönborn*.

53. *Recueil . . . Mayence*, p. 71.

54. Ibid.

55. After Turenne defeated the Brandenburgers and Imperials late in the winter of 1673, a small contingent of imperial soldiers remained in Germany instead of withdrawing into Bohemia with the bulk of the imperial army. In the spring they marched to garrison the elector of Trier's two Rhenish fortresses. See Persode de Maizery (a French agent in Frankfort) to Pomponne, 25 Apr. 1673, AAE, All. 271 supplement, fo. 145.

Grémonville (Louis XIV's special envoy to the imperial court) reported from Vienna (30 June 1673, AAE, Autriche 46, fo. 119) that a special Dutch envoy (Coenraad van Heemskerck) had been told by Leopold's government that an imperial army would probably be sent back into Germany.

56. Louis XIV to Gravel, 22 July 1673, AAE, All. 275, fo. 101.

57. See below, chap. 4.

58. Verjus de Crécy (French envoy in Berlin) to Pomponne, 4 Aug. 1673, AAE, Brandebourg 9, fo. 188.

59. Abbé de Gravel to Pomponne, 4 Aug. 1673, AAE, Mayence 13, fo. 232.

60. Robert de Gravel to Louis XIV, 10 Aug. 1673, AAE, All. 266, fos. 58–59.

61. Ibid., fo. 60.

62. Wilhelm von Fürstenberg to Pomponne, 5 Aug. 1673, AAE, Cologne 11, fos. 193–94. Abbé de Gravel, who was still in Mainz when Fürstenberg arrived there, found everyone in Germany suspicious of Fürstenberg. Gravel to Isaac de Pas, marquis de Feuquières (French ambassador to Sweden), 4 Aug. 1673, in Au-

guste A. Etienne-Gallois, ed., *Lettres inédites des Feuquières, 1631–1704* (hereafter *Lettres des Feuquières*), 2:218. See also Braubach, *Fürstenberg*, pp. 268–69.

63. Fürstenberg to Louis XIV, 4 Aug. 1673, AAE, Cologne 11, fos. 163–82.

64. Georges Pagès, *Contributions à l'histoire de la politique française en Allemagne sous Louis XIV*, p. 2. O'Connor ("Fürstenberg," pp. 127, 134) also emphasizes the close ties between Lionne and Wilhelm Egon and the similarity of their political ideas.

65. Turenne to Louvois, 18 July 1673, AG, A^1 347, no. 176.

66. Leopold I to Count F. E. Pötting (imperial ambassador to Spain), 12 July 1673, in *Privatbriefe Kaiser Leopold I an den Grafen F. E. Pötting, 1662–1673*, 2:337; Grémonville to Louis XIV, 17 July 1673, AAE, Autriche 46, fos. 155–56.

67. Louvois to Le Tellier, 25 July 1673, AG, A^1 316, fos. 74–75.

68. Memorandum of 5 July 1673, printed in A. F. Pribram, *Franz Paul von Lisola und die Politik seiner Zeit*, pp. 619–20.

69. Wilhelm von Fürstenberg to Pomponne, 11 Aug. 1673, AEE, Cologne 11, fo. 1210.

70. Louis XIV to Robert de Gravel, 27 July 1673, AAE, All. 275, fo. 103.

71. Condé to Louvois, 12 Dec. 1672, AG, A^1 281, nos. 205–9.

72. The duke fled into Germany with an army of 26,000 men. See Louis André, *Louis XIV et l'Europe*, pp. 127–28.

73. As a means of overcoming an impasse in the negotiations, the diplomats had intentionally left the extent of French jurisdiction in Alsace ambiguous when they drew up the Treaty of Münster. See Fritz Dickmann, *Der Westfälische Frieden*, pp. 482–85; Livet, *L'intendance d'Alsace*, pp. 385–86; Georges Bardot, *La question des dix villes impériales d'Alsace*, pp. 252–58.

74. Louvois to Condé, 19 Jan. 1673, AG, A^1 314, fo. 33.

75. Condé to Louvois, 30 Jan. 1673, AG, A^1 344, no. 108.

76. Livet, *L'intendance*, pp. 349–50. Charles-Armand had married Mazarin's niece, Hortense, and assumed the cardinal's surname.

77. Philippe de Montault, duc de Navailles, *Mémoires*, p. 268.

78. Louvois to Le Tellier, 16 Aug. 1673, AG, A^1 316, fos. 128–29.

79. Louis XIV, *Oeuvres*, 3:400–401. Louis wrote this in 1679 (Sonnino, "Mémoires de la guerre," p. 42).

80. Livet, *L'intendance*, pp. 370 ff. Chr. Pfister, "Louis XIV en Alsace: Le premier voyage (août–septembre 1673)," pp. 5–63.

81. Livet, *L'intendance*, p. 379; see also Bardot, *Villes d'Alsace*, pp. 257–58.

82. Gravel to Pomponne, 19 Aug. 1673, AAE, All. 266, fo. 81.

83. Charles-Armand de Mazarin also made his case for permitting a certain independence in Alsace directly to Robert de Gravel in Regensburg (Mazarin to Gravel, 27 Jan. 1673, AAE, All. 271, fo. 17).

84. Quoted in Livet, *L'intendance*, p. 122.

85. Louis XIV to Grémonville, 12 Aug. 1673, AAE, Autriche 46, fo. 251.

86. Louvois to Condé, 18 Aug. 1673, AG, A^1 316, fo. 138.

87. Louvois to Le Tellier, 22 Aug. 1673, AG, A^1 316, fo. 165; Louis XIV to Robert de Gravel, 26 Aug. 1673, AAE, A11. 275, fo. 20.

Louis sent a special emissary to the elector of Mainz to explain that he had decided to seize Trier only after it became "absolutely certain that the Spaniards had plans to place a garrison in the fortress. He [Louis] would have been neglecting his interests and all the imperatives of war, which are the most demanding laws in the world, if he had let that city fall into the hands of those who are so adverse to him." Instructions to Closier de Juvigny, 27 Aug. 1673, in *Recueil des instructions . . . Mayence*, p. 82.

88. Louis XIV to Gravel, 26 Aug. 1673, AAE, All. 275, fo. 120.

89. Louvois to Fourilles, 19 Aug. 1673, AG, A¹ 347, no. 334.

90. Ibid.

91. Fourilles to Louvois, 13, 17 Aug. 1673, AG, A¹ 325, fos. 257, 290.

92. Louvois to Montal, 1 Aug. 1673, AG, A¹ 312, no. 1.

93. Rousset (*Louvois*, 1:471) claims that a member of the staff of Monterey, governor of the Spanish Netherlands, informed Louvois about Monterey's plans to enter Trier with a body of troops, but Rousset does not document his source. René Pillorget ("La France et l'Electorate de Trèves au temps de Charles-Gaspard de la Leyen," p. 141) carelessly cites Rousset to demonstrate that Louis's seizure of Trier was a military necessity. I have found no evidence that Louvois had any information other than that provided to him by Fourilles.

94. Saint-Maurice, *Lettres*, 2:605.

95. Gilbert Burnet, *History of My Own Times*, 1:548.

96. Louvois to Gravel, 31 Aug. 1673, AG, A¹ 316, nos. 185–90.

97. Rochefort to Louvois, 27 Aug. 1673, in Henri Griffet, ed., *Recueil des lettres pour servir d'éclaircissement à l'histoire militaire du règne de Louis XIV*, 2:108–10.

98. See below, chap. 3.

99. Saint-Pouange to Louvois, 4 Sept. 1673, AG, A¹ 348, no. 21.

100. Louis XIV to Louvois, 7 Sept. 1673, AG, A¹ 348, nos. 30–32.

101. Gravel to Pomponne, 31 Aug. 1673, AAE, All. 274, fo. 110.

102. Pomponne to Gravel, 4 Sept. 1673, AAE, All. 266, fo. 92.

103. Turenne to Louvois, 29 Aug. 1673, AG, A¹ 347, no. 385.

104. Turenne to Louvois, 9 Aug. 1673, in P. H. Grimoard, ed., *Collection des lettres et mémoires trouvées dans les portefeuilles du maréchal de Turenne* (hereafter *Lettres de Turenne*), 2:312.

105. Courtin to Louvois, 7 Oct. 1673, AG, A¹ 328, fos. 73–74.

106. In 1673, it is possible Louis was also seeing one Mme. de Ludre (J. F. Michaud, "Ferry de Frolois de Ludre," *Biographie Universelle*, 25:454–55), prioress of a convent at Poussey in Lorraine and a lady-in-waiting to Louis's queen. In any case, *chansonniers* in Paris seized upon the possibility (BN, fonds français 12687, p. 151):

> *La Vallière was a commoner;*
> *Montespan came from the nobility;*
> *Mme. Ludre was a nun.*
> *All three serve only one man;*
> *He is the greatest of potentates,*
> *Who likes to assemble all the Estates.*

107. Saint-Maurice, *Lettres*, 2:527.

108. "It is said that the king will not leave on the 15th because Mme. de Montespan is in childbed and will not be up until the 25th, and if she is not the departure will be delayed even further" (ibid.).

109. Lisola to Hocher, 3 July 1673, in Onno Klopp, *Der Fall des Hauses Stuart*, 1:394.

110. "Since I wrote my note, the king sent for me. He was in Mme. de Montespan's quarters with M. de Louvois. He bade me enter and told me that because

the Spaniards might soon declare war I should send an express courier to Burgundy [with orders to prepare munitions in the province]." Seignelay to Colbert, 21 Aug. 1673, BN, nouvelles acquisitions 9504, fo. 188.

111. *Mémoires for the Instruction of the Dauphin*, p. 247.

112. Wolf, *Louis XIV*, p. xiii.

113. See below, chap. 3.

Chapter 3

1. Elector Frederick William allied with the Dutch in May 1672, promising military aid in return for financial subsidies. The following month, Frederick William and Emperor Leopold signed a defensive treaty for the protection of the empire; Louis XIV's army had technically violated German territory when Louis crossed the duchy of Cleves in his attack upon the Dutch. On Frederick William's tortuous diplomacy during this period see Georges Pagès, *Le Grand Electeur et Louis XIV, 1660–1688*, and Albert Waddington, *Le Grand Electeur Frédérick Guillaume de Brandenbourg, sa politique extérieure, 1640–88*.

2. See Julius Grossmann, "Raimund Montecuccoli, Ein Beitrag zur österreichischen Geschichte des siebzehnten Jahrhunderts, vornehmlich der Jahre 1672–1673," p. 417.

3. In this treaty (printed in Mignet, *Négociations*, 3:548–52), Leopold promised not to interfere in any war that Louis XIV might wage against England, Sweden, or the Dutch Republic, provided the French did not violate the Peace of Aix-la-Chapelle (1668).

4. Bernhard Erdmannsdörffer, *Deutsche Geschichte vom Westfälischen Frieden bis zum Regierungsantritt Friedrich's des Grossen, 1648–1740*, 1:573–75.

5. On Turenne's winter campaign see Camille G. Picavet, *Les dernières années de Turenne, 1660–1675*, and Ferdnand des Robert, *Les campagnes de Turenne en Allemagne, 1672–1674*.

6. Frederick William to Emperor Leopold, 20 Feb. 1673, in *Urkunden und Actenstücke zur Geschichte des Kurfürsten Friedrich Wilhelm von Brandenburg* (hereafter *UA*), 13:430.

7. Frederick William to Stratmann, 10 Mar. 1673, in ibid., p. 486.

8. See Meinders' instructions (12/13 May 1673) in ibid., pp. 502–6.

9. The treaty is known as the Treaty of Vossem because Meinders delivered Frederick William's ratification of the provisional articles to the French court at Vossem (just outside Brussels), 6 June 1673. On the negotiations that led to this treaty see Pagès, *Electeur*, pp. 298–328; Waddington, *Electeur*, pp. 284–312; Meinders's dispatches to Frederick William's court in *UA*, 13:506–40.

10. Louvois to Turenne, 6 June 1673, AG, A^1 315, fo. 284.

11. Although Frederick William resumed the war with France within a year, Pagès (*Electeur*, p. 330) points out that the elector was not simply buying time with the Treaty of Vossem but genuinely hoped that a general European peace would follow his accommodation with Louis XIV.

12. Louis XIV to abbé de Gravel, 18 Mar. 1673, AAE, Mayence 12, fo. 336.

13. Louvois to Turenne, 10 Apr. 1673, AG, A^1 315, fo. 124.

14. Turenne to Louvois, 29 Apr. 1673, AG, A^1 322, fo. 814.

15. Louvois to Turenne, 14 Mar. 1673, AG, A^1 314, fos. 230–36.

16. It seems apparent that most (if not all) diplomatic dispatches of any moment that were sent out over the king's signature were read to him word for word before they were drafted in final form for coding; see Sonnino, *Papacy*, p. 5.

17. Louis XIV to Robert de Gravel, 28 Apr. 1673, AAE, All. 275, fos. 60–61.

18. Grémonville to Louis XIV, 21 Apr. 1673, AAE, Autriche 45, fos. 268 ff.

19. Ibid., 27 Apr. 1673, ibid., fos. 273–75.

20. Pomponne to Grémonville, 13 May 1673, ibid., fo. 320.

21. Louvois to Turenne, 14 May 1673, AG, A¹ 315, fo. 224.

22. Ibid.

23. Turenne to Louvois, 2 May 1673, AG, A¹ 323, fo. 36.

24. Poduits (a spy of Turenne's) to Turenne, Apr. 1673, ibid., fo. 47.

25. Turenne to Louvois, 9 May 1673, ibid., fo. 213. The eastern frontier of France was vulnerable through Alsace, as Montecuccoli was to demonstrate in his campaign of 1675–76.

26. Abbé de Gravel to Louis XIV, 21 May 1673, AAE, Mayence 13, fo. 92.

27. Louvois to Turenne, 22 May 1673, AG, A¹ 315, fos. 244–45.

28. Pillorget, "France et Trèves," p. 138.

29. This is a possibility. Louvois wrote to Franz von Fürstenberg (27 May 1673, AG, A¹ 315, fo. 263): "The king has learned . . . that the garrison from Friedberg has marched toward Koblenz. . . . If it enters there, I will inform the elector of Trier that he had a choice of allowing a like number of the king's troops into the fortress or seeing his low lands devastated."

30. Louis XIV to Gravel, 22 May 1673, AAE, All. 275, fo. 66.

31. Grémonville to Robert de Gravel, 8 June 1673, AAE, Autriche 47, fo. 107.

32. Abbé de Gravel to Louis XIV, 21 May 1673, AAE, Mayence 13, fos. 92–93.

33. Abbé de Gravel to marquis de Feuquières (French ambassador to Sweden), 19 May 16 June 1673, in *Lettres des Feuquières*, 2:154, 162–63.

34. Turenne to Louvois, 23 May 1673, AG, A¹ 346, no. 269.

35. Franz von Fürstenberg to Pomponne, 26 May 1673, AAE, Cologne 11, fo. 65.

36. Wilhelm von Fürstenberg to Pomponne, 30 May 1673, ibid., fo. 73.

37. Ibid., fo. 74.

38. Robert de Gravel to Louis XIV, 7 June 1673, AAE, All. 265, fos. 132–35.

39. Ibid., fo. 132.

40. Grémonville was sending the same information to the French court (1 June 1673, AAE, Autriche 46, fo. 20).

41. Robert de Gravel to Pomponne, 7 June 1673, AAE, All. 265, fo. 149.

42. See Pomponne to Wilhelm von Fürstenberg, 23 May 1673, AAE, Cologne 11, fo. 51. Pomponne's defense of this policy is, however, markedly flat and may have been merely his official duty.

43. Wilhelm von Fürstenberg to Pomponne, 30 May 1673, ibid., fo. 74.

44. Louvois to Turenne, 14, 22 May, and 6 June 1673, AG, A¹ 315, fos. 223–25, 244–46, 284.

45. Louis XIV to Turenne, 6 June 1673, *Oeuvres*, 3:410.

46. Turenne to Louvois, 13 June 1673, AG, A¹ 347, no. 45.

47. Claude Badalo-Dulong (*Trente ans de diplomatie française en Al-*

lemagne, p. 206) errs in remarking that Louvois ordered Germany to be devastated by the French army in 1673.

48. The machinery established by the Le Telliers to supply French armies on campaign was designed to stop pillaging at home rather than abroad. See Louis André, *Michel Le Tellier et Louvois*, pp. 368–75.

49. Turenne to Gravel, 7 July 1673, quoted in Camille Picavet, *Les dernières années de Turenne, 1660–1675*, p. 360.

50. Louis XIV to Robert de Gravel, 28 Apr., 22 May 1673, AAE, All. 275, fos. 60–61, 66–67.

51. Pierre de Chassan to Louis XIV, 16 June 1673, AAE, Saxe 9, fo. 75; Verjus to Pomponne, 29 June 1673, AAE, Cologne 11, fos. 119–20.

52. Turenne to Louvois, 19 Jan. 1673, AG, A¹ 344, no. 63.

53. Persode de Maizery to Feuquières, 24 June 1673, *Lettres des Feuquières*, 2:168.

54. See Bertrand Auerbach, *La France et le Saint Empire romain germanique*, pp. 184–85.

55. Turenne to Louvois, 20 May 1673, AG, A¹ 346, no. 253.

56. Ibid.

57. Philippe Grimoard, *Histoire des quatres dernières campagnes du maréchal de Turenne en 1672, 1673, 1674, 1675.*

58. Napoleon I, *Mémoires écrits à Sainte-Hélène*, 5:94.

59. Picavet, *Les dernières années*, pp. 356–93.

60. Turenne to Louvois, 3 June 1673, AG, A¹ 324, fo. 10.

61. Maizery to Feuquières, 15 July 1673, *Lettres des Feuquières*, 2:209–10.

62. Turenne to Louvois, 15 July 1673, AG, A¹ 347, no. 169.

63. Turenne to Gravel, 2 July 1673, AAE, All. 271, fo. 282.

64. Turenne to Louvois, 12 July 1673, AG, A¹ 347, no. 154.

65. Louvois passed rumors that were circulating at the French court on to Turenne, who was in the field, which suggested that Turenne was not pursuing the Imperials as vigorously as he might. See Rousset, *Louvois*, 1:399–400; Picavet, *Les dernières années*, p. 323.

66. Louvois to Turenne, 29 July 1673, AG, A¹ 316, fo. 93.

67. Turenne to Louvois, 5 Aug. 1673, AG, A¹ 347, no. 274.

68. Ibid.

69. Louvois to Turenne, 9 Sept. 1673, AG, A¹ 316, fo. 219.

70. Plenipotentiaries to Pomponne, 8 Aug. 1673, AAE, All. 268, fos. 108–9.

71. See below, chap. 4.

72. See Louvois to Condé, 4 Aug. 1673, AG, A¹ 316, fo. 101; Louvois to Fourilles, 21 Aug. 1673, ibid., fo. 158; Louvois to Turenne, 2 Sept. 1673, ibid., fos. 192–93; Louvois to Turenne, 26 Sept. 1673, ibid., fo. 346.

73. Louvois to Turenne, 5 Sept. 1673, AG, A¹ 316, fos. 215–17.

74. Turenne to Louvois, 15 Sept. 1673, AG, A¹ 327, fos. 2–3.

75. Ibid., fo. 3.

76. Louvois to Turenne, 9 Sept. 1673, AG, A¹ 316, fos. 217–18.

77. Turenne's campaign of 1673 was one of several studied by Clausewitz (*Vom Kriege*, p. 798), which led him to conclude that in strategic maneuvers many specific and independent variables weigh more than abstract general rules in deciding the issue.

78. Quoted in Erdmannsdörffer, *Deutsche Geschichte*, 1:585.

79. See the letter posted in Eger on 20 Aug. 1673, in AAE, Mayence 13, fo. 253.

80. Abbé de Gravel to Louis XIV, 29 Aug. 1673, ibid., fo. 263.

81. Robert de Gravel to Louis XIV, 31 Aug. 1673, AAE, All. 266, fo. 89.

82. Williamson and Jenkins to Arlington, 12 Sept. 1673, in William Wynne, *Life of Sir Leoline Jenkins*, 1:98.

83. Louvois to Turenne, 9 Sept. 1673, AG, A¹ 316, fo. 215.

84. Turenne to Louvois, 15 Sept. 1673, AG, A¹ 327, fo. 4; Rousset, *Louvois*, 1:496; Picavet, *Les dernières années*, p. 365.

85. Charles de Marguetel de Saint-Évremond, "Parallèle de Condé et Turenne," *Oeuvres en prose*, 4:417.

86. Turenne to Louvois, 15 Sept. 1673, AG, A¹ 348, no. 76.

87. Ibid., 21 Sept. 1673, no. 110.

88. Alington to Arlington, 30 Sept. 1673, PRO, SP 78/138, fo. 104.

89. See Chamlay's letters to Louvois during the campaign in AG, A¹ 348.

90. Louvois to Turenne, 4, 21 Aug. 1673, AG, A¹ 316, fos. 106–7, 161.

91. Camus de Beaulieu (the intendant of Turenne's army) to Louvois, 22 Sept. 1673, AG, A¹ 327, fo. 252. Beaulieu kept up an extended correspondence with Louvois independently of Turenne.

92. Turenne to Louvois, 28 Sept. 1673, AG, A¹ 348, no. 150.

93. Ibid., 4 Oct. 1673, ibid., no. 189.

94. Ibid., 16 Oct. 1673, ibid., no. 255.

95. Alington to Arlington, 13 Oct. 1673, PRO, SP 78/138, fo. 125.

96. Turenne to Vitry (French special envoy in Munich), 22 Oct. 1673, AAE, All. 272, fo. 289.

97. Abbé de Gravel to Louis XIV, 16 Oct. 1673, AAE, Mayence 14, fos. 28–29.

98. Beaulieu to Louvois, 28 Oct. 1673, AG, A¹ 329, fo. 85.

99. Persode de Maizery to Vitry, 17 Oct. 1673, AAE, All. 272, fo. 265.

100. Turenne to Louvois, 21 Oct. 1673, AG, A¹ 348, no. 295.

101. Ibid., 6 Aug. 1673, *Lettres de Turenne*, 2:309–310.

102. Louvois to Turenne, 28 Oct. 1673, AG, A¹ 317, fo. 379.

103. Turenne to Louvois, 21 Oct. 1673, AG, A¹ 348, no. 295.

104. See abbé de Gravel's letters to Turenne and the French court in AAE, Mayence 14, fos. 44–77.

105. Turenne to Louvois, 26 Oct. 1673, AG, A¹ 329, fos. 21–23.

106. Winston S. Churchill, *Marlborough: His Life and Times*, 1:100.

107. Alington to Arlington, 29 Oct. 1673, PRO, SP 78/138, fo. 136.

Chapter 4

1. Violet Barbour, *Capitalism in Amsterdam in the Seventeenth Century*, pp. 111–12, 118–19.

2. When the Triple Alliance was renewed on 31 January 1670, Spain agreed to accept the burden of subsidizing Sweden in return for a Swedish commitment to help keep the French out of the Spanish Netherlands. See Rowen, *Ambassador*, pp. 94–101.

3. The provisions of the Treaty of Stockholm are given in Mignet, *Négociations*, 3:365–374.

4. In the instructions provided (7 Oct. 1672; *Recueil des instructions* . . .

Suède, p. 137) for the marquis de Feuquières when he was about to replace Honoré Courtin as French ambassador to Sweden, Louis XIV noted that he had accepted the Swedish offer to mediate.

5. K. H. D. Haley, *William of Orange and the English Opposition, 1672–74*, pp. 113–14.

6. Abraham de Wicquefort, *Histoire de Provinces-Unies des Païs Bas*, 4:631–32.

7. Louis XIV to Courtin (ambassador to Sweden in 1672), 14 Oct. 1672, AAE, Suède 41, fo. 114.

8. Ibid.

9. Ibid., 25 Nov. 1673, ibid., fo. 229.

10. Louis XIV to Feuquières, 6 Feb. 1673, in *Lettres de Feuquières*, 2:89. The *minute* of the king's dispatch (AAE, Suède 42, fo. 84) is interesting because in its original form it shows that Pomponne, who drafted the king's diplomatic dispatches, was more flexible than Louis. The *minute* reads: "to calm the suspicions of Sweden is my principal goal in this affair."

11. Louis XIV to Colbert de Croissy, 25 Feb. 1673, AAE, Angleterre 109, fo. 60.

12. Louvois to Luxembourg, 11 Mar. 1673, AG, A¹ 314, fo. 195.

13. Louvois to Turenne, 1 Apr. 1673, AG, A¹ 346, no. 1.

14. See Pierre de Ségur, *Le maréchal de Luxembourg et le prince d'Orange: 1666–1688*, chap. 7; Rousset, *Louvois*, 1:408–12.

15. Dutch military commanders were continuing to flood the countryside in spring 1673, although they had to kill protesting peasants to do so. See Prince Jean-Maurice of Nassau to the prince of Orange, 23 May 1673, in Gulielmus Groen van Prinsterer, ed., *Archives ou correspondance inédite de la maison d'Orange-Nassau*, 5:318–19.

16. Luxembourg to Louvois, 17 Mar. 1673, AG, A¹ 333, no. 142.

17. Louvois to Luxembourg, 25 Mar. 1673, AG, A¹ 314, fo. 271.

18. After Turenne's successful winter campaign, the imperial army had withdrawn into Bohemia.

19. Louvois to Rochefort (royal commander in Nancy), 31 Mar. 1673, AG, A¹ 345, no. 194.

20. Vitry to Pomponne, 24 May 1673, AAE, Bavière 8, fo. 143.

21. Louvois to Stoppa, 8 May 1673, AG, A¹ 315, fos. 200–201.

22. Jean Héraut de Gourville, *Mémoires*, 24:543.

23. Pomponne to Chaulnes and Courtin, 23 May 1673, AAE, A11. 270 bis, fo. 25.

24. Chaulnes and Courtin to Louis XIV, 30 May 1673, AAE, A11. 267, fos. 26–30; Max Braubach, *Kurköln: Gestalten und Ereignisse aus zwei Jahrhunderten rheinischer Geschichte*, p. 44.

25. Chaulnes and Courtin to Pomponne, 30 May 1673, ibid., fo. 32.

26. Courtin to Condé, 6 June 1673, Archives de Chantilly, papiers de Condé, P 47, fo. 132.

27. Chaulnes and Courtin to Pomponne, 3 June 1673, AAE, All. 267, fos. 44–45.

28. Williamson and Jenkins to Arlington, 16 June 1673, in Wynne, *Jenkins*, 1:14–15.

29. Chaulnes and Courtin to Pomponne, 10 June 1673, AAE, All. 267, fo. 54.

30. Louvois, quoted in Rousset, *Louvois*, 1:445.
31. Pomponne to plenipotentiaries, 9 June 1673, AAE, All. 270 bis, fo. 29.
32. *Recueil des instructions . . . Hollande*, 1:316.
33. Plenipotentiaries to Louis XIV, 24 June 1673, AAE, All. 267, fo. 94.
34. Although the "cautionary" towns that the English demanded on the Dutch coast were ostensibly to be held only as security until their other demands were met, it is clear that the English wanted a toehold on the Continent. See the pertinent clauses in the secret Treaty of Dover (Mignet, *Négociations*, 3:194) and Charles II's instructions to his plenipotentiaries, Williamson and Jenkins (Wynne, *Jenkins*, 1:4).
35. Williamson and Jenkins to Arlington, 30 June 1673, in Wynne, *Jenkins*, 1:21–22.
36. The brothers Fürstenberg were also at Maastricht for the siege (see Braubach, *Fürstenberg*, pp. 266–67).
37. Courtin to Louvois, 10 June 1673, AG, A^1 347, no. 34.
38. Ibid., 14 June 1673, ibid., no. 47.
39. This was information that Tott let out when he returned to Cologne. Plenipotentiaries to Pomponne, 8 July 1673, AAE, All. 267, fo. 126; Williamson and Jenkins to Arlington, 11 July 1673, in Wynne, *Jenkins*, 1:28.
40. This is how Louis recounted Tott's remarks in a dispatch sent 6 July to Colbert de Croissy in London (*Lettres des Feuquières*, 2:187–90).
41. Ibid., p. 191.
42. Louis XIV to plenipotentiaries, 7 July 1673, AAE, All. 270 bis, fo. 43.
43. See secret article 1 of the treaty in Mignet, *Négociations*, 3:366–67.
44. Louis XIV to Croissy, 6 July 1673, in *Lettres des Feuquières*, 2:192.
45. Williamson and Jenkins to Arlington, 13 July 1673, in Wynne, *Jenkins*, 1:32–33.
46. Albizzi, the papal nuncio in Vienna, remarked about Leopold: "If one may say so, I would like to see him place a little less trust in God, so that he would be more alert in the face of danger and decisive in dealing with it." Quoted in Oswald Redlich, *Geschichte Österreichs*, 6:113.
47. Courtin to Pomponne, 18 July 1673, AAE, All. 268, fo. 30; Pieter de Groot to Abraham de Wicquefort, 22 Aug. 1673, in Krämer, ed., *Lettres de Pieter de Groot*, p. 155.
48. Williamson and Jenkins to Arlington, 13 July 1673, in Wynne, *Jenkins*, 1:33.
49. Plenipotentiaries to Louis XIV, 18 July 1673, AAE, All. 268, fo. 18.
50. Plenipotentiaries to Pomponne, ibid., fo. 29.
51. Croissy to Louis XIV, 24 July 1673, AAE, Angleterre 107, fo. 113.
52. Plenipotentiaries to Pomponne, 5 Aug. 1673, AAE, All. 268, fo. 99.
53. Ibid., 8 Aug. 1673, ibid., fo. 105.
54. Williamson and Jenkins to Arlington, 7 Aug. 1673, in Wynne, *Jenkins*, 1:53.
55. Louis XIV to plenipotentiaries, 4, 10 Aug. 1673, AAE, All. 268, fos. 82–85, 113, 115.
56. 4 Aug. 1673, ibid., fo. 85.
57. 9 Aug. 1673, ibid., fo. 111.
58. Pomponne to plenipotentiaries, 10 Aug. 1673, ibid., fo. 115.
59. Plenipotentiaries to Louis XIV, 14 Aug. 1673, ibid., fos. 127–28.
60. Plenipotentiaries to Pomponne, 14 Aug. 1673, ibid., fo. 137.

61. Williamson and Jenkins to Arlington, 15 Aug. 1673, in Wynne, *Jenkins*, 1:63. However, Charles II's concessions at the bargaining table did not prevent him from continuing to plan a landing on the Dutch coast. See below, chap. 7.

62. Williamson and Jenkins to Arlington, 15 Aug. 1673, in Wynne, *Jenkins*, 1:64.

63. Croissy to Louis XIV, 7, 10 Aug. 1673, AAE, Angleterre 107, fos. 142, 150; Croissy to Pomponne, 10 Aug. 1673, ibid., fo. 153.

64. Louis XIV to plenipotentiaries, 17 Aug. 1673, AAE, All. 268, fos. 141–43.

65. Louvois to Louis Robert (intendant of the French army in the Netherlands), 20 Aug. 1673, AG, A¹ 316, fos. 152–53; Louvois to Courtin, 20 Aug. 1673, AG, A¹ 347, no. 341; Louis XIV to plenipotentiaries, 17 Aug. 1673, AAE, All. 268, fos. 141–43; Pomponne to plenipotentiaries, 17 Aug. 1673, ibid., fo. 45; Pomponne to Count Tott, 17 Aug. 1673, ibid., fo. 146.

66. Plenipotentiaries to Louis XIV, 21 Aug. 1673, ibid., fos. 165–66.

67. Williamson and Jenkins to William Lockhart (English ambassador with the French court), 14 Aug. 1673, in Wynne, *Jenkins*, 1:60.

68. Plenipotentiaries to Louis XIV, 19 Aug. 1673, AAE, All. 268, fos. 147–50.

69. A. F. Pribram, *Franz Paul von Lisola und die Politik seiner Zeit*, pp. 610–12.

70. Leopold I to Count Pötting (imperial ambassador to Spain), 12 July 1673, *Privatbriefe Kaiser Leopold I*, 2:337; Grémonville to Louis XIV, 30 June 1673, AAE, Autriche 46, fo. 119.

71. Pribram, *Franz Paul von Lisola*, pp. 620–22.

72. Plenipotentiaries to Pomponne, 23 Sept. 1673, AEE, All. 269, fo. 90.

73. Jean DuMont, ed., *Corps universel diplomatique du droit des gens*, 7: pt. 1, 240–44; Max Immich, *Geschichte des Europäischen Staatensystems, 1660–1789*, p. 78.

74. Louis XIV to plenipotentiaires, 23 Aug. 1673, AAE, All. 268, fo. 179.

75. Plenipotentiaries to Louis XIV, 25 Aug. 1673, ibid. fo. 192.

76. Plenipotentiaries to Louis XIV, 31 Aug. 1673, ibid., fo. 215.

77. Louvois to Condé, 4 Sept. 1673, AG, A¹ 316, fo. 200.

78. Louvois to Louis Robert, 7 Sept. 1673, ibid., fo. 206.

79. Louis XIV to plenipotentiaries, 10 Sept. 1673, AAE, All. 270 bis, fo. 100.

80. Pomponne to Feuquières, 5 Sept. 1673, AAE, Suède 43, fos. 113–14; Pomponne to Feuquières, 3 Nov. 1673, ibid., fo. 174.

81. Courtin to Louvois, 16 Sept. 1673, AG, A¹ 348, no. 81.

82. Louvois to Courtin, 21 Sept. 1673, AG, A¹ 316, fos. 302–3.

83. Louis XIV to plenipotentiaries, 26 Sept. 1673, AAE, All. 269, fos. 92 ff.

84. Louvois to Courtin, 8 Oct. 1673, AG, A¹ 317, fo. 85.

85. Wicquefort to De Groot, 18 Sept. 1673, Krämer, ed., *Lettres de Pierre de Groot*, p. 174.

86. Ibid., p. 175.

87. Courtin to Louvois, 19 Dec. 1673, AG, A¹ 331, fos. 378–79.

88. Louis XIV, *Mémoires*, p. 37.

89. After he had signed the Treaty of Stockholm in April 1672, for example, Courtin generously credited Pomponne with having done the important work:

"The treaty is the result of the esteem and good will that M. de Pomponne generated here during his first embassy" (Courtin to Louis XIV, 15 Apr. 1672, in Mignet, *Négociations*, 3:375).

90. Courtin to Pomponne, 19 Sept. 1673, AAE, All. 269, fo. 82.

91. Pomponne to Courtin, 26 Sept. 1673, ibid., fo. 98.

92. Pomponne to Colbert, 30 Sept. 1673, BN, mélanges Colbert 165 bis, fo. 738.

93. Courtin to Louvois, 3 Oct. 1673, AG, A¹ 348, no. 188.

94. Courtin to Pomponne, 14 Oct. 1673, AAE, All. 269, fo. 160.

95. Pomponne to Courtin, 21 Oct. 1673, AAE, All. 270 bis, fo. 137.

96. Dutch plenipotentiaries to Swedish ambassadors, 9 Oct. 1673, AAE, All. 272, fo. 244.

97. Louis XIV, *Mémoires*, p. 87.

98. *Recueil . . . Hollande*, 1:314.

99. Pomponne to plenipotentiaries, 10 Oct. 1673, AAE, All. 270 bis, fo. 125.

100. Courtin to Louvois, 4 Nov. 1673, AG, A¹ 349, no. 30.

101. Gravel to Vitry, 9 Oct. 1673, AAE, All. 272, fo. 249.

102. Louis XIV to plenipotentiaries, 18 Nov. 1673, AAE, All. 270, fos. 23–24.

103. Louvois to Courtin, 16 Nov. 1673, AG, A¹ 349, no. 130.

104. Louvois to Wilhelm von Fürstenberg, 5 Oct. 1673, AG, A¹ 317, fo. 61.

105. Louvois to Courtin, 16 Nov. 1673, AG, A¹ 349, no. 130.

106. Franz Paul von Lisola, *Détention de Guillaume de Fürstenberg*, p. 9.

107. Ibid., p. 94.

108. Lisola (ibid., p. 79) justified the seizure of Fürstenberg by describing him as a virtuoso of evil to compare with Milton's Satan: "He has violated the laws of the empire and employed all sorts of trickery, fraud and impostures, and perhaps also charms and spells, to oblige the elector [of Cologne] to make war against his friends and neighbors in the Empire." John T. O'Connor ("William Egon von Fürstenberg and French Diplomacy in the Rhineland Prior to the Outbreak of the War of the League of Augsburg in 1688," pp. 8, 34, 35) has pointed out that within the political context of seventeenth-century Europe the Fürstenberg brothers can hardly be branded traitors to Germany. Stephen Baxter (*William III and the Defense of European Liberty, 1650–1702*, p. 127) argues that the charges of treason leveled against Wilhelm Egon by Emperor Leopold had a "certain plausibility." See Braubach (*Kurköln*, pp. 67–70; *Fürstenberg*, pp. 283–86) for a detailed description of the kidnaping.

109. Chaulnes did good service for the crown in Brittany. In the "stamped paper" rebellion of 1675, a war that taxation helped to provoke, his good judgment contributed to taming the revolt. See Roland Mousnier, *Fureurs paysannes*, pp. 139–56.

110. Plenipotentiaries to Louis XIV, 14 Nov. 1673, AAE, All. 269, fos. 297–98.

111. Louis XIV to plenipotentiaries, 25 Nov. 1673, AAE, All. 270 bis, fos. 175–76.

112. Pomponne to plenipotentiaries, 26 Nov. 1673, ibid., fo. 179.

113. Courtin to Louvois, 5 Dec. 1673, AG, A¹ 330, fo. 341.

114. Ibid., fo. 343.

115. Courtin to Louvois, 8 Dec. 1673, AG, A¹ 331, fos. 90, 93.

116. Courtin to Pomponne, 5 Dec. 1673, AAE, All. 270, fo. 132.

117. Pomponne to plenipotentiaries, 28 Nov. 1673, All. 270 bis, fo. 181.
118. Louvois to Courtin, 19 Dec. 1673, AG, A¹ 349, no. 331.
119. Pomponne to Courtin, 19 Dec. 1673, AAE, All. 270 bis, fo. 220. Italics mine.
120. Louvois to Courtin, 17 Dec. 1673, AG, A¹ 317, fos. 766–67.
121. Herbert H. Rowen, "Arnauld de Pomponne: Louis XIV's Moderate Minister," pp. 531–49; Paul Sonnino, "Arnauld de Pomponne, Louis XIV's Minister for Foreign Affairs during the Dutch War," pp. 49–60.

Chapter 5

1. In the marriage contract, Marie's renunciation of her rights was made expressly contingent upon payment of the dowry (see article 4 of the contract in Henri Vast, *Les grands traités du règne de Louis XIV*, 1:179). It was probably the idea of Hugues de Lionne, who assisted Mazarin in negotiating the Peace of the Pyrenees and became Louis's foreign minister in 1661, to have Marie Thérèse's renunciation qualified with the phrase "moyennant le paiement effectif fait à S.M.T.C. des dits 500 mille écus d'or." See Vast, *Traités*, 1:179, n. 1.
2. See Antoine Bilain, *Traité des droits de la reyne très-chrétienne, sur divers états de la monarchie d'Espagne*; M. Dupuy, *Traitez touchant les droits du roy très-chrestien sur plusieurs estats et seigneuries possédés par divers princes voisins*.
3. See Rowen, *Ambassador*, esp. chap. 6.
4. Mignet, *Négociations*, 2:323–481; Jean Bérenger, "Une tentative de rapprochement entre la France et l'Empereur: le traité de partage secret de la Succession d'Espagne du 19 janvier 1668," pp. 291–314.
5. Herbert H. Rowen, "John de Witt and the Triple Alliance," pp. 1–14; Waldemar Westergaard, *The First Triple Alliance: The Letters of Christopher Lindenov, Danish Envoy to London, 1668–1672*, pp. 1–78.
6. On Louis XIV's desire to wage war with Spain in the early 1670s see Paul Sonnino, "Louis XIV and the Dutch War," pp. 155–56.
7. Louvois to Condé, 1 Nov. 1671, quoted in Mignet, *Négociations*, 3:665.
8. Although no primary documents, in the strict sense, have yet been adduced to prove that Louvois was largely responsible for convincing Louis XIV to reject the Dutchmen's preliminary peace offers in summer 1672, contemporaries thought that the war minister was responsible, and historians have agreed. See Wicquefort, *Histoire des Provinces-Unies*, 4:433–34; Antoine de Pas, marquis de Feuquières (eldest son of Isaac de Pas), *Memoirs of the Late Marquis de Feuquières*, 2:19–21; André, *Le Tellier*, p. 213; Mignet, *Négociations*, 4:32; Rousset, *Louvois*, 1:378; Rowen, "Pomponne," p. 542.
   I recently found an original letter that tends to support this consensus. Early in 1674, Isaac de Pas (marquis de Feuquières), the French ambassador in Sweden, wrote to Pomponne about the deteriorating situation in Germany: "I would like to learn from your lips . . . why the elector of Trier has been so mistreated . . . if I did not know that the same genius who refused peace with the Dutch is responsible" (Feuquiéres to Pomponne, 3 Feb. 1674, AAE, Suède 46, fo. 79).
9. See below, chap. 7.
10. Louis XIV to Louvois, 19 Dec. 1672, AG, A¹ 282, no. 141.
11. Ibid., 21 Dec. 1672, ibid., no. 73.

12. Ibid., 22 Dec. 1672, *Oeuvres*, 3:273. I could not locate this letter in AG, but it gives every appearance of being authentic.

13. Ibid., 23 Dec. 1672, AG, A¹ 291, no. 116.

14. "Since receiving . . . Your Majesty's orders about Franche-Comté, I have sent Sieurs de Ricous and de Rivière to reconnoitre the fortresses and to send me a complete report on the strength of the area" (Condé to Louis XIV, 27 Dec. 1672, AG, A¹ 282, no. 188).

15. Louis XIV to Louvois, 24 Dec. 1672, AG, A¹ 282, no. 140.

16. Ibid., 26 Dec. 1672, ibid., no. 186.

17. Ibid., 29 Dec. 1672, ibid., no. 251.

18. Louvois to Condé, 7 Jan. 1673, AG, A¹ 314, fo. 8.

19. Louvois to Turenne, 1 Apr. 1673, AG, A¹ 346, no. 3.

20. Louvois to Humières, 20 Apr. 1673, AG, A¹ 315, fo. 107.

21. *Recueil des instructions . . . Hollande*, 1:339.

22. Ibid., pp. 339–40.

23. Le Tellier to Louvois, 14 Apr. 1668, quoted in André, *Le Tellier*, p. 180.

24. Wolf, *Louis XIV*, pp. 231–32.

25. Vauban to Louvois, 19(?) Jan. 1673, AG, A¹ 337, no. 111. Nelly Girard d'Albissin (*Genèse de la frontière franco-belge: les variations des limites septentrionales de la France de 1659 à 1789*, p. 160) errs in dating this letter 4 Oct. 1675. Vauban wrote *another* letter on that date (see Gaston Zeller, *L'organisation défensive des frontières du Nord et de l'Est au XVIIe siècle*, p. 61), using the phrase "pré carré."

26. Vauban to Louvois, 22 Dec. 1673, AG, A¹ 340, no. 287. Italics mine.

27. Louvois to Vauban, 24 Jan. 1673, quoted in Rousset, *Louvois*, 1:431.

28. Condé to Louvois, 11 Jan. 1673, AG, A¹ 344, no. 33.

29. Zeller, *L'organisation défensive*, p. 61.

30. *Oeuvres*, 3:426–41.

31. Ibid., p. 434.

32. Louis XIV to Courtin and Barrillon, 25 Nov. 1673, AAE, All. 270 bis, fo. 176.

33. Girard d'Albissin, *Genèse de la frontière*, pp. 162–67; Zeller, *L'organisation défensive*, p. 109.

34. Girard d'Albissin, *Genèse*, chap. 5.

35. See above, chap. 2, n. 23.

36. See below, chap. 7.

37. *Oeuvres*, 3:303–4.

38. Navailles to Louvois, 4 June 1673, AG, A¹ 324, fos. 22–23.

39. Louvois to Navailles, 15 June 1673, AG, A¹ 315, fo. 303.

40. Villars to Louis XIV, 4 June 1673, quoted in Mignet, *Négociations*, 4:181.

41. Villars to Louis XIV, 2 Aug. 1673, AAE, Espagne 62, fo. 202.

42. Louis André, *Louis XIV et L'Europe*, pp. 55–56.

43. Alberti (Venetian envoy to England) to the doge and Senate, 21 July 1673, in *Calendar of State Papers and Manuscripts Relating to English Affairs Existing in the Archives and Collections of Venice and in other Libraries of Northern Italy* (hereafter CSPV), 38:76.

44. Louvois to Condé, 21 Aug. 1673, AG, A¹ 316, fos. 155–56.

45. Ibid., 30 Aug. 1673, ibid., fo. 181.

46. Ibid., 7 Sept. 1673, ibid., fo. 204.
47. Ibid., 4 Sept. 1673, ibid., fos. 200–201.
48. Louvois to Saint-Romain, 12 Sept. 1673, ibid., fos. 237–38.
49. Pomponne to Colbert, 13 Sept. 1673, AAE, Mémoires et Documents, France 298, fo. 17.
50. The declaration is given in AG, A^1 316, fos. 329–31.
51. Louvois to Turenne and Condé, 26 Sept. 1673, ibid., fos. 342 ff.
52. Ibid., fo. 342.
53. Turenne to Louvois, 21 Sept. 1673, AG, A^1 348, no. 110.
54. Condé to Louvois, 19 Sept. 1673, AG, A^1 327, fo. 135.
55. Louis had been exposed to the Spanish war at an early and impressionable age. See Wolf, *Louis XIV*, pp. 28–29.
56. Louvois to Condé, 26, 28 Sept. 1673, AG, A^1 316, fos. 342–44, 356–63.
57. Pomponne to plenipotentiaries, 26 Sept. 1673, AAE, All. 269, fo. 97.
58. Louis XIV to plenipotentiaries, 26 Sept. 1673, ibid., fos. 92 ff.
59. Louvois to Condé, 26 Sept. 1673, AG, A^1 316, fo. 343.
60. Louvois to Condé, 28 Sept. 1673, ibid., fo. 357.
61. Villars to Louis XIV, 14 Sept. 1673, AAE, Espagne 62, fos. 233 ff.
62. Condé to Estrades, 16 Oct. 1673, BN, fonds Clairambault 581, fo. 615.
63. Louvois to Condé, 16 Oct. 1673, AG, A^1 317, fo. 140.
64. Louvois to Rochefort, Charuel, and Navailles, 16 Oct. 1673, ibid., fo. 144.
65. Perwich (an English informant in Paris) to Arlington, 7 Oct. 1673, in *The Despatches of William Perwich*, p. 266.
66. Ibid., 18 Oct. 1673, ibid., p. 267.

Chapter 6

1. Most accounts of the Dutch War do not deal with this crucial withdrawal. The best account now available is in Pierre de Ségur, *Le maréchal de Luxembourg et le prince d'Orange: 1666–1688*, pp. 263–71.
2. Louis XIV's brief account of the French withdrawal from Holland (*Oeuvres*, 3:453–55) was not written until 1678, by which time Louis could conveniently forget about his setbacks of five years earlier. See Sonnino, "Mémoires de la guerre," p. 49.
3. Luxembourg to Louvois, 1 Sept. 1673, AG, A^1 326, fos. 137–38.
4. Louvois to Luxembourg, 13 Sept. 1673, AG, A^1 316, fos. 243–44.
5. Louvois to Condé, 17 Sept. 1673, ibid., fo. 266.
6. Louis XIV to Luxembourg, 20 Sept. 1673, ibid., fo. 298.
7. Luxembourg to Louvois, 12 Sept. 1673, AG, A^1 336, no. 26.
8. Louvois to Courtin, 21 Sept. 1673, AG, A^1 316, fo. 303.
9. Louvois to Luxembourg, 15 Oct. 1673, AG, A^1 336, no. 111.
10. Luxembourg to Louvois, 24 Oct. 1673, AG, A^1 328, fos. 645–50.
11. Turenne to Louvois, 4 Oct. 1673, AG, A^1 348, no. 189.
12. Louvois to Turenne, 20 Oct. 1673, AG, A^1 317, fos. 229–30.
13. Ségur (*Maréchal de Luxembourg*, p. 263) notes that Louvois had "several weeks of trouble," but then argues that toward the end of October Louvois "seemed to be pulling himself together, finding once again his coolness, perceptiveness and decisiveness." My argument is that Louvois was floundering all through October and November 1673.

14. Louvois to Condé, 15 Oct. 1673, AG, A¹ 317, fo. 129.
15. Condé to Louvois, 18 Oct. 1673, AG, A¹ 328, fo. 405.
16. Louvois to Condé, 18 Oct. 1673, AG, A¹ 317, fo. 186.
17. Condé to Louvois, 20 Oct. 1673, AG, A¹ 328, fo. 472.
18. Louvois to Rochefort, 20 Oct. 1673, AG, A¹ 317, fos. 242–43.
19. Louvois to Luxembourg, 21 Oct. 1673, ibid., fo. 253.
20. Louis XIV, *Oeuvres*, 3:454–55.
21. Louvois to Condé and Luxembourg, 22, 23 Oct. 1673, ibid., fos. 263–315.
22. Louis XIV to Luxembourg, 23 Oct. 1673, AG, A¹ 336, no. 127.
23. Louvois to Luxembourg, 23 Oct. 1673, ibid., fos. 301–2.
24. See Luxembourg to Louvois, 17 Nov. 1672 (quoted in Rousset, *Louvois*, 1:393), in which Luxembourg seemed to relish describing the burning of peasant dwellings in which men, women, and children were sleeping.
25. The wanton destruction and the atrocities that had accompanied the French conquest of Dutch territory in 1672 were largely prevented during the withdrawal of 1673. Louvois ordered Luxembourg (24 Oct. 1673, AG, A¹ 317, fo. 331) to collect a "furious" sum of money from the Dutch in return for not looting or burning the towns. The French could no longer allow their soldiers to pillage; they needed money to sustain the war. For a firsthand account of the French withdrawal from Utrecht see Wicquefort, *Histoire des Provinces-Unies*, 4:603–12.
26. Luxembourg to Louvois, 27 Oct. 1673, AG, A¹ 329, fo. 38.
27. See the letters from Louis Robert (Luxembourg's intendant) to Louvois (10, 14 Nov. 1673, AG, A¹ 340, nos. 45, 62) in which Robert remarks that the war minister had miscalculated the strength of Luxembourg's army and describes the chaos in Utrecht as the French prepared to evacuate the city.
28. Louvois to Turenne, 1 Nov. 1673, AG, A¹ 317, fos. 426–27.
29. Turenne to Louvois, 10 Nov. 1673, AG, A¹ 329, fo. 286.
30. Reveillon, the commander of the French garrison that had defended Bonn, described these details to Louvois in a lengthy dispatch: Reveillon to Louvois, 6 Dec. 1673, AG, A¹ 343, no. 273.
31. Oswald Redlich, *Weltmacht des Barock: Österreich in der Zeit Kaiser Leopold I*, p. 124.
32. Chassan to Pomponne, 8 Dec. 1673, AAE, Saxe 9, fo. 251.
33. Louvois to Verjus (French envoy in Berlin), 20 Dec. 1673, quoted in Georg B. Depping, *Geschichte des Krieges der Münsterer und Cölner im Bündnisse mit Frankreich, gegen Holland in den Jahren 1672, 1673 und 1674*, p. 300.
34. Louis XIV to Feuquières, 24 Nov. 1673, AAE, Suède 43, fo. 208.
35. Perwich to Arlington, 15 Nov. 1673, PRO, SP 78/138, fo. 160.
36. Feuquières, *Memoirs*, 1:125.
37. Courtin to Louvois, 21 Oct. 1673, AG, A¹ 328, fos. 540–42.
38. See Braubach, *Kurköln*, pp. 1–2, 15–16; *Fürstenberg*, pp. 275–76.
39. Turenne to Louvois, 14 May 1673, AG, A¹ 323, fo. 308.
40. "Mémoire pour servir d'instruction au sieur Verjus, envoyé extraordinaire de Sa Majesté en Allemagne," 19 Mar. 1673, in *Recueil des instructions . . . Prusse*, pp. 192–96.
41. Wilhelm von Fürstenberg to Pomponne, 6 Apr. 1673, AAE, Cologne 10, fo. 443.

42. Max Heinrich to Louis XIV, 2 May 1673, AAE, Cologne 11, fo. 13.
43. Franz von Fürstenberg to Pomponne, 2 May 1673, ibid., fo. 18. One week later, however, Franz Egon, adept in the serpentine politics of the Rhenish states, wrote disingenuously to the bishop of Münster about the great advantage it would be to have Brandenburg out of the war (William Kohl, *Christoph Bernhard von Galen*, p. 382, n. 68).
44. Louis XIV to Max Heinrich, 23 May 1673, AAE, Cologne 11, fo. 50.
45. Pomponne to Wilhelm von Fürstenberg, 23 May 1673, ibid., fo. 51.
46. Louvois first served on Louis XIV's high council as interim foreign minister after Lionne's death in September 1671. Pomponne returned from his embassy in Stockholm to take charge of the foreign ministry in January 1672. Rousset (*Louvois*, 1:341) remarks that after this experience as foreign minister Louvois "never ceased to influence diplomacy."
47. Louvois to Wilhelm von Fürstenberg, 8 Apr. 1673, AG, A¹ 315, fos. 53–54.
48. Courtin to Louvois, 4 Nov. 1673, AG, A¹ 349, no. 30.
49. Louvois to Wilhelm von Fürstenberg, 30 Oct. 1673, AG, A¹ 317, fos. 389–90.
50. Courtin to Louvois, 23 Nov. 1673, AG, A¹ 349, no. 179. The countess was apparently an unusually generous woman, for Courtin also remarked to Louvois (ibid.) that exempting her estates "will also please M. Sparr [a Swedish diplomat], one of our negotiators who is just as in love as Prince Wilhelm."
51. Ibid., 17 Feb. 1674, in Depping, *Geschichte des Krieges*, p. 321.
52. See below, chap. 7.
53. Williamson and Jenkins to Arlington, 17 Nov. 1673, in Wynne, *Jenkins*, 1:162–63.
54. See below, chap. 7.
55. Rousset (*Louvois*, 1:501) argued that Louvois's "vigorous resolution" concerning the evacuation of the Dutch Netherlands is an honor to his "intelligence, good sense and cool-headedness." This one of Rousset's few lapses in judgment in his unsurpassed biography of the war minister.
56. Courtin to Louvois, 26 Nov. 1673, in Depping, *Geschichte des Krieges*, pp. 293–94.
57. See above, chap. 5, n. 8.
58. Louis XIV to Louvois, 22 Dec. 1672, AG, A¹ 282, no. 101.
59. Louvois to Condé, 29 Jan. 1673, AG, A¹ 344, no. 65.
60. Louvois to Louis XIV, 18 July 1673, AG, A¹ 316, fo. 42.
61. Louis XIV to Louvois, 19 July 1673, AG, A¹ 324, fo. 378.
62. Saint-Maurice, *Lettres*, 2:586. Louvois's father, Le Tellier, had suffered a stroke in December 1672 and was not yet functioning at full capacity (André, *Le Tellier*, p. 220).
63. Louis XIV to Louvois, 7 Sept. 1673, AG, A¹ 348, nos. 30–32.
64. Saint-Maurice, *Lettres*, 2:606.
65. Ibid.
66. Condé wrote to Louvois from Flanders (6 Sept. 1673, AG, A¹ 312, no. 56): "I confess that it is a little mortifying for me ... to be as useless as I have been during this campaign."
67. See Luxembourg to Condé (5 Sept. 1673, quoted in Henri d'Orleans, duc d'Aumale, *Histoire des princes de Condé, pendant les XVIe et XVIIe siècles*, 8:404–5): "You know this country [Utrecht]; one should not be abandoned here

the way I am. M. de Louvois informs me that I have a large number of infantry, but he is including those that are being used to garrison fortresses and outposts, and he shall see that almost none remain for any campaigning."

68. All their contemporaries agreed upon this. See, for example, Mme. de Sévigné to Mme. de Grignan, 29 Dec. 1673, in Marie de Rabutin-Chantal de Sévigné, *Lettres*, 3:339; Louis-Henri de Loménie, comte de Brienne, *Mémoires*, 2:284; Louis Hector, duc de Villars, *Mémoires*, p. 30.

69. Ezechiel Spanheim, *Relation de la cour de France en 1690*, p. 187; Charles Auguste, marquis de La Fare, *Mémoires et réflexions sur les principaux événements du règne de Louis XIV*, pp. 272–73; André, *Le Tellier*, pp. 234–36.

70. Villars, *Mémoires*, p. 30.

71. Gourville to Condé, 11 Jan. 1674, Archives de Chantilly, papiers de Condé, P 56, fo. 19.

72. Condé requested a command for his son (Condé to Louvois, 6 Sept. 1673, Archives de Chantilly, papiers de Condé, P 52, fos. 64–65) and in the spring of 1674 Louvois wrote to Condé (9 May 1674, AG, A¹ 380, fo. 19) from the royal army that had invaded Franche-Comté: "M. le Duc is satisfying the king here in every respect. And the faithful servants of Your Highness, among whom I believe I have the honor of being included, could not wish for more." Louvois's tone in dealing with Condé was far more respectful than in spring 1673.

73. Rousset, *Louvois*, 1:512.

74. Villars, *Mémoires*, pp. 30–31.

75. Louvois to Courtin, 23 Jan. 1674, AG, A¹ 379, no. 78.

76. Perwich to Arlington, 10 Dec. 1673, PRO, SP 78/138, fo. 169.

77. BN, fond français 12687, p. 205.

78. See Turenne's letter to Louis XIV of January 1674 (*Oeuvres de Louis XIV*, 3:424–25), in which Turenne recounts a conciliatory conversation he had with the war minister. Although this letter has never been found in the archives, and there is some doubt as to its authenticity, it seems that when Louvois and Turenne concluded that their row was a standoff, each decided that it was in his best interests to reconcile their differences.

Chapter 7

1. Quoted in F. P. G. Guizot, *History of Oliver Cromwell and the English Commonwealth*, 2:222.

2. Maurice Lee Jr., *The Cabal*, pp. 95–97; Rowen, "Triple Alliance," pp. 1–14.

3. See the provisions of the Treaty of Dover in Mignet, *Négociations*, 3:187–99. On the complex negotiations preceding the treaty see Lee, *The Cabal*, pp. 101–12; Rowen, *Ambassador*, chap. 9. In December 1670 a second treaty was signed; this was the *traité simulé*, or phony treaty, which did not include the clauses pertaining to Charles II's proposed conversion to Roman Catholicism and which was designed to prevent an immediate uproar in England. See Mignet, *Négociations*, 3:256–65.

4. K. H. D. Haley (*The First Earl of Shaftesbury*, pp. 316–17) has pointed out that Shaftesbury's speech stemmed from political calculation rather than hatred of the Dutch, but in any case it was a successful speech in the Commons.

5. K. H. D. Haley, *William of Orange and the English Opposition, 1672–74*, pp. 97–98.

6. John Evelyn, *Diary*, p. 585.

7. Alberti to the doge and Senate, 30 June 1673, *CSPV*, 38:68.

8. Haley, *English Opposition*, p. 98.

9. Croissy to Colbert, 5 Mar. 1673, AAE, Angleterre 109, fo. 120.

10. Gilbert Burnet, *History of My Own Times*, 2:18.

11. Croissy to Pomponne, 5 Mar. 1673, AAE, Angleterre 106, fo. 123.

12. Pomponne to Croissy, 5 Apr. 1673, ibid., 109, fo. 126.

13. Louis XIV to Croissy, 13 Mar. 1673, AAE, Angleterre 109, fos. 94–96.

14. Croissy to Louis XIV, 20 Mar. 1673, ibid., 106, fo. 152.

15. Croissy to Colbert, 30 Mar. 1673, ibid., 109, fo. 121.

16. Pomponne to Verjus, 25 Mar. 1673, AAE, Brunswick-Hanovre 2, fo. 412.

17. *Recueil . . . Hollande*, 1:311, 319, 343.

18. Louis XIV to Croissy, 6 July 1673, in *Lettres des Feuquières*, 2:193.

19. Louis XIV to plenipotentiaries, 7 July 1673, AAE, Allemagne 270 bis, fos. 43 ff.; ibid., 9 Aug. 1673, ibid., 268, fo. 111.

20. Alberti to the doge and Senate, 14 July 1673, *CSPV*, 38:71.

21. "We all went after dinner to see the formal, & formidable Camp, on Black-heath, raised to invade Holland, or as others suspected for another designe etc." (Evelyn, *Diary*, p. 587). The fanatical Protestants in England suspected that Charles II had plans to use military force to impose Catholicism on the country. Charles never had any such plans, of course.

22. Lockhart to Arlington, 25 July 1673, PRO, SP 78/137, fo. 231.

23. Louvois to Condé, 1 July 1673, AG, A¹ 316, fos. 1–2.

24. Louvois to Turenne, 10 July 1673, quoted in Rousset, *Louvois*, 1:467.

25. Sluis was the most important of these towns. Article 7 of the secret treaty (Mignet, *Négociations*, 3:194) guaranteed it to England once the French and English had won the war.

26. Courtin to Condé, 1 Aug. 1673, AG, A¹ 325, fos. 137–39.

27. Williamson and Jenkins to Arlington, 8 Aug. 1673, in Wynne, *Jenkins*, 1:57.

28. Ibid., 1 Aug. 1673, ibid., p. 47.

29. Lockhart to Williamson and Jenkins, 4 Aug. 1673, PRO, SP 78/138, fo. 250. Italics mine.

30. Courtin to Pomponne, 8 Aug. 1673, AAE, All. 268, fo. 108.

31. See Charles de la Roncière, *Histoire de la marine française*, 5:550–51.

32. Rupert to Arlington, 29 May 1673 (O.S.), in *Calendar of State Papers Domestic (hereafter CSPD)*, 15:309.

33. "It only remains for me to rejoice with you over your recent splendid action" (Colbert to Estrées, 12 June 1673, AN, Série marine B⁴ 305, fo. 352).

34. Croissy to Colbert, 22 June 1673, BN, mélanges Colbert 164, fo. 573.

35. Stephen Baxter, *William III and the Defense of European Liberty, 1650–1702*, p. 104.

36. Martel's "Journal," AN, Série marine B⁴ 5, fo. 81.

37. From Prince Rupert's relation of the battle, *CSPD*, 15:521.

38. Pieter Geyl, *The Netherlands in the Seventeenth Century*, pt. 2, pp. 142–43.

39. Colbert to Saint-Aignan, 21 June 1673, in Clément, ed., *Lettres*, 3:493.

40. See *CSPD*, 15:520–21.

41. Croissy to Colbert and Seignelay, 28 Aug. 1673, BN, mélanges Colbert 165 bis, fo. 452.

42. Eugene Suë, *Histoire de la marine française*, vol. 2, bk. 5, chap. 1.

43. See especially "Mémoire pour servir à l'information sécrette de ce qui s'est passé dans l'armée navalle pendant le dernière campagne 1673" (AN, série marine B⁴ 5, fos. 198 ff.).

44. Louis XIV to plenipotentiaries in Cologne, 9 Aug. 1673, AAE, Allemagne 268, fo. 111.

45. Croissy to Colbert, 31 Aug. 1673, BN mélanges Colbert 165 bis, fo. 502.

46. Croissy to Colbert and Seignelay, 7 Sept. 1673, ibid., fos. 558, 560.

47. Croissy to Seignelay, 11 Sept. 1673, ibid., fos. 592—93.

48. Colbert to Croissy, 13 Sept. 1673, AN, série marine B² 23, fo. 132.

49. Cf. Martel's "Journal," AN, série marine B⁴ 5, fos. 79 ff.; Martel to Croissy, 6 Sept. 1673, ibid., fos. 166 ff.; "Relation of the French Squadron, sent to Prince Rupert by Monsr. Martel, Vice Admiral," *CSPD*, 15:529—31. See also Croissy to Colbert, 18 Sept. 1673 (BN, mélanges Colbert 165 bis, fo. 709), where Croissy implied that Rupert took advantage of Martel's political naivete and used him to make the French admiral, Estrées, look bad.

50. "Mémoire pour servir à l'information," AN, série marine B⁴ 5, fo. 198.

51. Colbert to Estrées, 20 Sept. 1673, in Clément, ed., *Lettres*, 3:pt. 1, 507, n. 2.

52. Henry Ball to Williamson, 8 Sept. 1673, in W. D. Christie, ed., *Letters Addressed from London to Sir Joseph Williamson while Plenipotentiary at the Congress of Cologne*, 1:191.

53. Ibid., 15 Sept. 1673, ibid., 2:13.

54. Croissy to Colbert, 14 Sept. 1673, BN, mélanges Colbert 165 bis, fo. 631.

55. Alberti to the doge and Senate, 8 Sept. 1673, *CSPV*, 38:106.

56. Wicquefort to de Groot, 21 Sept. 1673, in Krämer, ed., *Lettres de Pierre de Groot*, p. 181.

57. Croissy to Colbert, 30 Mar. 1673, AAE, Angleterre 109, fo. 120.

58. See Croissy to Louis XIV, 7, 10 Aug. 1673, AAE, Angleterre 107, fos. 142, 150; Croissy to Pomponne, 10 Aug. 1673, ibid., fo. 153.

59. Croissy to Colbert, 18 Sept. 1673, BN, mélanges Colbert 165 bis, fo. 649.

60. Alberti to the doge and Senate, 13 Oct. 1673, *CSPV*, 38:138.

61. Croissy to Louis XIV, 20 Nov. 1673, quoted in Mignet, *Négociations*, 4:233.

62. Alberti to the doge and Senate, 10 Nov. 1673, *CSPV*, 38:170.

63. See Lee, *The Cabal*, pp. 224—25; Keith Feiling, *British Foreign Policy, 1660—1672*, pp. 352—53.

64. The marriage by proxy had taken place in Modena in early October 1673 (Paolo Sarotti [Venetian resident in Milan] to the doge and Senate, 11 Oct. 1673, *CSPV*, 38:134—35). John Evelyn remarked (5 Nov. 1673 [o.s.], *Diary*, p. 594) that "the youths of the Citty burnt the Pope in Effigie after they had made procession with it in greate triumph; displeased at the D [York]: for altering his Religion, & now marrying an Italian Lady etc:."

65. Croissy to Louis XIV, 27 Nov. 1673, AAE, Angleterre 108, fo. 134.

66. Ibid., 22 Dec. 1672, ibid., 104, fos. 221—23.

67. Alberti to the doge and Senate, 10 Nov. 1673, *CSPV*, 38:170.
68. John Wilmot, earl of Rochester, *Poems*, p. 111. Carewell was a popular English form of the name of Louise Renée de Kéroualle, duchess of Portsmouth, a French girl whom Louis XIV had presented to Charles II at the time of the Treaty of Dover. She became one of Charles's favorite mistresses. Teague was a contemptuous name for an Irish Roman Catholic.
69. Quoted in Feiling, *British Foreign Policy*, p. 356.
70. Alberti to the doge and Senate, 17 Nov. 1673, *CSPV*, 38:174.
71. See Haley, *English Opposition*.
72. Croissy to Pomponne, 14 Sept. 1673, AAE, Angleterre 107, fos. 207–8.
73. Croissy to Pomponne, 25 Sept. 1673, ibid., fo. 22.
74. Lee, *The Cabal*, p. 237. Italics mine.
75. Aubeville to Pomponne, 26 Sept. 1673, AAE, Portugal 12, fos. 233–36.
76. Louis XIV to Croissy, 2 Oct. 1673, AAE, Angleterre 110, fos. 118–20.
77. Croissy to Louis XIV, 30 Oct. 1673, ibid., 108, fos. 55–56.
78. Aubeville to Louis XIV, 4 Dec. 1673, AAE, Portugal 12, fo. 269.
79. Alberti to the doge and Senate, 20 Sept., 3 Nov. 1673, *CSPV*, 38:121, 163.
80. Ibid., 20 Oct. 1673, ibid., 143.
81. Pomponne to Gravel, 15 Feb. 1674, AAE, Allemagne 275, fo. 20.
82. Du Mont, *Corps*, 7: pt. 1, 253–54.
83. See Lee, *The Cabal*, chap. 3.

Chapter 8

1. De Witt, quoted in Lavisse, *Histoire de France*, 7: pt. 2, 281.
2. Rousset (*Louvois*, 1:517–40) gives the entire text of Louis's memoir for the campaign of 1672. Paul Sonnino has masterfully analyzed the manuscript of this memoir and demonstrated ("Mémoires de la guerre," pp. 29–50) that it was written in 1678.
3. "The ambassadors [from the States General] offered all the towns in the Generality lands. . . . It could be said that the States General, in offering all of the Generality towns to France, would have made the king master of the United Provinces and of all the Low Countries" (Wicquefort, *Histoire des Provinces-Unies*, 4:433).
4. "The least progress that you could make there [near Naarden] would be a mortal blow to the Dutch" (Louvois to Condé, 12 May 1673, AG, A^1 315, fo. 219).
5. Victor-L. Tapié, "Quelques aspects de la politique étrangère de Louis XIV," p. 6. William F. Church ("Louis XIV and Reason of State," p. 387) has remarked that "even in this war [the Dutch War], which he [Louis] undertook for highly personal reasons, he associated these with the interests of the state."
6. Courtin to Louvois, 16 Sept. 1673, AG, A^1 348, no. 81.
7. Colbert to Croissy, 6 Dec. 1673, AN, série marine B^2 23, fos. 175–76.
8. Pierre Goubert, *Louis XIV et vingt millions de français*, pp. 85–95; Lavisse, *Histoire de France*, 7: pt. 1, 177–205.
9. Cole remarked (*Colbert and a Century of French Mercantilism*, 1:445): "By this time [1671] it had become clear that a war was almost inevitable, a war of which the peace-loving Colbert approved, a war brought on as much (perhaps more) by economic rivalry as by Louis's avidity for conquest or by any political

considerations." However, Paul Sonnino ("Arnauld de Pomponne, Louis XIV's Minister for Foreign Affairs during the Dutch War," p. 50) has questioned whether Colbert *ever* supported Louis's plans for war against the Dutch.

10. Colbert to Jean Talon, 4 June 1672, in Clément, ed., *Lettres*, 3: pt. 2, 542.

11. Colbert to Louis XIV, 14 Aug. 1673, ibid, 2: pt. 1, lxxxvii. Of course, it was no coincidence that in 1673 Louis attempted to increase royal revenues by extending, for the first time, the *régale* to all the provinces of France (see H. G. Judge, "Louis XIV and the Church," p. 249).

12. Perwich to Arlington, 7 Oct. 1673, PRO, SP 78/138, fo. 114.

13. Ibid., 18 Oct. 1673, ibid., fo. 134.

14. Cole, *Colbert and French Mercantilism*, 2:551.

15. See duke of Chaulnes (royal governor in Brittany) to Colbert, 16 June 1675, In Georg B. Depping, ed., *Correspondance administrative sous le règne de Louis XIV*, 1:258; Mousnier, *Fureurs paysannes*, p. 134. The stamp tax also created a furor in Languedoc, where the merchants in the provincial estates objected vehemently to the new impost (Bishop of Mirepoix to Colbert, 11 Dec. 1673, in Depping, ed., *Correspondance*, 1:303–4).

16. Perwich to Arlington, 10 Dec. 1673, PRO, SP/138, fo. 168.

17. Lavisse, *Histoire de France*, 7: pt. 1, 176.

18. Church, "Louis XIV and Reason of State," p. 370.

19. Hatton, "Louis XIV and His Fellow Monarchs," pp. 164–65, 174–75.

20. Charles de Secondat, baron de Montesquieu, *De l'esprit des Lois*, 2:6.

21. Thomas Paine, *Common Sense and Other Political Writings*, p. 10.

22. Pierre Goubert, *L'ancien régime*, 2:114.

23. Ibid., 2:113.

24. John C. Rule, "Louis XIV, Roi-Bureaucrate," pp. 3–101.

25. John B. Wolf, "Louis XIV, Soldier-King," p. 196.

26. Joseph Schumpeter, *Imperialism and Social Classes*, p. 77.

27. Louis XIV to Louvois, 27 Dec. 1672, AG, A^1 282, no. 204. See also Louis's description of the siege at Maastricht (*Oeuvres*, 3:325–90) as a revealing document on the king's frame of mind at this time.

28. Louis XIV to Condé, 31 Dec. 1672, AG, A^1 282, no. 267.

29. Saint-Simon remarked (*Mémoires*, 28:38–39, 392) upon Louis's tendency to become absorbed with minutiae rather than the substance of affairs.

30. Emmanuel Le Roy Ladurie, *Les paysans de Languedoc*, 2:602. Sometimes it seems that, in its enthusiasm, the Annales school goes too far to discount such events as wars. See, for example, Goubert, *L'ancien régime* (1:40–41), where he seems to say that warfare in seventeenth-century France had a deleterious effect on the population *exclusively* in those provinces where fighting occurred, thus glossing over the consequences of extra taxation, economic dislocation, the billeting of troops, the spread of diseases, etc.

31. Voltaire, *The Age of Louis XIV*, p. 126.

32. Zeller, *Les temps modernes*, p. 49.

Bibliography

1. Manuscript Sources

Paris:
Archives des Affaires Etrangères (AAE)
  1. Correspondance Politique
    Allemagne: 265–70, 270 bis, 271, 271 supplément, 272, 272 supplément, 273–75.
    Angleterre: 106–11.
    Autriche: 45–47.
    Bavière: 2, 7–9.
    Brandebourg: 8, 9.
    Brunswick-Hanovre: 2.
    Cologne: 10, 11.
    Espagne: 62.
    Hollande: 92.
    Mayence: 11–14.
    Portugal: 12.
    Saxe: 9–11.
    Suède: 41–46.
  2. Mémoires et Documents
    France: 298.
    Hollande: 26.

Archives Nationale (AN)
Série Marine, B²: 21–23; B⁴: 5, 305.
Bibliothèque Nationale (BN)
  1. Fonds Clairambault: 581.
  2. Fonds Français: 12686–88.
  3. Mélanges Colbert: 164, 165, 165 bis.
  4. Nouvelles Acquisitions Françaises: 9504, 9505.
Vincennes:
Archives de la Guerre (AG)
Série A¹: 281, 282, 314–17, 322–31, 337, 340, 343–49, 379, 380, 410.
Chantilly:
Archives de Chantilly
Série P. (Papiers de Condé): 46–56.
London:
Public Record Office (PRO)
State Papers 78: 137, 138.

2. Printed Sources

Bilain, Antoine. *Traité des droits de la reyne très-chrétienne sur divers états de la monarchie d'Espagne*. Paris, 1667.
Brienne, Louis Henri de Loménie, comte de. *Mémoires*. Edited by F. Barrière. 3 vols. Paris: Ponthieu et Cie, 1828.
Burnet, Gilbert. *History of My Own Times*. Edited by Osmund Airy. 2 vols. Oxford: Clarendon Press, 1897–1900.

Calendar of State Papers of the Reign of Charles II, Domestic Series, Vol. 15 edited by F. H. Blackburne Daniell. London: Longmans, 1902.

Calendar of State Papers and Manuscripts Relating to English Affairs Existing in the Archives and Collections of Venice and in Other Libraries of Northern Italy. Vol. 38 edited by Allen B. Hinds. London: Longmans, 1941.

Christie, William Dougal, ed. Letters Addressed from London to Sir Joseph Williamson while Plenipotentiary at the Congress of Cologne. 2 vols. London: Camden Society, 1874.

Clément, Pierre, ed. Lettres, instructions et mémoires de Colbert. 7 vols. Paris: Imprimerie Royale, 1861–82.

Depping, Georg B., ed. Correspondance administrative sous le règne de Louis XIV. 4 vols. Paris: Imprimerie Royale, 1850–55.

Dumont, Jean, ed. Corps universel diplomatique du droit des gens. 8 vols. Amsterdam, 1726–31.

Dupuy, M. Traitez touchant les droits du Roy très chrestien sur plusieurs estats et seigneuries possédées par divers prince voisins. Rouen, 1670.

Etienne-Gallois, Auguste Alphonse, ed. Lettres inédites des Feuquières, 1631–1704. 5 vols. Paris: Leleux, 1845–46.

Evelyn, John. Diary. Edited by E. S. de Beer. London and New York: Oxford University Press, 1959.

Fénelon, François de Salignac de la Mothe. Ecrits et lettres politiques. Edited by C. Urbain. Paris: Editions Bossard, 1920.

Feuquières, Antoine de Pas, marquis de. Memoirs of the Late Marquis de Feuquières. 2 vols. London, 1737.

Griffet, Henri, ed. Recueil des lettres pour servir d'éclaircissement à l'histoire militaire du règne de Louis XIV. 4 vols. The Hague, 1740–41.

Grimoard, P. H., ed. Collection des lettres et mémoires trouvées dans les portefeuilles du maréchal de Turenne. 2 vols. Paris, 1782.

Groen van Prinsterer, Gulielmus, ed. Archives ou correspondance inédite de la maison d'Orange-Nassau. 2d series, 1584–1688. 5 vols. Utrecht, 1835–96.

Krämer, F. J. T., ed. Lettres de Pierre de Groot à Abraham de Wicquefort (1668–74). The Hague: M. Nijhoff, 1894.

La Fare, Charles Auguste, marquis de. Mémoires et réflexions sur les principaux événements du règne de Louis XIV. In Nouvelle collection des mémoires pour servir à l'histoire de France. Edited by J. F. Michad and J. J. F. Poujoulat. Série 3, vol. 8. Paris, 1839.

Leopold I. Privatbriefe Kaiser Leopold I an den Grafen F. E. Pötting, 1662–1673. Edited by A. F. Pribram and Moriz von Pragenau. 2 vols. in 1. Vienna: C. Gerold's Sohn, 1903–4.

Lisola, Franz Paul, Freiherr von. Détention de Guillaume, prince de Fürstenberg nécessaire pour maintenir l'authorité de l'empereur, la tranquillité de l'empire et pour procurer une paix juste, utile, et nécessaire. Amsterdam, 1674.

——. Remarques sur le discours du Commandeur de Grémonville. The Hague, 1673.

Louis XIV. Mémoires for the Instruction of the Dauphin. Translated and edited by Paul Sonnino. New York: Free Press, 1970.

——. Oeuvres. Edited by Ph. H. Grimoard and Ph. A. Grouvelle. 6 vols. Paris, 1806.

Navailles, Philippe de Montault, duc de. Mémoires. Amsterdam, 1701.

Pellisson-Fontanier, Paul. Lettres historiques. 3 vols. Paris, 1729.

Perwich, William. The Despatches of William Perwich, English Agent in Paris,

1669–1677. Edited by M. Beryl Curran. London: Royal Historical Society, 1903.

Pomponne, Simon Arnauld, marquis de. *Mémoires.* Edited by J. Mavidal. 2 vols. Paris: Huet, 1868.

Primi-Visconti. *Mémoires sur la cour de Louis XIV.* Translated and edited by Jean Lemoine. Paris: Calmann-Levy, 1908.

Recueil des instructions données aux ambassadeurs et ministres de France depuis les traités de Westphalie jusqu'à la Révolution française. Vol. 1, *Autriche,* edited by Albert Sorel. Paris: Alcan, 1884. Vol. 2, *Suède,* edited by Albert Geffroy. Paris: Alcan, 1885. Vol. 16, *Prusse,* edited by Albert Waddington. Paris: Alcan, 1901. Vol. 18, *Diet germanique,* edited by Bertrand Auerbach. Paris: Alcan, 1912. Vol. 22, *Hollande–1* (1648–98), edited by Louis André and Emile Bourgeois. Paris: E. de Bocard, 1922. Vol. 25, *Angleterre–2* (1660–98), edited by J. J. Jusserand. Paris: E. de Bocard, 1929. Vol. 26, *Venise,* edited by Pierre Duparc. Paris: Centre National de la Recherche Scientifique, 1958. Vol. 28, *Etats allemands,* pt. 1, *Mayence,* edited by Georges Livet. Paris: Centre National de la Recherche Scientifique, 1962. Pt. 2, *Cologne,* edited by Georges Livet. Paris: Centre National de la Recherche Scientifique, 1963. Pt. 3, *Trèves,* edited by Georges Livet. Paris: Centre National de la Recherche Scientifique, 1966.

Saint-Evremond, Charles de Marguetel, seigneur de. *Oeuvres en prose.* Edited by René Ternois. 4 vols. Paris: Marcel Didier, 1962–69.

Saint-Maurice, Thomas François, marquis de. *Lettres sur la cour de Louis XIV.* Edited by Jean Lemoine. 3 vols. Paris: Calmann-Lévy, 1911–12.

Saint-Simon, Louis de Rouvroy, duc de. *Mémoires.* Edited by A. de Boislisle. 41 vols. Paris: Hachette et Cie, 1879–1928.

Sévigné, Marie de Rabutin-Chantal de. *Lettres.* Edited by M. Monmerqué. 14 vols. Paris: Hachette et Cie, 1862–66.

Spanheim, Ezechiel. *Relation de la cour de France en 1690.* Edited by Ch. Schefer. Paris: Société de l'Histoire de France, 1882.

Temple, William, Sir. *Works.* 4 vols. Edinburgh, 1754.

Urkunden und Actenstücke zur Geschichte des Kurfürsten Friedrich Wilhelm von Brandenburg. Vol. 13 edited by Reinhold Brode. Berlin, 1864.

Van Malssen, P. J. W., ed. *Louis XIV d'après les pamphlets répandus en Hollande.* Amsterdam: H. J. Paris, 1937.

Vast, Henri, ed. *Les grands traités du règne de Louis XIV.* 3 vols. Paris: A. Picard, 1893–99.

Villars, Louis-Hector, duc de. *Mémoires.* Edited by the marquis de Vogüé. Paris: Société de l'Histoire de France, 1884.

Wicquefort, Abraham de. *Histoire des Province-Unies des Païs-Bas.* Edited by M. L. Ed. Lenting and C. A. Chais van Buren. 4 vols. Amsterdam: F. Muller, 1861–74.

Wilmot, John, earl of Rochester. *Poems.* Edited by Vivian De Sola Pinto. Cambridge, Mass.: Harvard University Press, 1953.

Wynne, William. *Life of Sir Leoline Jenkins.* 2 vols. London, 1724.

3. Secondary Works

André, Louis. *Louis XIV et l'Europe. L'évolution de l'humanité,* no. 64. Paris: Albin Michel, 1949.

————. Michel Le Tellier et l'organisation de l'armée monarchique. Paris: Alcan, 1906.

————. Michel Le Tellier et Louvois. Paris: A. Colin, 1942.

Auerbach, Bertrand. La diplomatie française et la cour de Saxe (1648–1680). Paris: Hachette, 1888.

————. La France et le Saint Empire romain germanique. Paris: H. Champion, 1912.

Aumale, Henri Eugene Philippe, duc d'. Histoire des princes de Condé pendant les XVIe et XVIIe siècles. 7 vols. Paris: Calmann-Levy, 1863–96.

Badalo-Dulong, Claude. Trente ans de diplomatie française en Allemagne: Louis XIV et l'Electeur de Mayence (1648–1678). Paris: E. Plon, 1956.

Barbour, Violet. Capitalism in Amsterdam in the Seventeenth Century. Baltimore: Johns Hopkins University Press, 1950.

Bardot, Georges. La question des dix villes impériales d'Alsace. Paris: A. Picard et Fils, 1899.

Baxter, Douglas. Servants of the Sword: French Intendants of the Army, 1630–70. Urbana: University of Illinois Press, 1976.

Baxter, Stephen. William III and the Defense of European Liberty, 1650–1702. London: Longmans, 1966.

Bérenger, Jean. "Une tentative de rapprochement entre la France et l'Empereur: le traité de partage secret de la Succession d'Espagne du 19 janvier 1668." Revue d'histoire diplomatique 74 (1965): 291–314.

Bohmer, H. "Forschungen zur französischen Bündnispolik im 17 Jahrhundert: Wilhelm Egon von Fürstenberg und die französische Diplomatie in Deutschland, 1668–1672." Rheinische Vierteljahrsblätter 4 (1934): 225–59.

Braubach, Max. "Eine Wirtschaftsenquête am Rhein im 17 Jahrhundert." Rheinische Vierteljahrsblätter 13 (1949): 51–86.

————. Kurköln; Gestalten und Ereignisse aus zwei Jahrhunderten rheinischer Geschichte. Münster: Aschendorff, 1949.

————. Wilhelm von Fürstenberg (1629–1704) und die französische Politik im Zeitalter Ludwigs XIV. Bonn: L. Röhrscheid, 1972.

Church, William F. "Louis XIV and Reason of State." In Louis XIV and the Craft of Kingship. Edited by John C. Rule. Columbus: Ohio State University Press, 1969, pp. 362–406.

————. Louis XIV in Historical Thought: From Voltaire to the Annales School. New York: Norton, 1976.

————. Richelieu and Reason of State. Princeton, N.J.: Princeton University Press, 1972.

Churchill, Winston S. Marlborough: His Life and Times. 5 vols. New York: Charles Scribner's Sons, 1933.

Clausewitz, Karl von. Vom Kriege. Bonn: Dümmler, 1966.

Cole, Charles Weolsey. Colbert and a Century of French Mercantilism. 2 vols. New York: Columbia University Press, 1939.

Depping, Georg B. Geschichte des Krieges der Münsterer und Cölner im Bündnisse mit Frankreich, gegen Holland in den Jahren 1672, 1673 und 1674. Münster: Theissing, 1840.

Des Robert, Ferdinand. Les campagnes de Turenne en Allemagne (1672–1675). Nancy: Sidot Frères, 1883.

Dickmann, Fritz. Der Westfälische Frieden. Münster: Aschendorff, 1965.

Döberl, Michael. Bayern und Frankreich, vornehmlich unter Kurfürst Ferdinand-Maria. 2 vols. Munich: C. Haushalter, 1900–3.

Elzinga, Simon. *Het voorspel van dan oorlog van 1672: De economisch-politieke betrekkingen tusschen Frankrijk en Nederland in de jaren 1660–1672.* Haarlem: H. D. Tjeenk, Willink & Zoon, 1926.

Erdmannsdörffer, Bernhard, *Deutsche Geschichtge vom Westfälischen Frieden bis zum Regierungsantriff Friedrich's des Grossen, 1648–1740.* 2 vols. Berlih: G. Grote, 1892–93.

Feiling, Keith. *British Foreign Policy, 1660–1672.* London: Macmillan, 1930.

Flassan, Gaëtan de Raxis de. *Historie générale et raisonnée de la diplomatie française.* Paris, 1811.

Frederick the Great. *History of My Own Times.* Translated by Thomas Holcroft. London, 1789.

Fruin, Robert, *De oorlog van 1672.* Groningen: Wolters-Noordhoff, 1972.

Geyl, Pieter. Review of *Het voorspel van dan oorlog van 1672*, by Simon Elzinga. In *History*, new series 13 (1928): 162–63.

―――. *The Netherlands in the Seventeenth Century.* Pt. 2, *1648–1715.* New York: Barnes and Noble, 1966.

Gillot, Hubert. *Le règne de Louis XIV et l'opinion publique en Allemagne.* Nancy: A. Crepin-Leblond, 1914.

Girard d'Albissin, Nelly. *Genèse de la frontière francobelge: les variations des limites septentrionales de la France de 1659 à 1789.* Bibliothèque de la Société d'Histoire du Droit des Pays Flamands, Picards, et Wallons, no. 26. Paris: A. & J. Picard, 1970.

Goubert, Pierre. *L'ancien régime.* 2 vols. Vol. 1, *La société.* Vol. 2, *Les pouvoirs.* Paris: Armand Colin, 1969, 1973.

―――. *Louis XIV et vingt millions de français.* Paris: Arthème Fayard, 1966.

Grimoard, P. H. *Histoire des quatre derniers campagnes du maréchal de Turenne en 1672, 1673, 1674, 1675.* Paris, 1782.

Grossmann, Julius. "Der Kaiserliche Gesandte Franz von Lisola im Haag, 1672–73." In *Archiv für österreichische Geschichte* 51 (1873): 3–193.

―――. "Raimund Monteccucoli, Ein Beitrag zur österreichischen Geschichte des siebzehnten Jahrhunderts, vornehmlich der Jahre 1672–1673." In *Archivfür österreichische Geschichte* 57 (1879): 399–462.

Grotius, Hugo. *The Law of Peace and War.* Translated by Francis Kelsey. Washington, D.C.: Carnegie Institution, 1925.

Guizot, F. P. G. *History of Oliver Cromwell and the English Commonwealth.* Translated by Andrew R. Scobie. 2 vols. Philadelphia: Blanchard and Lea, 1854.

Haley, K. H. D. *The First Earl of Shaftsbury.* Oxford: Clarendon Press, 1968.

―――. *William of Orange and the English Opposition, 1672–74.* Oxford: Clarendon Press, 1953.

Hatton, Ragnhild. "Louis XIV and His Fellow Monarchs." In *Louis XIV and the Craft of Kingship.* Edited by John C. Rule. Columbus: Ohio State University Press, 1969, pp. 155–95.

―――. and Bromley, J. S., eds. *William III and Louis XIV: Essays 1680–1720 by and for Mark Thompson.* Liverpool: Liverpool University Press, 1968.

Hill, David Jayne. *A History of Diplomacy in the International Development of Europe.* 3 vols. New York: Longmans, Green, 1911.

Höynck, Paul Otto. *Frankreich und seine Gegner auf dem Nimwegener Friedenskongress.* Bonn: L. Röhrscheid, 1960.

Immich, Max. *Geschichte des europäischen staatensystems von 1660 bis 1789.* Reprint of 1905 edition. Munich: R. Oldenburg, 1967.

Jal, Auguste. *Abraham Du Quesne et la marine de son temps.* 2 vols. Paris: H. Plon, 1873.

Judge, H. G. "Louis XIV and the Church." In *Louis XIV and the Craft of Kingship.* Edited by John C. Rule. Columbus: Ohio State University Press, 1969, pp. 240–64.

Klopp, Onno. *Der Fall des Hauses Stuart und die Succession des Hauses Hannover in Gross-Britannien und Irland.* 14 vols. Vienna: W. Braumüller, 1875–88.

Kohl, Wilhelm. *Christoph Bernhard von Galen: Politische Geschichte des Fürstbistums Münster, 1650–1678.* Münster: Verlag Regensberg, 1964.

La Roncière, Charles G. de. *Histoire de la marine française.* 5 vols. Paris: E. Plon, Nourrit et Cie, 1899–1920.

Lavisse, Ernest. *Histoire de France depuis les origines jusqu'à la Révolution française.* Vol. 7, *Louis XIV de 1643 à 1685.* Paris: Hachette, 1911.

Lee, Maurice. *The Cabal.* Urbana: University of Illinois Press, 1965.

Le Roy Ladurie, Emmanuel. *Les paysans de Languedoc.* 2 vols. Paris: Imprimerie Nationale, 1966.

Livet, Georges. *L'intendance d'Alsace sous Louis XIV, 1648–1715.* Paris: Belles Lettres, 1956.

————. "Louis XIV and the Germanies." in *Louis XIV and Europe.* Edited by Ragnhild Hatton. Columbus: Ohio State University Press, 1976, pp. 60–81.

Lossky, Andrew. "France in the System of Europe in the Seventeenth Century." *Proceedings of the Western Society for French History* 1 (Flagstaff, Ariz., 1974): 32–48.

————. "Some Problems in Tracing the Intellectual Development of Louis XIV from 1661 to 1715." In *Louis XIV and the Craft of Kingship.* Edited by John C. Rule. Columbus: Ohio State University Press, 1969, pp. 317–44

Mahan, Alfred T. *The Influence of Sea Power on History, 1660–1783.* 13th ed. Boston: Little, Brown, 1897.

Mandrou, Robert. *La France aux XVIIe et XVIIIe siècles.* Paris: Presses Universitaires de France, 1967.

Martin, Ronald D. "The Marquis de Chamlay and the Dutch War." *Proceedings of the Western Society for French History* 1 (Flagstaff, Ariz., 1974): 61–72.

————. "The Marquis de Chamlay, Friend and Confidential Advisor to Louis XIV: The Early Years, 1650–1691." Ph.D. dissertation, University of California, Santa Barbara, 1972.

————. *Weltmacht des Barock, Osterreich in der Zeit Kaiser Leopolds I.* Vienna: R. M. Rohrer, 1961.

Mentz, Georg. *Johann Philipp von Schönborn, Kurfürst von Mainz, Bischof von Würzburg und Worms, 1605–1673.* 2 vols. in 1. Jena: G. Fischer, 1896–99.

Michaud, J. F. *Biographie Universelle.* 45 vols. in 23. Paris: Ch. Delagrave et Cie, 1843.

Mignet, F. A. M. *Négociations relatives à la succession d'Espagne sous Louis XIV.* 4 vols. Paris, 1835–42.

Montesquieu, Charles de Secondat, baron de. *De l'esprit des Lois.* Edited by Jean Brethe de la Gressaye. 3 vols. Paris: Belles Lettres, 1950–58.

Mousnier, Roland. *Fureurs paysannes: les paysans dans les révoltes du XVIIe siècle (France, Russie, Chine).* Paris: Calmann-Lévy, 1967.

————. *Les XVIe et XVIIe siècles. Histoire générale des civilisations,* vol. 4. Paris: Presses Universitaire de France, 1961.

Napoleon I. *Mémoires écrits à Sainte-Hélène*. Edited by Désiré Lacroix. 5 vols. Paris Garnier Frères, 1905.

O'Connor, John T. "Louis XIV's Strategic Frontier in the Holy Roman Empire." *Proceedings of the Western Society for French History* 3 (Denver, 1975): 108–17.

————. "Wilhelm Egon von Fürstenberg, a German Agent in the Service of Louis XIV." *French Historical Studies* 5 (1967): 119–46.

————. "William Egon von Fürstenberg and French Diplomacy in the Rhineland Prior to the Outbreak of the War of the League of Augsburg in 1688." Ph.D. dissertation, University of Minnesota, Minneapolis, 1965.

Ogg, David. *England in the Reign of Charles II*. 2 vols. Oxford: Clarendon Press, 1934.

Pagès, Georges. *Contributions à l'histoire de la politique française en Allemagne sous Louis XIV*. Paris: Société Nouvelle de Librairie de d'Edition, 1905.

————. *Le Grand electeur et Louis XIV, 1660–1688*. Paris: Société Nouvelle de Librairie et d'Edition, 1905.

————. "L'histoire diplomatique du règne de Louis XIV." *Revue d'histoire moderne et contemporaine* 7 (1905–6): 653–58.

————. *Louis XIV et l'Allemagne (1661–1715)*. Paris: Centre de Documentation Universitaire, 1937.

Paine, Thomas. *Common Sense and Other Political Writings*. Edited by Nelson F. Adkins. Indianapolis and New York: Bobbs-Merrill, 1953.

Pfister, Christian. "Louis XIV en Alsace: Le premier voyage (août–septembre 1673)." *Saisons d'Alsace* 17 (1953):5–63.

Picavet, Camille. *La diplomatie française au temps de Louis XIV (1661–1715); institutions, moeurs et coutumes*. Paris: Alcan, 1930.

————. *Les dernières années de Turenne (1660–1675)*. Paris: Calmann-Lévy, 1919.

Piccioni, Camille V. *Les premiers commis des affaires étrangères au XVIIe et au XVIIIe siècles*. Paris: E. de Bocard, 1928.

Pillorget, René. "La France et l'électorat de Trèves temps de Charles-Gaspard de la Leyen II (1653–1679)." *Revue d'histoire diplomatique* 78 (1964): 118–47.

Pribram, A. F. *Franz Paul, freiherr von Lisola und die Politik seiner Zeit*. Leipzig: Veit, 1894.

Redlich, Oswald. *Geschichte Osterreichs*. Vol. 6, *Osterreichs Grossmachtbildung in der Zeit Kaiser Leopolds I*. Gotha: F. A. Perthes, 1921.

Rousset, Camille. *Histoire de Louvois et de son administration politique et militaire*. 4 vols. Paris: Didier, 1862–63.

Rowen, Herbert H. "Arnauld de Pomponne: Louis XIV's Moderate Minister." *American Historical Review* 61 (1956): 531–49.

————. "John de Witt and the Triple Alliance." *Journal of Modern History* 26 (1954): 1–14.

————. *The Ambassador Prepares for War: The Dutch Embassy of Arnauld de Pomponne, 1669–1671*. The Hague: M. Nijhoff, 1957.

Rule, John C. "Louis XIV, Roi-Bureaucrate." In *Louis XIV and the Craft of Kingship*. Edited by John C. Rule. Columbus: Ohio State University Press, 1969, pp. 3–101.

Sagnac, Philippe, and Saint-Léger, Alexandre de. *La prépondérance française: Louis XIV, 1661–1715. Peuples et civilisations*, vol. 10. Edited by Louis Halphen and Philippe Sagnac. Paris: Presses Universitatire de France, 1949.

Schumpeter, Joseph. *Imperialism and Social Classes*. Translated by Heinz Norden and edited by Paul M. Sweezy. New York: A. M. Kelley, 1951.

Sée, Henri. "Que faut-il penser de l'oeuvre économique de Colbert." *Revue historique* 152 (1926): 181–93.

Ségur, Pierre de. *Le maréchal de Luxembourg et le prince d'Orange, 1666–1678*. Paris: Calmann-Lévy, 1902.

Smith, Adam. *The Wealth of Nations*. Edited by Bruce Mazlish. Indianapolis and New York: Bobbs-Merrill, 1961.

Sonnino, Paul. "Arnauld de Pomponne, Louis XIV's Minister for Foreign Affairs during the Dutch War." *Proceedings of the Western Society for French History* 1 (Flagstaff, Ariz., 1974): 49–60.

_____. "Hugues de Lionne and the Origins of the Dutch War." *Proceedings of the Western Society for French History* 3 (Denver, 1975): 68–78.

_____. "Louis XIV and the Dutch War." In *Louis XIV and Europe*. Edited by Rahnhild Hatton. Columbus: Ohio State University Press, 1976, pp. 153–78.

_____. "Louis XIV's Mémoires pour l'histoire de la guerre de Hollande." *French Historical Studies* 8 (1673): 29–50.

_____. *Louis XIV's View of the Papacy (1661–1667)*. Berkeley and Los Angeles: University of California Press, 1966.

Sorel, Albert. *Essais d'histoire et de critique*. Paris: E. Plon, 1883.

_____. *L'Europe et la Révolution française*. Pt. 1, *Moeurs politiques et les traditions*. 4th ed. Paris: E. Plon, Nourrit et Cie, 1897.

_____. *Nouveaux essais d'histoire et de critique*. Paris: E. Plon, Nourrit et Cie, 1898.

Suë, Eugène. *Histoire de la marine française*. 2d ed. 4 vols. Paris, 1844.

Tapié, Victor-L. "Louis XIV's Methods in Foreign Policy." In *Louis XIV and Europe*. Edited by Rahnhild Hatton. Columbus: Ohio State University Press, 1976, pp. 3–15.

_____. "Quelques aspects de la politique étrangère de Louis XIV." *XVIIe siècle* 46–47 (1960): 1–28.

Vattel, Emmerich de. *The Law of Nations or the Principles of Natural Law Applied to the Conduct and to the Affairs of Nations and Sovereigns*. Translated by Charles G. Fenwick from the 1758 edition. New York: Oceana Reprints, 1964.

Voltaire. *The Age of Louis XIV*. Translated by Martyn P. Pollack. New York: E. P. Dutton, 1961.

Waddington, Albert. *Le Grand Electeur Frédéric Guillaume de Brandebourg, sa politique extérieure, 1640–1688*. 2 vols. Paris: E. Plon, Nourrit et Cie, 1905–8.

Westergaard, Waldemar. *The First Triple Alliance: The Letters of Christopher Lindenov, Danish Envoy to London, 1668–1672*. New Haven, Conn.: Yale University Press, 1947.

Wilson, Charles. *The Dutch Republic*. New York: McGraw-Hill, 1968.

Wolf, John B. *Louis XIV*. New York: Norton, 1968.

_____. "Louis XIV, Soldier-King." In *Louis XIV and the Craft of Kingship*. Edited by John C. Rule. Columbus: Ohio State University Press, 1969, pp. 196–223.

Zeller, Gaston. *Aspects de la politique française sous l'ancien régime*. Paris: Presses Universitaire de France, 1964.

————. "Deux mémoires inédits du Grand Condé sur l'Alsace." *Revue historique* 140 (1922): 208–17.

————. "La monarchie d'ancien régime et les frontières naturelles." *Revue d'histoire moderne* 8 (1933): 305–33.

————. *Les temps moderne: de Louis XIV à 1789. Histoire des relations internationales*, vol. 3. Edited by Pierre Renouvin. Paris: Hachette, 1955.

————. *L'organisation défensive des frontières du Nord et de l'Est au XVIIe siècle*. Paris: Berger-Levrault, 1928.

————. "Politique extérieure et diplomatie sous Louis XIV." *Revue d'histoire moderne* 6 (1931): 124–43.

Index

A

Absolutism, royal: Louis XIV and, 35,
167, 171, 178
Aix-la-Chapelle, city of, 89
Aix-la-Chapelle, Peace of (1668), 10,
19, 105, 112; character of frontier
created by, 14; ambition of allies to
undo, 95; Louis XIV's distaste for,
97; not unfavorable for France, 98;
concluded War of Devolution, 111;
Turenne shocked by, 116; Charles II
declares Spaniards violated, 119,
188 (n. 23); French claim Spaniards
violated, 123
Alberti, Girolamo, Venetian envoy in
England, 156; sees problems in the
Anglo-French alliance, 165–66; reports England paralyzed by approaching session of Parliament,
166; reports English fear of war
with Spain, 167
Albizzi, Francesco, papal nuncio in
Vienna: remarks about Emperor
Leopold's indecision, 197 (n. 46)
Alfonso, dispossessed king of Portugal:
attempt to regain throne, 169
Alsace, 4, 25, 66–67, 73, 96; transferred to Louvois's jurisdiction, 26;
Condé sent to appraise situation in,
34; Vauban inspects fortifications of,
34; cities of (Decapolis), 35–37,
109, 129; Louvois goes to appraise
situation in, 35; Navailles sent to

appraise situation in, 35; Louis XIV
marches into, 36, 43, 45, 122; rela-
tionship to French crown, 37;
French need to secure, 38; Louis
XIV returns from, 41; fortifications
in, 146. *See also* Münster, Treaty of
Amsterdam, 165, 173; protected by
flooded polders, 13; surrounded by
water, 17; Luxembourg attempts to
reach across frozen polders, 81
Andernach: French-held bridge over
Rhine River at, 67
Anglo-Dutch commercial wars, 152,
185 (n. 8)
Anglo-French relations, 13, 33, 83–98
passim, 151–71 passim
Annales school: interpretation of Louis
XIV's reign, 182; enthusiasm for its
method, 209 (n. 30)
Anne of Austria, Louis XIV's mother
and regent of France, 151
Arcy, René Martel, marquis d', 27
Ardennes: Louis XIV passes through,
25
Arlington, Lord, Charles II's secretary
of state for foreign affairs, 169;
correspondence with English ambas-
sadors at Cologne Conference, 69,
89, 90, 92; correspondent in Turenne's army, 73, 75; correspondent in
Paris, 127, 138, 177–78; dislike of
French alliance, 157–61; foreign

[221]

policy based on friendship with Spain, 171

Arras: Louis XIV's army passes through, 55

Artagnan, Charles de Batz-Castelmore, count d': killed at siege of Maastricht, 20

Aschaffenburg: strategic bridge over Main River at, 69, 72–74

Ath, village in Flanders, 126

Atlantic fleet, French: commanded by the count d'Estrées, 164

Aubeville, Nicolas de Sève d', French ambassador in Portugal: uncovers plot, 169; confirms complicity of Charles II in plot, 170

Austria, 101

B

Baden, Switzerland: Swiss Diet meets in, 122

Bad Kreuznach in Rhenish Palatinate: Turenne's army passes through, 136

Balance of power: Robert de Gravel's view of, 103; Louis XIV fails to understand, 103; England and, 151

Baltic Sea: Dutch fleet and, 77

Barrillon, Paul de, French ambassador at Cologne Conference, 83–107 passim

Bavaria, 64; French envoy in, 82

Beaulieu, Camus de, intendant in Turenne's army: correspondence with Louvois, 73, 195 (n. 91)

Berlin, 49

Beverningk, Hieronymous van. See Van Beverningk, Hieronymous

Bissy, Sieur de, French soldier, 38

Blackheath Common: assembly point for English troops, 156

Bohemia: rendezvous of imperial army in, 31–33; imperial army stationed in, 53–65 passim; imperial army marches out of, 68; newsletters from, 69

Bonn, capital of electorate of Cologne, 63, 136; threatened by Dutch and imperial armies, 133; captured by

allied armies, 137; defended by French garrison, 137, 203 (n. 30); importance of loss of, 137–39

Bouchain, fortress in Spanish Netherlands: Louis XIV plans to attack, 118

Bourbon family, 3; enemy of Hapsburgs, 34, 54; treaty with Hapsburgs, 38; aided Dutch in war for independence, 111; enemy of Spain, 116

Bourbon, Louise-Françoise de, bastard daughter of Louis XIV and Mme. de Montespan, 44

Brandenburg, elector of. See Frederick William, elector of Brandenburg

Brandenburg, electorate of, 16, 28, 29, 180; county of Mark belongs to, 51; reconciled with France, 51–64 passim; logical enemy of Cologne, 139–41

Breda: negotiations at in 1666, 83, 85

Breisach, French fortress on Rhine River, 34, 35, 96, 138; Louis XIV travels to, 36

Brittany: duke de Chaulnes, governor of, 105; meeting of estates in, 105; tax revolt in, 199 (n. 109)

Brühl, 84; Courtin meets Franz von Fürstenberg in, 18

Brussels, 28, 51, 94, 113; Louis XIV threatens, 19; Lisola headquartered at, 44; Navailles advocates attack on, 119

Burgundy, Louis de France, duke of, Louis XIV's grandson: tutored by Fénelon, 10

Burnet, Bishop Gilbert: comments on psychology of princes, 7; comments on battle of Texel

C

Cadrature: Vauban advocates for northern frontier of France, 116–17

Cadiz: French ship sunk in harbor of, 115

Cambrai, fortress in Spanish Netherlands: Louis XIV plans to attack, 118

Canada: deprived of funds by Dutch War, 176

Carlos II, king of Spain: death anticipated, 111–12; half-witted, 120

Carmelite monastery in Cologne: negotiations held in, 85

Cato: quoted by Shaftesbury, 152

Chamlay, Jules-Louis, marquis de, Louvois's man in Turenne's army, 72

Chantilly, château of prince of Condé, 17

Charleroi, French fortress in Flanders, 39; Dutch lay siege to, 19, 112–13, 146; siege at motivates Louis XIV to act, 113–14, 146; Spaniards assist Dutch at siege of, 113–15, 117, 119, 121, 123

Charles I, king of England: executed in 1649, 151; husband of Louis XIV's aunt, 151

Charles II, king of England, 151–71 passim; issues declaration favorable to French, 19, 119; Louis XIV attempts to manipulate, 24; and Cologne Conference, 88, 90, 92, 144; does not require pressure from Parliament to quit French alliance, 144, 170–71; and Triple Alliance of 1668, 152; prepares Louis XIV for anti-Dutch alliance, 152; abandons French alliance, 153; and Declaration of Indulgence, 154–56; and Treaty of Dover, 154, 187 (n. 2); Louis XIV tries to deceive, 157–58; plans landing on Dutch coast, 161, 198 (n. 61); sold Dunkirk to French, 163; forced to seek peace with Dutch, 166; perceives Louis XIV's taste for war, 168; fools Croissy, 168–70; engaged in Portugese plot 169–70; crafty politician, 170; makes separate peace with Dutch, 171; proposed conversion to Roman Catholicism, 205 (n. 3); no plans to impose Catholic religion on England, 206 (n. 21); receives French girl from Louis XIV, 208 (n. 68)

Charles IV, duke of Lorraine: enemy of Louis XIV, 34, 41; captures Ehren-

breitstein, 41; duchy seized by French, 48, 102; joins anti-French alliance, 95; fled into Germany, 190 (n. 72)

Charles VIII, king of France, 173

Charles XI, king of Sweden: equates survival of Dutch Republic with that of Sweden, 87

Chassan, Pierre de, French diplomat, 138

Chaulnes, Duke Philipe de, 89; heads French delegation at Cologne Conference, 79, 83, 84; leaves Cologne Conference, 105; works against tax rebellion in Brittany, 199 (n. 109)

Churchill, John, future duke of Marlborough: at siege of Maastricht, 20; perhaps served in Turenne's army, 75

Clausewitz, Karl von: studied Turenne's campaign of 1673, 194 (n. 77)

Cleves, duchy of: possession of Brandenburg, 52

Clifford, Lord Thomas, English minister of state: forced to resign from government because of religion, 167

Colbert, Jean-Baptiste, 101, 113, 123, 147, 163–65; and Dutch War, 5, 6; vigorous minister, 8; preoccupied with finances, 9, 21; and development of French navy, 160–61; praises De Ruyter, 162; displeased with Dutch War, 175–76; economic program destroyed by Dutch War, 176–78; Louis XIV rejects vision of for France, 178; concept of French state, 179; tariff policy of, 181; opposed to Dutch War, 185 (n. 11). *See also* Mercantilism

Colmar, 43; leading city of Alsace, 35; walls of demolished, 36; complains to Imperial Diet, 37

Cologne, elector of. *See* Maximilian Heinrich, elector of Cologne

Cologne, electorate of, 17, 18, 60, 142–44, 147; vulnerable to imperial army, 72–73, 75, 133, 135–36; invaded by imperial army, 127, 137; contiguous to territories of Brandenburg, 139; interests of ignored by French, 140–41, 171

Cologne, free imperial city of: negotiations held in, 28, 67, 79–109 passim, 115, 118, 121, 122, 138–39, 144; made neutral for Cologne Conference, 84; special courier route created to, 147

Cologne Conference, 77–109 passim, 158, 160; Louis XIV's harsh terms at, 28; stigmatized as uninteresting, 79; Louis XIV's purposes at, 99; reasons for failure of, 102–4; end of, 104; Louis XIV limits negotiations at, 115

Company of the North: ruined by Dutch War, 177

Compiègne: Louis XIV advances to, 113, 146; Louis XIV plans to leave, 114

Condé, fortress in Spanish Netherlands: Louis XIV plans to attack, 118

Condé, Louis II de Bourbon, prince of, 82, 84, 96, 114, 119, 123, 125, 130, 157, 180; makes strategic recommendations, 14–15; commands army, 16; warned by Courtin not to overshadow the king, 17; ordered into Holland, 23; leaves Utrecht, 24; warns Louvois about strength of empire, 34; sent to appraise French position in Alsace, 34; recommends action in Alsace, 35, 37; returns from Alsace, 35; compared with Turenne, 70; urges rectification of northern frontier, 117; relegated to menial duties, 121–22, 148; faces strategic problems in Low Countries, 124; reports that Spaniards have begun war, 126; begins hostilities with Spaniards, 127; stationed in Flanders, 133; rejects Louvois's requests, 133; guards Flemish frontier, 134–35; request rebuffed by Louvois, 146; and anti-Louvois cabal, 149; presides over war council, 150; ordered into Flanders, 157; writes spurious letter to deceive the English, 158–59; urged

to advance into Holland, 173; requests command for son, 205 (n. 72)

Conseil d'en haut: foreign affairs principal responsibility of, 9. *See also* High council

Continent, 165; French position on, 67; Swedes do not wish to see English on, 88; Switzerland at crossroads of, 123; England removed from affairs of, 151; Louis XIV does not want English on, 163; war on Louis XIV's personal affair, 171

Copper pontoons: invented 1672, 189 (n. 44)

Corbie, year of: Louis XIV affected by, 124

Courtin, Honoré: warns Condé about Louis XIV's desire to dominate 1673 campaign, 17; negotiates with Franz von Fürstenberg, 18; comments on fall of Maastricht, 22; critic of royal policy, 43, 99, 102–3, 174–75, 177–78; discouraged with negotiations in Cologne, 95–96; left as head of French delegation at Cologne Conference, 105; Louis XIV enraged with, 105–6; friend of Louvois, 145; admonishes Louvois, 145; tricks English diplomats at Cologne Conference, 158; jokes with Condé about Louis XIV, 158; warns Pomponne about fragility of English alliance, 159–60; speaks generously of Pomponne, 198 (n. 89)

Courtrai: Louis XIV passes through, 55

Coysevox, French sculptor: his bas-relief of Louis XIV at Versailles, 129

Crécy, Louis Verjus, count de: negotiates treaty between France and Cologne, 139–40

Crete: French assist Venetians against Turks on, 119

Crèvecoeur: evacuated by French army, 134

Croissy, Colbert de, French ambassador in England, 87, 153–71, 207 (n. 49); sent instructions on how to deal with Charles II, 88; reports Charles II willing to reduce demands

on Dutch, 90; suggests French demands on Dutch be reduced, 92; confrontation with Spanish ambassador in London, 121; and revocation of Declaration of Indulgence, 155; reports English opinion on French alliance, 163–65; decides Anglo-French alliance is finished, 165–66; wants to leave England, 166; fooled by Charles II, 168–70
Cromwell, Oliver: alliance with France, 151

D

Decapolis: did not welcome French rule, 34; Condé recommends discipline of, 35; Robert de Gravel recommends treating diplomatically, 37. *See also* Alsace, cities of
Declaration of Indulgence, 154–56; Charles II's revocation of, 155–56
De Groot, Pieter: exiled from Dutch Republic, 21–22; a leader of States party, 187 (n. 3); Dutch ambassador at Doesburg, 187 (n. 3)
De Ruyter, Michiel, Dutch admiral: and battle of Texel, 98, 160–62; praised by Colbert, 162
Devolution, law of: and Louis XIV's claim to Spanish territories, 110–11
Devolution, War of (1667–68), 77; a test for Louis XIV, 10; ended by Peace of Aix-la-Chapelle, 111; and Turenne, 115
De Witt, brothers, Johan and Cornelis: grisly fate of, 85; murdered, 160, 187 (n. 3)
De Witt, Johan, 7; tried to solve problem of Spanish Netherlands, 111; comments on Louis XIV, 172
Diet. *See* Imperial Diet; Switzerland, diet of cantons
Doesburg: negotiations held at, 13, 82, 146; Louis XIV rejects Dutch offers at, 112
Dover, Treaty of (1670), 187 (n. 2), 208 (n. 68); signed by England and France, 152; and Catholicism in England, 154; guarantees Dutch

towns to English, 197 (n. 34); *traité simulé*, 205 (n. 3)
Dresden, 138
Du Moulin, Pierre, anti-French propagandist: author of *England's Appeal*, 153; propaganda machine of, 168
Dunkirk: Charles II sold to France, 1662, 163
Du Pas, French governor of Naarden: Louis XIV orders court martial of, 130
Dutch Brabant, 24, 91, 157
Dutch coastal towns: demanded by English, 24, 88–89, 154, 156–57, 197 (n. 34), 206 (n. 25); Charles II drops demand for, 92
Dutch Gelderland, 13, 91, 92
Dutch Netherlands, 15, 16, 80, 118, 129, 130; war in a frustration, 82; war in futile, 90; Luxembourg commands French army in, 131. *See also* United Provinces of the Dutch Republic
Dutch War, xiv, 9, 19, 25, 37, 47, 55, 62, 79, 100, 109, 115, 117, 133, 145, 154, 159; dynastic causation of explained, 4; economic causation of attempted, 5, 185 (n. 7); becomes war of attrition, 10; evolves into larger war, 11; successful first phase of, 14; changing nature of, 26, 127, 134, 174; not served by attack on Trier, 42; fought largely on German soil, 51; Louis XIV contemplates ending, 80; ended at Nijmegen (1678), 97; an "unfortunate mess" says Courtin, 99; begins to go sour, 106; Louis XIV planned, 112; northern frontier at end of, 119; opening campaign of well known, 129; Colbert displeased with, 175; destroys Colbert's economic program, 176–78; brings out division in royal government, 178–79; subjective nature of, 180–81; "the greatest mistake of the reign," 183
Dynasticism: basis for politics during Old Regime, 3–4; Louis XIV and, 110–12

E

East India Company (French): ruined by Dutch War, 177
East Indies, Dutch, 162
Eastern frontier of France: Louis XIV leads army to, 25–27; Louis XIV plans to strengthen, 27, 34–35, 38, 45; area of potential danger for France, 43, 110, 172, 174, 193 (n. 25); Turenne seeks to secure, 73. *See also* Alsace; Lorraine; Münster, Treaty of
Eger: rendezvous point for imperial army, 32
Ehrenbreitstein: imperial troops garrisoned in, 27; Elector Max Heinrich flees to, 41
Emperor, Holy Roman. *See* Leopold, Emperor
Empire, Holy Roman. *See* Germany; Holy Roman Empire of the German Nation
Enghien, Henri-Jules de Bourbon, duke d', son of prince of Condé: Condé seeks command for, 149
England, 87, 92, 144, 147, 169; made war for commercial reasons, 6; demands Dutch coastal towns, 85; and Triple Alliance of 1668, 111; and France, 112, 151–71 passim; Spain recognized Commonwealth in, 151; anti-French opinion in, 152–55, 165–68; anti-Catholic opinion in, 153–55, 167; privy council in, 167; makes peace with Dutch Republic, 167. *See also* House of Commons; London; Parliament
England, king of. *See* Charles I; Charles II
England's Appeal: anti-French pamphlet by Pierre Du Moulin, 153–54
Enlightenment: ideas on bellicose nature of monarchy, 179
Estrades, Godefroi, count d': made governor of Maastricht, 22; refuses to go to Cologne Conference, 79
Estrées, François-Annibal, count d', 168, 207 (n. 49); leads French squadron of Anglo-French fleet,

160–61; actions during battle of Texel, 162–63; Rupert condemns conduct of, 163–65; Martel writes savage criticism of, 164–65
Evelyn, John: comments on religious situation in England, 153
Fénelon, François de Salignac de la Mothe: criticizes Louis XIV's war policies, 10
Feuquières, Antoine de Pas, marquis de: analyzes capture of Bonn, 138
Feuquières, Isaac, marquis de: appointed ambassador to Sweden, 80; relative of Pomponne's, 100–101, 195 (n. 4)
First partition treaty (1668), 111, 186 (n. 29)
Flanders, 14, 15, 19, 24, 39, 40, 44, 54, 55, 110, 114, 115, 116, 117, 130, 133, 134, 146, 157, 180, 181; Monterey cannot meet challenge of combat in, 23; Louvois sent to appraise situation, 113; Alliance of The Hague and frontier of, 123; Louis XIV thinks of war with Spain there, 125; war with Spain begins there, 126; Condé guards frontier of, 134–35, 148
Fortresses: proposed exchange of in Netherlands, 89–90, 105; Vauban views for external and domestic purposes, 117
Fourilles, chevalier de, 31, 38, 39, 191 (n. 93); ordered to march into electorate of Trier, 26–27
France, 24, 25, 27, 40, 45, 48, 81, 98, 105, 110, 113, 172, 176, 180; foreign policy of, 3–11 passim, 26, 42, 60, 77, 79, 95, 97, 99, 141–42, 145, 153, 159, 171, 175, 181–82; did not make war for commercial reasons, 6; economy of hurt by Dutch War, 10, 176–78; Vauban's notion of, 14, 116–17; Louis XIV and, 16, 172–83 passim; and German princes, 56–75 passim; treaty with Sweden, 77; Courtin fears isolation of, 96; England ally of, 112; and Spain, 112–33 passim; and Cologne, 139–47 passim; and

England, 151–71 passim; Colbert's dream for, 178; differing views of in royal government, 179. *See also* Eastern frontier; Northern frontier

Franche-Comté of Burgundy (Spanish), 24, 55, 73, 110–11, 115–16, 119, 123; Condé gathers intelligence on, 113–14, 201 (n. 14); proposals for invasion of reviewed, 121–22; invasion plans for abandoned, 124–25, 130

Francis I, 6, 34

Franco-Dutch Treaty (1662), 186 (n. 1); obliges France to protect Dutch from foreign aggressors, 152

Franconia, 29, 58–72 passim, 136; Fürstenberg brothers oppose Turenne's advance into, 60; Turenne leads army into, 69; Turenne and Montecuccoli maneuver in, 69–72, 124

Frankfurt-am-Main, 61–75 passim

Frederick Henry, prince of Orange, 17

Frederick the Great, 179–80, 189 (n. 44)

Frederick William, elector of Brandenburg, 28–29, 48, 49, 51–64 passim, 80, 82, 139–41, 192 (nn. 1, 10); does not want emperor as patron of German princes, 29; makes peace with Louis XIV, 30, 49–64 passim; opposed to Dutch War, 116

French army: logistics of, 61–62, 64, 68, 70, 72, 194 (n. 48)

French Revolution, 63, 100

Fresno, Marquis Pedro Fernández del, Spanish ambassador in England: confrontation with Croissy at Whitehall, 121

Freud, Sigmund, 5, 7

Friedberg, 193 (n. 29); imperial regiment holed up in, 55–57

Friesland, 80

Froissart, Jean: describes medieval chivalry, 43

Fronde, 84, 122, 151

Fulda, imperial abbey of, 56

Fürstenberg, Franz Egon von, bishop of Strasbourg, 58, 84, 95, 145; complains about Dutch garrison in

Maastricht, 18; prophecies prove accurate, 59; opposes Turenne's march into Franconia, 60; called Bishop Bacchus by enemies, 89; entertains Cologne society, 89; wants to be coadjutor of Cologne, 140; writes to Pomponne, 140–41; Courtin tells Louvois to placate, 142; whispers secrets to English ambassadors, 159; devious politician, 204 (n. 43)

Fürstenberg, Wilhelm Egon von, 32, 58, 84, 139–41, 144, 145, 159, 190 (n. 64); signs new treaty between France and Cologne, 18; condemns French policy in Germany, 30–31; elector of Mainz warns about consequences of French invasion of Trier, 33; prophecies prove accurate, 59; opposes Turenne's march into Franconia, 60; abducted by imperial soldiers in Cologne, 79, 104; helps persuade Louis XIV to accept "third party" in Germany, 103; abused by Louvois, 141–42; Courtin suggests that Louvois placate, 142–43; as mercenary diplomat, 142–43; characterized as devil by Lisola, 199 (n. 108)

G

Galen, Bernhard Christoph von, bishop of Münster: tires of war in alliance with France, 96

Gallus amicus non vicinus, Dutch proverb expressing attitude toward France, 111

Generality Lands (of Dutch Republic), 21, 92, 208 (n. 3); Maastricht part of, 17

German princes: react to French invasion of Trier, 28–29, 33; drawn to emperor, 33, 66, 137–38; and France, 34, 51, 53; anger at Turenne's advance into Franconia, 58–59, 66

Germany, 4, 14, 16, 22, 23, 27, 30, 32, 40–43, 45, 80, 82, 84, 85, 123–34 passim, 138, 155, 157, 159, 168,

171; French army intended for, 15; Turenne's army in, 24, 25, 31, 47–75, 114, 120–38 passim, 157, 181; French aggression into, 28–29; military circles of, 29, 30, 57, 62, 66; anti-French sentiment in, 30–31, 61–63, 64, 66, 68–69; conflict between Bourbons and Hapsburgs over, 38, 54; military situation in, 91; Swedes supposed to aid French in, 96–97; failure of French policy in, 137–41; French interests in, 143. *See also* Franconia; Imperial Diet

Ghent: Louis XIV's army threatens, 19

Gobelin tapestry, 129

Gourville, Jean Héraut de: serves as reconciler between Louvois and Condé, 149

Grana, marquis of, commander of imperial regiment in Cologne, 84

Grave, fortress in Spanish Netherlands: Louis XIV plans to attack, 118

Gravel, abbé de: represents France in meeting of Imperial Circles in Mühlhausen, 29–30; represents France in Mainz, 52; reports from Mainz that the elector is troubled by French actions, 57; receives reports from agents in Bohemia, 69; reports bishop of Würzburg is peace loving, 71; observes imperial army from Mainz, 75; finds Germans suspicious of Wilhelm von Fürstenberg, 189 (n. 62)

Gravel, Robert de, French representative at Imperial Diet, 26, 28, 33, 36, 37, 40, 42, 46, 53, 54, 59, 60, 65, 171; comments on French victory at Maastricht, 22; disagrees with Louis XIV's decision to advance into Lorraine, 25; criticizes royal policy toward Trier, 30; unable to understand Louis XIV's policy in Germany, 39; suffers heart attack in Regensburg, 41; ordered to justify presence of French army in Germany, 56–57, 61, 64–65; qualities as diplomat, 188 (n. 35), 189 (n. 52)

Gravesend: Charles II holds council of war at, 161

Grémonville, Jacques Bretel, chevalier de, French special envoy in Vienna, 38, 101; reports emperor not intimidated by French victory at Maastricht, 31–32; reports imperial army ordered to withdraw into Bohemia, 53–54; reports that imperial army will return to Germany, 57, 59, 189 (n. 55); signs first partition treaty in Vienna, 111

Groningen, Dutch province, 80

Groot, Pieter de. *See* De Groot, Pieter

Grotius, Hugo: comments on international law, 188 (n. 2)

Gun Powder Plot, 168

H

Haguenau, city in Alsace: Condé characterizes as needing discipline, 35

Hanover, 143

Hapsburgs (Austrian), 37, 38, 52, 53, 99, 111; enemy of Bourbons, 34, 54; party of Alliance of The Hague, 95; Louis XIV wishes to expand frontiers at expense of, 116; attempts to unify Germany, 137; Richelieu tried to break power of, 151; Louis XIV forces into alliance with Spanish Hapsburgs, 181

Haren, Willem van. *See* Van Haren, Willem

Heemskerck, Coenraad van, Dutch diplomat: sent to Vienna to plead the Dutch case, 94

Heidelberg: Turenne's army must cross bridges at, 74–75

Henriette Marie of France, Louis XIV's aunt and queen of England, 151

Hérouard, Major: gives account of English navy, 163

Henry IV, king of France, 22

Hesse-Darmstadt, count of, 56

High council, 52–53, 74, 92, 145, 149, 176; Louis XIV and, 8; composition of 9, 19, 141, 204 (n. 46); functions of, 9; opinions in, 32, 40, 108–9, 196 (n. 10). *See also* Royal government

Histoire événementielle: recent contempt for, xiii

Holland, province of, 22, 25, 80, 82, 124, 138, 180; flooded polders protect, 14; French troops allocated for, 15; Condé order into, 23, 173; Turenne proposes evacuation of, 132; Louis XIV comments on evacuation of, 134

Holy Roman Empire of the German Nation, 33. *See also* Germany

Holy Roman Emperor. *See* Leopold I, Emperor

Hocher, Johann Paul von, Imperial Chancellor, 31, 32, 44

House of Commons, 153; Shaftesbury's speech in, 152; wants peace with the Dutch, 167. *See also* Parliament

Humières, Louis de Crévent, marshal d', 24

Hungarians, 32–33, 48

I

Ile de France, 117; heartland of France, 110

Ill River Valley: Louis XIV marches into

Imperial army: rendezvous of in Bohemia, 31–32; withdrawal of into Bohemia, 53, 55, 57, 63, 196 (n. 18); eludes Turenne, 70–71; joins Dutch army, 137; captures Bonn, 139. *See also* Montecuccoli, Count Raimund; Imperials

Imperial Council: war faction gaining predominance in, 31

Imperial Diet, 25, 28, 29, 59, 61, 64, 103, 171; Gravel French envoy at, 22; Gravel argues French cause in, 33; Gravel faces Colmar's complaints in, 37; pro-imperial members of shout down Gravel, 41; Gravel to justify the presence of Turenne's

army in Germany, 56–57; declares *Reichskrieg* against France, 137

Imperials, 54, 67, 69, 74, 171, 189 (n. 55); events in Europe work out in their favor, 33; Turenne leads campaign against, 49; in Thuringia, 55; withdrawal into Bohemia, 57, 63; and propaganda, 61; onus for war in Germany fell on, 62; Turenne's duty to stop, 70; French negotiations to divert, 101; bishop of Würzburg supports, 124; exploit Bonn's capture, 138. *See also* Imperial army

Insurance Company, 177

J

James, duke of York, 168–69, 207 (n. 64); supports his brother Charles II, 92; practicing Roman Catholic, 154; causes problems for brother, the king, 155; commander of the fleet, 160; forced to resign because Catholic, 160; attends war council, 161; Catholic wife of, 167

Jansenists: Pomponne's family belongs to, 8

Jenkins, Sir Leoline: English ambassador at Cologne Conference, 84, 89, 159

K

Kaiserwerth, 139

Kerkum, 19

Kijduin. *See* Texel, battle of, 98

Koblenz, 33, 55, 57, 137; imperial troops stationed in, 27

L

La Fère: fortifications at, 117

Lahn River, 57, 64, 69

La Vallière, Louise de la Beaume-le-Blanc de, mistress of Louis XIV, 43, 191 (n. 106)

League of Augsburg, War of the: Fénelon deplores conditions of France during, 10

Lens, 122
Leopold, Emperor, 22, 28, 37, 43, 45, 52, 53, 54, 56, 57, 58, 59, 62, 65, 84, 96, 97, 102, 105, 123, 138, 143, 180; prepares to aid Dutch, 27; Frederick William does not want him as protective patron of German princes, 29; not intimidated by French victory at Maastricht, 31; formulates restrained and shrewd policy, 32; policy more effective than Louis XIV's, 33; aids Dutch, 34; signs secret treaty of neutrality with French, 38; enters war on Dutch side, 48; agrees to support Frederick William, 49; withdraws army into hereditary lands, 55; threatens to march army across Germany, 60–61; intervenes in Louis XIV's war, 63; procrastination of, 88, 197 (n. 46); signs secret treaty of partition, 111; and Alliance of The Hague, 171; signs defensive treaty for protection of the empire, 192 (n. 1)
La Reynie Nicolas-Gabriel de, lieutenant general of police in Paris: proclaims war with Spain in Paris, 127
Le Tellier, Michel, 23, 32, 39, 61, 113, 145; convalesces from stroke, 9; stroke leaves partially paralyzed, 114, 146, 204 (n. 62); intervenes to save son's career, 149
Levant Company (French): Dutch War ruins, 177
Leyden, Karl Gaspard von der, elector of Trier, 43, 64; and French invasion of his electorate, 28–29; emperor has right to protect, 33; French devastate his lands, 56; invites imperial troops to garrison Koblenz, 57; his bridge over Rhine, 137
Liège, 22, 52, 118
Liège, bishop of, electoral prince Max Heinrich of Cologne, 17, 18, 98, 129
Lille, 54, 55
Lionne, Hugues de, 30, 31, 36, 100, 111, 112; death of, 8, 176; succeeded by Pomponne, 9; and Wilhelm von Fürstenberg, 60, 190

(n. 64); said aim of France to keep Hapsburgs divided, 99; waning influence upon Louis XIV, 186 (n. 24); and Peace of Pyrenees, 200 (n. 1)
Lira, Don Emmanuel de, 105
Lisbon, 169–70
Lisola, Franz Paul von, 33, 54, 85, 104, 139, 153, 199 (n. 108); intercepts Louis XIV's letters to his mistress, 44; imperial ambassador at The Hague, 93; diplomacy in the Netherlands, 94; tries to lure away French allies, 95
Lobkowitz, Wenzel Eusebius, prince of: the pro-French member of Leopold's government, 31–32; discredited by Montecuccoli and Lisola, 54
Lockhart, William, English ambassador in France, 92, 157, 159
London, 77, 79, 80, 88, 89, 95, 151–71 passim; French and Spanish ambassadors have row in, 120–21; public opinion in, 163; Rupert comes up from fleet to, 164–65; effigy of pope burned in, 168
Lorraine, 4, 24, 45, 122, 123, 147; French troops to hold, 14; transferred to Louvois's jurisdiction, 26; occupied by French, 34; French court moves to, 44; Louis XIV's campaign in, 66–67; Montecuccoli threat to, 73; Louis XIV headquartered in, 93; Louis XIV views as part of France, 102–4
Lorraine, duke of. See Charles IV, duke of Lorraine
Louis XIV: personality of, 5–8, 17, 21, 28, 36, 41, 43–45, 56, 63, 98, 124, 173, 180–81; pursuit of *gloire*, 6–7, 25, 43, 67, 98, 173–75, 178–81; attack on Dutch Republic, 13, 129; irritation with Dutch, 13, 186 (n. 1); rejects Dutch offers at Doesburg, 13, 112, 146, 173, 200 (n. 8); admiration for Dutch, 14, 187 (n. 5); strategy for 1673, 14, 17, 28, 42–43, 82–83, 114–20; military memoirs of, 16, 119, 173, 186 (n. 1),

187 (nn. 5, 12), 200 (n. 2), 208 (n. 2); and elector of Cologne, 17–19, 139–44; taste for siege warfare, 17; manipulative foreign policy of, 19, 79–80, 96, 98, 139–40, 143–45, 157–59; women of, 19, 43–45, 125, 191 (nn. 106, 108, 110), 191 (n. 110); at siege of Maastricht, 20–22, 86–87; desire for war with Spain, 23, 121; plans for march to eastern frontier, 24; march into Lorraine, 25; orders invasion of electorate of Trier, 27–28; antagonizes German princes, 28–29, 33, 34; headquartered in Nancy, 34, 68, 123; sends Condé to appraise situation in Alsace, 34; abilities those of a *rôi bureaucrate* not a *roi commandant*, 36, 179; march into Alsace, 36–37; secret treaty of neutrality with emperor, 38; plans for siege of Trier, 38–39; justification for attacking Trier, 39–40; impatient with siege at Trier, 41; subjective nature of policies, 43–45, 179–80; makes peace with Brandenburg, 51–52, 54; wishes to avoid trouble in Germany, 51–53; decides to advance Turenne, 55–56; trouble formulating cohesive foreign policy, 56, 62, 81–82; absorption in own campaign, 66–67; agrees to peace conference in Cologne, 79, 82; changing view of Dutch, 80–81, 116; underestimates Dutch, 83; confused by Swedish ambassador, 87–88; and Charles II, 88, 119, 144, 151–71 passim; bargaining position of at Cologne Conference, 91–98; misjudges the Dutch, 95; failure of foreign policy of, 99–100, 144–45, 171, 173–83; *Mémoires* for the instruction of the dauphin, 102; views about Lorraine and France, 102–4; no concept of balance of power, 103; anger with Courtin and Barrillon, 105–6, 118; dynastic claim in Spanish Netherlands, 110–11; wishes to invade Spanish Netherlands, 110–19; *Projet pour 1674*, 118; desire to dominate 1673 campaign, 121, 122, 126, 158; wishes to invade Franche-Comté, 122–23; prepares declaration of war against Spain and cancels it, 123; declares war on Spain, 127, 169; returns to St. Germain, 125–26; orders court martial of Du Pas, 139; feelings about Dutch conquests, 131–32; decides to withdraw armies from Dutch Republic, 134–35; dependence on Louvois, 145–48; anger at Louvois, 147; and Treaty of Dover, 154; pays dowry for duke of York's Catholic wife, 167; view of in England, 167–68; De Witt characterizes, 172; and reason-of-state, 174–75, 181–82, 208 (n. 5); rejects Colbert's vision for France, 178; regrets Dutch War, 178; Janus-faced, 179; belittles Turenne, 181; love of minutiae, 182, 209 (n.. 27); exposed to war when very young, 202 (n. 55); presents French girl to Charles II, 208 (n. 68); extends *régale*, 209 (n. 11)

Louvois, François-Michel le Tellier, marquis de, 9, 19, 22, 23, 29, 31, 37, 38, 40, 42, 52, 53, 62, 64, 65, 68, 71, 74, 75, 80, 81, 92, 96, 97, 102, 103, 106, 107, 116–127 passim, 134, 135, 177, 180, 191 (n. 93), 204 (n. 67); vigor of as minister, 8; close advisor to Louis XIV, 11, 24, 28, 40, 109, 114, 118, 130–31, 141, 146–47; reconnoiters Moselle Valley, 24; procedes to Nancy, 26; defenses of eastern frontier, 28; writes to Le Tellier, 32; sends Navailles to appraise situation in Alsace, 35; takes Navailles to see Louis XIV, 35; orders siege of Trier, 39; misjudges strength of Trier, 41; involved in diplomacy, 18, 51, 145; invites Turenne to devastate central Germany, 56; orders Turenne to maintain discipline in army, 60; creator of "new army," 61; row with Turenne, 63, 69–70, 75, 148–50, 194 (n. 65); promises to support Turenne, 66; personality of, 67, 69–70, 82,

108–9, 141; attempts to bully Turenne, 69–70; his men in Turenne's army, 72–73; contempt for Dutch, 85; Courtin's friend and confidant, 97, 103, 106–7; Courtin warns about war, 99; position in government threatened, 100, 149; effective politician, 101; describes king's mentality, 104; writes honestly to Courtin, 108; describes Pomponne's anguish, 109; interim foreign minister, 112, 141, 187 (n. 15), 204 (n. 46); sent by king to appraise situation in Flanders, 113; writes tantalizing letter to Turenne, 114–15; secret correspondence with Luxembourg, 132; in desperate straights, 133, 202 (n. 13); misjudges French army in Netherlands, 136, 203 (n. 27); consequences of his miscalculations, 138; abuses Wilhelm von Fürstenberg, 141–42; detested by Wilhelm von Fürstenberg, 143; ineptness as diplomat, 143–44; rising power of, 145–48, 176; Louis XIV's anger with, 147; generals plot against, 148–50; relations with Condé, 149, 205 (n. 72); position in government reaffirmed, 150; persuades Louis XIV to reject Dutch offers, 200 (n. 8); orders money extorted from Dutch, 203 (n. 25); Rousset comments on, 204 (n. 55)

Louvre, 120
Low Countries. *See* Netherlands
Ludre, Ferry de Frolois de: possibly the king's mistress, 191 (n. 106)
Luxembourg, 24, 39
Luxembourg, François-Henri de Montmorency-Bouteville, duke of, 119, 121, 133, 138, 180, 204 (n. 67); tries to cross ice to Amsterdam, 81; commands French army in Utrecht, 130; confused by Louis XIV's muddled strategy, 131; corresponds secretly with Louvois, 132; ordered to evacuate Holland and march to Rhine, 134–36; does not conspire against Louvois, 149; sadistic streak in, 203 (n. 24); extorts money from Dutch, 203 (n. 25); Louvois misjudges strength of his army, 203 (n. 27)

M

Maastricht, 42, 43, 44, 51, 54, 62, 64–65, 66, 85, 86, 88, 92, 118, 125, 126, 129, 147, 148, 168; French plans to attack and conquer, 16–26; French expect its conquest to improve their position, 22; Louis XIV's campaign after conquest of, 45; Louis XIV offers to relinquish, 98; Louis XIV wishes to be known as conqueror of, 119; Spanish ministers advocate war over issue of, 120; Louis XIV would rather give up Paris or Versailles than, 131; Louvois's position enhanced by siege of, 146; Count Tott visits Louis XIV at, 156
Madrid, 33, 38, 114, 120, 121, 126
Maes, 138
Main River, 30, 55, 68, 69, 70, 72–75, 136; Turennes's approach to, 61, 64, 65; Turenne cannot hold down Germany both north and south of, 66; Turenne maneuvers with Montecuccoli along, 123
Mainz, city of, 136; abbé de Gravel watches imperial army from, 75
Mainz, elector of. *See* Metternich, Lothar Friedrich von; Schönborn, Johann Philipp von
Maizery, Persode de, French agent in Frankfurt: describes alarm created in Germany by Turenne's approach to Main River, 64; keeps Turenne informed of Montecuccoli's activities, 73–74
Malines: law of devolution in, 110
Margaret Theresa, deceased wife of Emperor Leopold, 32
Maria Ana, queen mother in Spain: nominally in charge of regency council for Carlos II, 120
Maria-Zell, pilgrimage town for Emperor Leopold, 32, 33

Marie Thérèse, queen of France, 43, 110; her marriage to Louis XIV and French foreign policy, 3, 200 (n. 1)

Mark, countess of: mistress of Wilhelm von Fürstenberg, 142–43, 204 (n. 50)

Mark, county of, 52, 64, 141; possession of Brandenburg, 51

Marseilles, 178

Martel, marquis de, second in command of French squadron, 162; writes condemnation of Estrées, 164; damages French interests, 165; political naivete used by English, 207 (n. 49)

Marx, Karl, 5

Mary of Modena, duke of York's second wife, 167

Maximilian Heinrich, elector of Cologne, 58, 60, 142–44, 159; bishop of Liège and *de jure* sovereign of Maastricht, 17; treaty with Louis XIV, 18, 139; manipulated by Louis XIV, 19, 24, 139–41; flees Cologne, 41; French ally, 63, 125, 136, 139–40; enemy of Brandenburg, 139; feels deserted by Louis XIV, 139; frightened by approach of allied armies, 139; feels abused by French, 140–43; interests ignored by France, 171

Mazarin, Duke Charles-Armand de: encourages sense of independence in Alsace, 35; married Mazarin's niece and assumed cardinal's surname, (n. 76); writes to Robert de Gravel concerning Alsace, 190 (n. 83)

Mazarin, Jules, Cardinal, 4, 8, 9, 29, 30, 35, 36, 177; returned to France at end of Fronde, 84; Lionne reiterates divide-and-conquer policy of, 94; taught fear of diplomatic isolation, 112; alliance with England greatest achievement of, 151; Louis XIV's policy and, 172–74; team trained by no longer runs French government, 176; Louis XIV undoes achievements of, 181; negotiated Peace of Pyrenees, 200 (n. 1)

Meinders, Franz von, secretary of state in Brandenburg: negotiates treaty between France and Brandenburg, 49–51

Mercantilism: Colbert and, 5–6, 176–78, 181, 185 (nn. 7, 8); not cause of Dutch War, 5–6, 176–78, 181, 185 (nn. 7, 8), 208 (n. 9)

Metternich, Lothar Friedrich von, elector of Mainz (1673–75), 64, 69, 72, 75; important neutral prince in Germany, 27; Wilhelm von Fürstenberg sent to placate, 30; warns Fürstenberg about invasion of Trier, 33; French want to arrange a German settlement, 52; abbé de Gravel reports troubled, 57; wishes to remain neutral, 73; and negotiations over Trier, 190 (n. 87)

Metz, 25

Meulen, Adam-François van der: Louis XIV has paint royal victory at Maastricht, 20

Meuse River, 16, 19, 22, 83, 91, 92, 118, 134

Middleground, 161

Monarchical government: inherently bellicose, 179

Monmouth, James Scott, duke of: fights at Maastricht and describes trench warfare, 20

Mons, fortress in Spanish Netherlands: Louis XIV plans to attack, 118

Montecuccoli, Count Raimund, 58, 59, 65, 68, 69, 72, 73, 126, 136; influence in Imperial Council rising, 31; leads imperial army into Germany, 33; ordered by emperor to go slow, 48; plans war for emperor, 53; works to discredit Lobkowitz, 54; maneuvers against Turenne along Main River, 61; has no intention to fight, 70; eludes Turenne, 71; stops in Frankfurt, 74; maneuvers in Franconia, 123–24; invades Cologne and Münster, 127, 137; sends flotilla down Rhine, 136; seizes Bonn, 137; advance of affects peace talks, 138

Monterey, count of, governor of Spanish Netherlands, 38–39, 113, 114, 115, 121–24; aids Dutch during siege of Charleroi, 19; Louis XIV wants him to start war, 23; and Lisola, 94; eager for war, 120

Montespan, Françoise-Athenäis de Rochechouart, marquise de: Louis XIV's sexual partner, 43; king wishes to play conquering hero for, 44; superb and demanding mistress, 45; accompanies the king's campaign, 124–25; pregnancy delays campaign, 191 (n. 108); campaign quarters serve as council chamber, 191 (n. 110)

Moselle River, 24–27, 36, 55, 65, 157; Louis XIV leads army toward, 23; French court moves along, 34; king's army immobilized on, 42

Mühlhausen, 29

Munich, 103

Münster, bishop of. See Galen, Christoph Bernhard von, bishop of Münster

Münster, bishopric of, 85, 143, 154; ally of France, 73; Montecuccoli invades, 127; enemy of Brandenburg, 139

Münster, Treaty of, 49; and Alsace, 34, 35, 190 (n. 73); See also Westphalia, Peace of

N

Naarden: prince of Orange besieges and recaptures, 98, 130

Namur, fortress in Spanish Netherlands: heads list of places Louis XIV wishes to attack, 118

Namur, province in Spanish Netherlands: law of devolution in, 110

Nancy, 34, 36, 68, 93, 96, 123, 147, 157, 159; Louis XIV plans to go to, 24, 26; royal campaign headquarters in, 35, 68

Nantes, 178

Naples: part of France's share of Spanish inheritance according to secret treaty of partition, 111

Nassau, count of, 56

Natural frontiers: Sorel's theory of, 4

Navailles, Philippe, duke of, 37; sent to Alsace to appraise situation, 35; disgraced assisting Venetians on Crete, 119

Navarre, 111

Nec pluribus impar, Louis XIV's motto, 10, 98

Neckar River: Turenne's army must cross, 75

Netherlands, 15, 22, 27, 48, 51, 54, 55, 63, 71, 83, 85, 87, 105, 113, 119, 121, 125, 143, 157; rising water level in, 23, 157; war in could not be isolated, 53; vulnerable to imperial army, 72; Louis XIV's first attack upon, 77; frozen polders in melt, 81; French army bogged down in, 82; Lisola active in, 94; intendant of French army in, 96; Lorraine gateway to, 102; Condé faces problems in, 124; French occupying force in, 131; Louvois misjudges strength of French army in, 136; French troops immobilized holding, 145; Triple Alliance intended to stop French expansion into, 152. See also Dutch Netherlands; Spanish Netherlands; United Provinces of the Dutch Republic

Neuburg, duke of. See Philip William, duke of Neuburg

Neuss, fortress on the Rhine River, 139

Newcastle, 161

Nijmegen, Peace of, 104; French forced to pay heavy price for territories acquired at, 95, 182; coalition compels Louis XIV to accept compromise settlement at, 97; French rewarded at expense of Spaniards and not Dutch at, 173; Louis XIV's position at time of, 183

North Sea, 24, 88, 161–62; Dutch navy fends off Anglo-French fleet in, 33

Northern frontier of France, 25, 54, 114; "pell-mell" of fortresses along, 14; dangerously close to Paris, 110, 172, 174; Louis XIV's view of, 116–19; Vauban's view of, 116–19. See also Aix-la-Chapelle, Peace of; Spanish Netherlands

O

Oise River, 113, 117
Old Regime, 83, 100, 150; French
   foreign policy during, 3–6; jurists
   debate harmless passage during, 19
Orange, Frederick Henry, prince of, 17
Orange, William III, prince of, 83,
   113, 115, 124, 135, 136, 138, 146,
   152, 161, 168–69, 179; to join
   forces with Montecuccoli, 74; con-
   solidation of power in Dutch Republic, 94; recaptures Naarden, 98;
   attempts to capture Charleroi, 112;
   invests Naarden, 130; Louvois belittles, 134; forces of invest Bonn, 137;
   reconciles De Ruyter and Tromp,
   160

P

Paine, Thomas: indictment of monarchy, 179
Palatinate, elector of, 75
Paris, 25, 38, 83, 95, 120, 127, 136,
   138, 150, 156, 176, 177, 178; reaction in to victory at Maastricht, 21;
   protection of, 110; threatened by
   Spanish *tercios*, 124; Louis XIV
   would rather relinquish than Maastricht, 131
Parliament, 152–71 passim; anti-
   French and anti-war, 90; approaching session of paralyzes England, 92;
   does not want war with Spain, 119;
   Charles II's problems with, 144;
   Shaftesbury's speech in, 152; discus-
   ses religious issue, 155; Charles II
   concedes some points to, 156; passes
   Test Act, 160. *See also* House of
   Commons
Parma, Alexander Farnese, duke of:
   conqueror of Maastricht, 21
Paul, French military engineer: Vau-
   ban's promising young assistant
   killed at Maastricht, 20
Pedro, regent of Portugal: plot to overthrow quashed, 169–70
Pellison-Fontanier, Paul: royal his-
   toriographer accompanies Louis
   XIV's campaign, 19

Peñaranda, Gaspar de Bracamonte,
   count of, Spanish minister opposes
   war with France, 120
Perwich, William, secretary to the English embassy in Paris, 177, 178
Petites-Maisons: Parisian insane
   asylum, 164
Philip I, king of Spain, father-in-law of
   Louis XIV, 3, 110, 120
Philippines: would go to France according to first partition treaty, 111
Philippsburg, fortress on Rhine River,
   34, 67, 68, 123, 138; pontoon
   bridge at, 24; Turenne must
   backtrack through, 74, 75, 136
Philip William, duke of Neuburg: signs
   treaties of amity with both Brandenburg and France, 49; worried lest
   Turenne march into Franconia, 58;
   prophecies to Fürstenbergs prove
   true, 59
Picardy, 117, 126
Pignerol, 14
Polders: Dutchmen flood, 13, 196 (n.
   15); bog down French armies,
   14–15, 81; protect Amsterdam and
   The Hague, 14, 16; Luxembourg
   tries to advance over frozen, 81
Pomponne, Simon Nicolas Arnauld,
   marquis de, 19, 22, 27, 29, 32, 36,
   37, 42, 46, 49, 54, 59, 60, 67,
   90–92, 100–101, 104, 118, 123,
   125, 138, 146, 153, 155, 156, 159,
   163, 168–69, 171, 196 (n. 10);
   becomes royal foreign minister after
   Lionne's death, 8; views on European states' system differ from those
   of Louis XIV, 9; corresponds with
   Fürstenbergs, 30–31, 58, 139–41;
   opposed to attack on Trier, 40–41;
   signs Treaty of Vossem, 51; orders
   abbé de Gravel to convince elector of
   Mainz to arrange a German peace,
   52; corresponds with Courtin, 83,
   84, 89; reminds plenipotentiaries
   about king's position on Lorraine,
   102; attacked by Courtin, 106–8; in
   agreement with Courtin on policy,
   109; works under great strain
   against opinions of Louvois and

Louis XIV, 109; prepares for invasion of Franche-Comté, 122; views France differently than Louis XIV, 179; performs official duties unenthusiastically, 193 (n. 42); Courtin mentions generously, 198 (n. 89)

Portsmouth, Louise Renée de Kéroualle, duchess of: presented to Charles II by Louis XIV at time of Treaty of Dover, 208 (n. 68)

Portugal, 169, 170

Pré carré: means squared field, 116; Vauban advocates for northern frontier, 116, 117, 201 (n. 25)

Protestant religion, 153, 167

Puritans: Spain swallowed distaste for in recognizing Commonwealth, 151; Venetian envoy could not understand, 167

Pyrenees: passes through into France, 24

Pyrenees, Peace of the (1659), 123; frontiers established by, 95; Marie Thérèse renounces all claims to Spanish inheritance in marriage contract included in, 110; Spanish Hapsburgs no longer threat after, 152; Lionne helped Mazarin negotiate, 200 (n. 1)

Régale: Louis XIV extends to all provinces of France, 209 (n. 11)

Regensburg, meeting place of Imperial Diet, 40, 56, 60, 61, 64, 65, 69; anti-French sentiment in, 41

Reichskrieg: Imperial Diet declares against France, 137

Rheims, 178

Rhine River, 19, 34, 42, 48, 55, 62, 64, 66, 67, 71, 72, 96, 105, 133, 134, 135, 138, 141, 181; possible "natural frontier" for France, 4; French bridges over, 24, 67, 74, 123, 136; strategic confluence with Main River, 27, 30, 75; imperial army might march toward, 43, 57, 60, 88; Turenne to prevent imperial army from approaching, 70; elector of Mainz's bridge over, 73; French crossing of in 1672, 129; Montecuc-

coli sends flotilla down, 136; French domination of broken, 137, 145

Rhineland, 45, 125; Turenne's army bogged down in, 136

Richelieu, Armand-Jean du Plessis, cardinal de, 9; foreign policy of, 4, 36, 99, 151, 172, 174; Louis XIV dislikes relationship of with Louis XIII

Robert, Louis, French intendant in the Netherlands, 96

Rochefort, Henri-Louis, marquis de: leads attack on Trier, 38, 40; commands occupying forces in Trier, 133

Rochester, John Wilmot, earl of: versifies anti-French feelings of English, 167–68

Rocroi, 122

Roussillon, 95; French army for, 14, 24

Royal Charles, English flagship, 161

Royal government: structure of, 9, 26, 150; dissension in, 30, 32, 40, 174–79; war council of, 150; financial problems of, 166, 176–78, 209 (nn. 10, 15). See also *Conseil d'en haut*; High council

Rupert, prince of the Palatinate, 165; commander of Anglo-French fleet, 160–62; denounces Estrées's conduct during battle of Texel, 163–64

Ruyter, Michiel de. *See* De Ruyter, Michiel

S

Saar, 136

Sadoc, French financier, 101

Saint-Dié: Louis XIV's army passes through, 36

Saint-Germain-en-Laye, 14, 19, 25, 43, 44, 48, 49, 53, 54, 77, 82, 113, 114, 125, 126, 138, 146, 155

Saint-Gotthard: Montecuccoli's most famous victory at, 137

Saint-Maurice, Thomas-François Chabod, marquis de: remarks that Pomponne is "timorous," 8; claims that Pomponne was opposed to attack on Trier, 40; comments on Montespan's fertility, 44; comments on Louvois's power in government, 147

Saint-Quentin, 126

Saint-Roman, Melchior de Héron de, French ambassador in Switzerland, 122–23

Saxony, duke of, 138

Scheldt River, 19, 55, 91, 118, 124

Scheveningen, 161

Schönborn, Johann Philipp von, elector of Mainz (1647–73): death of, 27, 189 (n. 52)

Schwarzenberg, Johann Adolf von, imperial minister, 31

Seignelay, Jean-Baptiste Colbert, marquis de, 164

Sélestat, 36, 43

Seven Provinces, De Ruyter's flagship, 154, 161, 162

Shaftesbury, Anthony Ashley Cooper, earl of: advocates destruction of Dutch Republic in Parliament, 152; anti-Dutch speech motivated by political calculation, 205 (n. 4)

's-Hertogenbosch, 21

Sicily, 111

Siege warfare: at Maastricht, 21–23; at Trier, 38–41; at Bonn, 137

Sluis, Dutch coastal town, 206 (n. 25)

Smith, Adam: economic interpretation of Dutch War given by, 5

Soest: Turenne's headquarters in Germany, 51

Somme River, 124

Spain, 3, 28, 91, 105, 106, 129, 131, 138, 151, 162, 169; Louis XIV eager for war with, 23, 180; and Alliance of The Hague, 95, 102; and exchange of territories in Netherlands, 96; and war with France, 110–27 passim; war with and evacuation of Holland, 132, 173; England's largest trading partner, 167; English foreign policy based on friendship with, 171

Spain, king of. *See* Carlos II

Spanish Brabant, 52; law of devolution in, 110

Spanish Flanders, 125

Spanish Netherlands, 23, 38, 54, 94, 112, 113, 115, 124, 133; Louis XIV's dynastic interest in, 4, 10; frontier of created by Peace of Aix-la-Chapelle, 14, 112; Condé sees as basic problem, 15; Louis XIV marches into, 19; logical target for French expansion, 25, 110–11, 116; exchange of territory proposed in, 90, 96, 105; Louis XIV jealous of conquests in, 106; Louis XIV's plans for, 118; renewed war begins in, 126. *See also* Aix-la-Chapelle, Peace of; Northern frontier

Spanish Succession: importance of in Louis XIV's foreign policy, 3–4, 110–11, 200 (n. 1)

Spragge, Edward, English vice admiral, 161–62

Stamp tax: raises furor in France, 177, 209 (n. 15)

States General of the Dutch Republic, 32–33, 57, 88, 90, 102, 208 (n. 3); sends delegates to talk peace with Louis XIV, 13; behind in subsidies owed to Brandenberg, 49; allies with Hapsburgs and Lorraine, 95; Pomponne thinks will accept French peace offers, 156; De Ruyter's orders from, 161

States party (in Dutch Republic): murder of De Witt brothers and demise of, 94

Stockholm, 80, 100

Stockholm, Treaty of (1672), 87, 195 (n. 3); Sweden signs with France, 77; Swedes are loath to honor, 80; obliges Sweden to fight with France, 88; Feuquières's task to persuade Swedes to honor, 101; Courtin gives Pomponne credit for, 198 (n. 89)

Strasbourg, bishop of. *See* Fürstenberg, Franz Egon von, bishop of Strasbourg

Stratmann, Dietrich von, duke of Neuburg's vice-chancellor: begins negotiations between France and Brandenburg, 49

Swabia, 66

Sweden, 79, 96, 105, 125, 143; French

fear to alienate, 23; works to arrange peace conference, 77; Louis XIV hopes to bring into war on French side, 80, 97, 98, 99, 101; wishes to preserve Dutch Republic, 87; becomes feeble, 88; Pomponne misjudges, 109; and Triple Alliance (1668), 111; opposes Dutch War, 116; loath to honor treaty with France, 154; does not want English on Continent, 156

Swiss Guards, 36

Switzerland: members of diet of bribed by French 122–23

T

Tauber River: Turenne's logistical base in Franconia, 72

Temple, Sir William: comments on Louis XIV and France, 7–8, 98

Tercios, Spanish infantry, invaded France, 124

Test Act (1673): forbids Roman Catholics from holding public office in England, 153; duke of York and Lord Clifford forced to resign from government because of, 160, 167

Texel, battle of: De Ruyter holds off combined Anglo-French fleet at, 98, 161–62; Anglo-French alliance weakened by, 144; English reaction to, 154; political repercussions of, 163–68; occasion for English rejection of French alliance, 171

Thames, River, 161

The Hague, 17, 77, 79, 88, 90, 91, 93, 99, 173; protected by flooded polders, 13–14, 81; Heemskerck returns to with encouraging news, 94; Triple Alliance signed at, 111

The Hague, Alliance of (1673): anti-French alliance of Dutch, Austrian Hapsburgs, Spanish Hapsburgs, and duke of Lorraine, 95, 123

Thionville, 25, 34, 65; Louvois joins king at, 26; French headquarters in, 32

Third Republic, 4

Thirty Years' War, 52, 68, 180

Thuringia, 55

Tott, Count Claudius, 100, 103; heads delegation of Swedish mediators at peace talks, 85; at Cologne Conference, 86–92; makes ominous visit to Louis XIV at Maastricht, 156

Tournai, 19, 44, 124

Traité simulé. See Dover, Treaty of

Transitus innoxius (harmless passage): Louis XIV's through Spanish Netherlands, 19; Grotius and Vattel on, 188 (n. 22)

Treason: seventeenth-century concept of, 199 (n. 108)

Trier, elector of. *See* Leyden, Karl Gaspard von der, elector of Trier

Trier, electorate of, 45, 55, 56, 66, 67, 68, 71, 109, 129, 130, 133. 136, 137, 148, 168; Louis XIV plans to place French troops in, 24–27; French invasion of, 28–29; criticism of invasion of, 30–33; French besiege capital city of, 38–41; invasion of did not serve Dutch War, 42; invasion of might be justified, 43; could be vulnerable to imperial army, 73; Louis XIV angry with Louvois over siege of capital of, 147

Triple Alliance (1668), 160, 168; entry of Sweden into, 77; England and Dutch Republic later joined by Sweden, 111; Dutch use to oppose Louis XIV, 112; participation of Charles II in, 152; helped persuade Louis XIV to accept peace in 1668, 186 (n. 29); renewal of the, 195 (n. 2)

Tromp, Cornelis: reconciliation with De Ruyter, 160; action during battle of Texel, 161

Turenne, Henri de la Tour d'Auvergne, vicomte de, 17, 19, 23, 24, 31, 33, 40, 41, 46, 84, 120, 125, 126, 139, 157, 189 (n. 55), 194 (n. 65); strategic recommendations for 1673 campaign, 14, counted on to stop imperial army in Germany, 15; in Germany to observe imperial army, 16; to spread news in Germany of French victory at Maastricht, 22; French army in eastern France to

support, 25; feelings about French relations with Trier, 42; Louis XIV's campaign leaves isolated, 45; campaign in Germany, 47–75; ordered to leave Brandenburg's territories, 56–57; does not underestimate emperor, 58; marches into Franconia, 59; criticism of his march into Franconia, 60; his army in Germany advantage to Imperials, 61; assumes superb attitude, 65; perceives anti-French sentiment in Germany, 66; importance of his mission in Germany, 67; compared with Condé, 70; rift with Louvois, 70; wants to fight Montecuccoli, 71; outmaneuvered by Montecuccoli, 71–74; movement toward Philippsburg, 75; receives tantalizing letter from Louvois, 114; advance into Spanish Netherlands during War of Devolution, 115–16; maneuvers on Main River, 123; strategic problems faced in Germany, 124; questions judgment of Louis XIV and Louvois, 132; trapped in Franconia, 136; consequences of abortive campaign of, 137–38; leads anti-Louvois cabal, 148–50; erred in judgment during 1673 campaign, 150; belittled by Louis XIV, 181; 1673 campaign of studied by Clausewitz, 194 (n. 77); letter of concerning reconciliation with Louvois, 205 (n. 78)
Turks, 32–33, 48

U

United Provinces of the Dutch Republic, 14, 18, 48, 80, 81, 87, 89, 90, 99, 145; Louis XIV's attack on, 9–10, 13, 112, 129; sends delegates to talk peace with French, 13; Spain recognized independence of, 17; Brandenburg and Austria enter war in favor of, 48; behind in subsidies to Brandenburg, 49; Sweden wishes to preserve independence of, 77; Louis XIV considers settlement with, 80; war against becomes burden for France, 81; fate of dependent on emperor, 88; alliance with Austria, Lorraine, and Spain, 95; and Triple Alliance (1668), 112; Louis XIV's first victories in, 112; Louis XIV considers destroying, 116; French armies withdraw from, 134–35; and Treaty of Dover, 152; England prepares to attack, 156–57; Dutch navy preserves, 162; Charles II's separate peace with, 171; failure of Louis XIV's attack upon, 183
Utrecht, 23, 24, 81, 134, 135; flooded polders in, 14; French propaganda in, 82; Luxembourg stationed in, 121, 130; evacuation of, 136, 203 (n. 27); Condé stationed in, 148

V

Valois, French royal family, 34
Van Beverningk, Hieronymous, Dutch diplomat, 88–89, 93; heads Dutch delegation to Cologne Conference, 85
Van Haren, Willem, Dutch diplomat at Cologne Conference, 88, 93
Vattel, Emmerich de: comments on international law, 188 (n. 22)
Vauban, Sébastien le Prestre de, 17, 146; sends strategic recommendations to Louis XIV, 14; directs siege of Maastricht, 20; tours defenses of eastern frontier, 28; inspects fortifications in Alsace, 34; helps plan attack on Trier, 40; advocates *pré carré* for northern frontier, 116–17
Venice, Senate of, 166
Versailles, château of, 9, 126, 127, 129, 131, 132, 170, 177
Verjus de Crécy. *See* Crécy, Louis-Verjus, count de
Vienna, 25, 28, 31, 32, 38, 44, 48, 53, 54, 55, 57, 59, 60, 88, 94, 101, 138
Villars, Louis-Hector, duke of, French ambassador in Spain, 126, 149; reports Frenchmen being harassed in Madrid, 120
Visconti, Primi: comments on Louis XIV's government, 8

Vitry, François-Marie, duke of, French ambassador in Bavaria, 82, 103
Volmar, Issak von, imperial diplomat, 37
Voltaire, François-Marie Arouet, 183
Vossem, 19, 28, 51; ratification of peace between France and Brandenburg delivered at, 62, 64, 192 (n. 9)
Vossem, Treaty of: haggling over wording of, 51; Frederick William of Brandenburg serious about, 192 (n. 11)

W

Waal River, 91
Woerden: French evacuate, 134
Weser River, 51
West Indies, 177
Westphalia: Turenne's campaign in, 49, 64
Westphalia, Peace of, 27, 34, 51, 53, 137; France as guarantor of, 61. *See also* Münster, Treaty of
Wetzlar: Turenne's headquarters in Germany, 64, 65, 69
Whitehall Palace, 121, 153, 164, 165. *See also* London

Wicquefort, Abraham de: comments on Cologne Conference, 79; comments on attitudes in Dutch Republic, 99; views on battle of Texel, 165
Wijk, suburb of Maastricht, 19
William III. *See* Orange, William III, prince of
Williamson, Joseph, English ambassador at Cologne Conference, 84, 85, 89–91, 165
Witt, Johan de. *See* De Witt, Johan
Wolsey, Cardinal Thomas, 151
Würzburg, bishop of: an uncommitted prince, 56; throws support to emperor, 124
Würzburg, bishopric of: Turenne maneuvers near, 55, 68–74

Y

York, James, duke of. *See* James, duke of York

Z

Zeeland, 16, 156, 158, 162
Zürich, 122

ഗരെ

The Author

Carl J. Ekberg is associate professor of history
at Illinois State University

The Book

Composition and design by
The University of North Carolina Press

Text set in Stempel V-I-P Sabon

Text stock, sixty-pound Olde Style
by S. D. Warren Company

Endsheet stock, Multicolor Textured Algarve Gray
by Process Materials Corporation

Binding cloth, Roxite Vellum B 51546
by The Holliston Mills, Incorporated

Printing and binding
by Vail-Ballou Press, Incorporated

Published by The University of North Carolina Press